Revolutionary Activism in the 1950s & 60s

Revolutionary
Activism
IN THE 1950S & 60S

Ernest Tate, A Memoir

Volume 1, Canada 1955–1965

Photographs by Michel Lambeth

Preface by Derrick O'Keefe

RESISTANCE BOOKS
London

Published by Resistance Books, PO Box 62732, London, SW2 9GQ. Resistance Books is the publishing arm of Socialist Resistance, a revolutionary Marxist organisation that is the British section of the Fourth International. Resistance Books publishes books jointly with the International Institute for Research and Education in Amsterdam and independently. Further information about Resistance Books, including a full list of titles currently available and how to purchase them, can be obtained by writing to the address above.

Ernest Tate Vol 1: Revolutionary memories
ISBN 978-0-902869-69-1
EAN: 9780902869691

Editing & Final Proof Reading by Derrick O'Keefe
Book Design & Electronic Prepress by Lawrence
Michel Lambeth photographs are from Library Archives Canada

The text of this book is set in Minion Pro, a type designed in the U.S. in 1990 by Robert Slimbach.

Printed in the Britain by Lightning Source.

Publisher's Foreword

RESISTANCE BOOKS IS PLEASED TO BE PUBLISHING THIS WORK. WE THINK it's an important contribution to the history of the left in Britain and Canada during a unique period, a political narrative of Ernest Tate's life as a socialist activist during the fifteen-year period from 1955 to 1970. In volume one he tells us about his arrival in Toronto in 1955 as a working-class immigrant from Northern Ireland and about how he quickly became engaged in radical politics. He provides us with interesting details of what political life was like in those years in a small revolutionary organization, the Socialist Educational League (SEL), which was affiliated to the Fourth International. We get to see how it was organized and we get a glimpse of some of its leading personalities as they sought to increase support for their ideas among working people. He underlines the importance of the American Socialist Workers Party (SWP) to its early years. One of the SEL's major activities was to organize cross-country tours to sell its monthly paper, the *Workers Vanguard*, across the vast expanse of Canada, tours that sometimes lasted up to six months. In a time when there was no Internet, it was often the only way to keep in touch with its supporters.

The ten-year period covered in volume one, from 1955 to 1965, was important for the left. The Canadian version of McCarthyism—although not as virulent as that in the United States, but equally as reactionary—had begun to recede, and a new radical consciousness had begun to emerge—almost surreptitiously, Ernest writes—that was influenced both by the victory of the Cuban Revolution in 1959, and the birth of the New Democratic Party in 1961. Regarding Cuba, a long chapter describes how, in order to defend that country's revolution and in response to the growing interest in it by Canadians, especially young people, the SEL initiated the setting up of the Fair Play for Cuba Committee. It became, as the author says, one of the most important campaigns to defend Cuba in the English-speaking world. This is the first time a comprehensive description of the Committee's work—and its difficulties—including the story of its remarkable leader, Verne Olson, have appeared. The birth of the New Democratic Party (NDP), a process that took a couple of years, posed new problems and opportunities for revolutionary socialists. There were many discussions about how they should relate to a party that had a social democratic programme and was further to the right than the old Cooperative Commonwealth Federation (CCF) which it had replaced. Those debates find their expression here.

Also described are the activities of revolutionary socialists in the trade unions, not easy in a period of low working-class consciousness. A couple of chapters provide us with important details about how the League for Socialist Action (LSA) organized its members in the unions, especially in the large transport companies in Ontario, those organized by the Teamsters' union. The LSA found itself at the head of a large rank-and-file opposition that had been deeply angered and frustrated by a trusteeship imposed upon it by Washington. Every contract renewal in those years saw widespread industrial action by the drivers, some that almost paralyzed the Ontario and Quebec economies for weeks at a time. This is the first time that story has been written giving the militants' side of that struggle.

Volume two covers Ernest Tate's political experiences in Britain when he was on assignment from the LSA to assist in the reorganization of the Fourth International's section. He describes his activities with the Bertrand Russell Peace Foundation, the birth of the International Marxist Group and the Vietnam Solidarity Campaign, including the tremendous effort to organize the famous Bertrand Russell International War Crimes Tribunal, the latter finally triumphing over both the opposition of American imperialism and the Soviet bureaucracy. In volume two, he also revisits the debates in the Fourth International about the guerrilla struggle in Latin America and provides a report, based upon recent information, about the tragic destruction in the seventies of a heroic guerrilla movement in Argentina led by Robert Santucho. The volume ends with Ernest Tate's return to Canada and his eventual parting of the ways with the LSA.

We are fortunate to have a preface to this volume written by Derrick O'Keefe, a writer and a leader in the Canadian anti-war movement. He is also the author of a Verso book, *Michael Ignatieff: The Lesser Evil?* and the co-writer of Afghan MP Malalai Joya's political memoir, *A Woman Among Warlords: The Extraordinary Story of an Afghan Who Dared to Raise Her Voice.* We are also extremely lucky to have a preface to volume two written by Phil Hearse. A long-time Marxist and revolutionary leader, Phil was part of the student radicalization of the period the memoir covers and he was an active participant in some of the events described. One of the early founders of the Vietnam Solidarity Campaign (VSC) and International Marxist Group (IMG), he became one of the IMG's central leaders, including representing it on the leadership bodies of the Fourth International. His well-known website, *Marxsite*, and his writings circulate widely in the radical left in Britain and internationally. Readers, we are sure will find his assessment of those years insightful, as he provides an overview and draws a balance sheet of what was achieved by the revolutionary left in those tumultuous times.

Dedication

THE COMRADES LISTED BELOW, WHOSE NAMES APPEAR IN THIS BOOK, are no longer with us. They devoted their lives completely to the struggle for socialism. At various times they had a large influence on my life and are an important part of the story told here. I dedicate it to their memory:

Reg and Ruth Bullock (Canada)

Ross Dowson (Canada)

Pierre Frank (France)

Joe and Reba Hansen (U.S.A.)

Pat Jordan (Britain)

Tom and Karolyn Kerry (U.S.A.)

Ernest Mandel (Belgium)

Verne and Ann Olson (Canada)

Patricia (Pat) Schulz (Canada)

Ray Sparrow (Art Sharon) (U.S.A.)

Paddy Stanton (Canada)

A Word of Thanks

WRITING THIS BOOK WOULD HAVE BEEN ALMOST IMPOSSIBLE WITHOUT the help of my companion, Jess MacKenzie. Her patience and good humour were essential in helping me see it through to the end. Efficient at chasing down wayward facts and important information, she also photographed countless pages of archives for me on our many travels. Carefully reading each draft chapter after I had written it, she found my many errors and managed to curb my excesses. Aside from having an important part in the following story, she was also invaluable in finally getting it into print.

In the process of preparing this work, we consulted various archives in several countries, such as Library Archives Canada (LAC) the International Institute of Social History (IISH), Amsterdam, Warwick University Archives, Coventry, Britain and the Taminent Library in New York. Often working under the pressures of severe budget cuts, the staff of these important institutions was invariably helpful and cooperative. Of special importance were the folks at the Bertrand Russell Archives at McMaster University, Hamilton, Ontario. That's where we had the good fortune to meet Dr. Kenneth Blackwell, a key architect of the collection. He helped guide us through it, bringing to our attention important materials that we might have otherwise overlooked. We're grateful for his assistance. I also thank Richard Fidler for having read the chapters on Cuba and the birth of the New Democratic Party (NDP) and his comments about them.

Also valuable to us was the time we spent at the International Institute for Research and Education (IIRE) in Amsterdam, an independent research institution that is supported by the Fourth International. There we had the able assistance of Marijke Colle, its Director, and Hendrik Patroons, in finding our way through its archives.

Finally, I wish to thank the comrades of Resistance Books in London for taking the risk and having the courage to publish the final product.

Preface

NOT LONG AGO, I OVERHEARD A PROMINENT SOCIAL DEMOCRATIC POLITICIAN in British Columbia repeating an old saw sometimes attributed to Winston Churchill, "Any man who is not a socialist at age twenty has no heart. Any man who is still a socialist at age forty has no head." He was offering this line to the editor of the *Vancouver Sun*—a joking way to put a right-wing journalist at ease. The implication was clear: despite a left-wing public image, rest assured he understood the limits of things and could be trusted on to deliver reasonable and moderate policies.

The limits of debate in mainstream media and society at large are exceedingly narrow, and everyone these days it seems must rush to prove their moderation and reasonableness. In practice this means that—rhetorical flourishes and youthful exuberance aside—one must pay due tribute to big business and avoid threatening the prerogatives of corporate power. For a politician, it means letting a right-winger know you might be left-wing, but you're not one of those left-wingers. I offer this anecdote to illustrate the rotten state of political life today. The popularity of this cliche that suggests one must inevitably become more right-wing as one gets older is a sign of the deep cynicism of politicians and their ilk.

Against this cynical "common sense," fortunately, new generations are once again being won over to radical ideas. The Occupy Wall Street movement brought back the language of class struggle into popular circulation. Socialism is no longer a dirty word in North America. An openly socialist candidate was just elected to city council in Seattle. More and more environmentalists are reaching explicitly anti-capitalist conclusions. Young people are again seeking out the rich traditions of Marxist ideas —a new left is again taking shape to meet the daunting challenges of our times.

This memoir by Ernie Tate is a valuable resource for these new generations coming into political life. First, because this memoir contains a trove of movement history for us here in Canada, much of it documented in depth for the first time. For instance, Ernie recounts the formation of the Fair Play for Cuba Committee in Canada, and the singular contribution of Verne Olson. The solidarity movement built around defence of the Cuban Revolution helped to attract thousands in Canada to socialist ideas. Ernie also recounts his participation in the Cooperative Commonwealth Federation (CCF) and then the New Democratic Party (NDP), with a chapter focusing on the debates around the 1961 formation of that social democratic party. The political landscape has shifted a great deal in the half century since, but the discussions and dilemmas related to the NDP are still with us in Canada. This first volume of Ernie's memoir is an important contribution to the history of the Canadian left. Volume two covers his time as a socialist organizer in the UK, where he participated in the sometimes byzantine factional struggles of the Trotskyist movement, while also interacting with some of the towering figures of 20th century scholarship and progressive activism, including Bertrand Russell, Ernest Mandel and Isaac Deutscher.

Perhaps even more important than the particular historical details, this book tells the story of a life lived in the struggle for a better world. Ernie Tate's life shows us that age doesn't have to mean a gradual slide to the right. Age can just mean an accumulation of experience and wisdom—more compassion, less dogma and better political judgment. After growing up in poverty in Northern Ireland—leaving school at the age of 14 to work in factories—Ernie came to Canada and began his life of socialist activism in the mid-1950s, not long after the height of Cold War anti-communism. His career as a militant organizer began in those lean times for the left, but was then followed by the tumultuous youth radicalization of the 1960s and early 70s.

The past three decades of Ernie Tate's life and activism are sketched only briefly. He provides a rough outline of his disagreements with the leadership of the small socialist organization to which he belonged, and explains his reasons for eventually leaving active membership. This memoir recounts honesty the challenges and failures of socialist groups, unions and other progressive organizations. Despite these experiences, he has remained an active socialist, never wavering from his beliefs and ethics. This is a real achievement, and worth noting. Capitalism works to grind us down in our working life but also in our moral life. It takes strength of personality, in addition to collective organization, to resist cynicism.

I first met Ernie and his wife Jess close to a decade ago, through mutual friends in Toronto. They both exude warmth and humility—I felt an instant sense of comradeship. It's an honour to write a preface to this volume of Ernie's memoir. I hope more of his generation and his stature— the real organizers—write their memoirs. The left has in many ways adapted to the youth fetishization so rampant under capitalism, and so we pay too little attention to learning our own history or honouring the wisdom of our movement's elders.

We have a lot to learn. It's not easy to change the world; it's not, and it never has been, easy to wrest political power from the brutal and selfish ruling classes. But I think learning what previous generations have been through helps steel us for the long battle, helps us keep perspective and understand ourselves better.

This memoir also reminds us that there is dignity and joy in the struggle for a better world. And for all the trials and tribulations of the left, we are part of a real and proud tradition. Whatever their age, everyone with a heart to feel and a head to think should be a socialist.

Derrick O'Keefe
December 2013

Michel Lambeth

Ross Dowson at an organizing meeting in the basement of the Toronto Labour Bookstore, 569 Yonge Street during SEL's 1956 Toronto Mayoralty campaign.

Table of Contents

Introduction

*T*HE YEARS I WRITE ABOUT IN THESE PAGES WERE INDEED, HEADY and optimistic times for socialists, especially as we neared the latter part of the Sixties. Many of us even began to toss around the idea of "socialism in our time" because the political conditions seemed to be very promising as the ruling classes in many countries appeared to be losing whatever little moral authority they possessed over people. At any moment, one could expect news of an uprising somewhere in the world that put socialism on the agenda. There hasn't been a radical period like it. Those fifteen years saw the rise of the black civil rights movement in the United States, the beginning of the Quebecois struggle for independence in Canada, the victory of the Cuban Revolution and the rise in North America and Britain of massive resistance to the Vietnam War—which undoubtedly, helped bring an end to that war. In Paris, the tumultuous events of May 1968 were but a symptom of a general rise in political consciousness throughout Europe that even reached into Czechoslovakia, where mass opposition to Stalinism ran so deep, the Warsaw Pact countries under Moscow's leadership, invaded that country with hundreds of thousands of troops to violently suppress it.

It was a period of momentous radical upsurge that even saw new actors stride onto the stage of history. Masses of women demanded equality for the first time in a new feminist upsurge. Large sectors of the population—especially the youth—began to question the very logic of capitalism at a time when relatively small Marxist groups found a new and ever larger audience for revolutionary ideas and who, because of their political skill, agility, and passionate sense of solidarity with the colonial revolution, were able to help bring thousands people onto the streets in major cities everywhere in angry protests against the foreign policies of their governments.

This account is not a "history" of our organization during those years. Of necessity, I have been selective, and include only those activities that may be of special interest to the reader, or those activities in which I had been especially involved. I do not deal with all our campaigns of those years, only the major ones. For example, very little is mentioned here about our activities—very important ones—in developing solidarity with the Algerian revolution, nor do I say much about our work in Canada and Britain to support Neville Alexander, a black South African intellectual of the Unity Movement, jailed by the apartheid regime. Neither do I say anything about our work in Britain to defend Obi Egbuna, a black Nigerian militant, jailed on the basis of a manuscript of a novel the police had seized when they searched his home. They alleged it contained detailed plans for carrying out violence against the state.

Instead, what I have tried to do, not merely relying on my memory but backed up by research in several major public archives, is to give some idea of what it was like to be a new member and subsequently a leader of a revolutionary organization. I was a young unsophisticated class-conscious worker, who knew virtually nothing about socialism, a genuine neophyte, when I became a member of a small group that turned out to be part of the Fourth International that had been founded by Leon Trotsky in the thirties. I joined it not long after most of its members had been expelled from the Cooperative Commonwealth Federation (CCF), which the group's members had joined on the basis that the CCF, a social democratic party "represented a form of labour party" in Canada. The group was in the process of setting up the Socialist Education League (SEL) and producing the first issue of its monthly journal, the *Workers Vanguard*, when I came across it for the first time. I describe the group's daily life, how it functioned in some detail and even how it ran its membership meetings. I include its major personalities and its political activity as it tried to increase its influence and the special efforts it made to try and make up for the fact that as an organization, it only existed in two cities, Toronto and Vancouver.

For example, to compensate for this lack of representation elsewhere, every two years it organized a tour across the vast interior of Canada that often lasted up to six months. I participated in several of these and I have tried to describe what that entailed.

I also discuss how our organization viewed the formation of the New Democratic Party (NDP) at the beginning of the Sixties as it replaced the CCF, and how the change was resisted by the CCF in the west, which had moved to the left under Hazen Argue on the issues of the North Atlantic Treaty Organization (NATO), and the nationalization of industry. I also describe our experiences in the trade unions, especially the International Brotherhood of Teamsters where we became the centre of a rank-and-file caucus in opposition to a Jimmy Hoffa-imposed trusteeship. This put us in the position of leading several Ontario wide wildcat strikes, some of which lasted many weeks and did not end too well. As far as I know, this is the first time this record has been written up in any detail.

The Cuban Revolution when it took place at the end of the fifties, although a bit of a surprise, was nevertheless, a big deal for us. I describe how we organized to defend it against a right-wing propaganda offensive designed to quarantine it from the Canadian people. One of the most successful campaigns of its kind in the English-speaking world, there was broad support for it in the unions, in the newly formed NDP and on university campuses. Under the leadership of Verne Olson and his wife Ann, both of whom I knew personally and who were among the more experienced members of our group, we set up the Fair Play for Cuba Committee (FPCC). I relate some of the difficulties that Verne ran into in dealing with representatives of the Cuban government when the Committee was in the process of organizing students to tour the island. How we carried out our support for Cuba, would become a template later for how we built opposition to the Vietnam War.

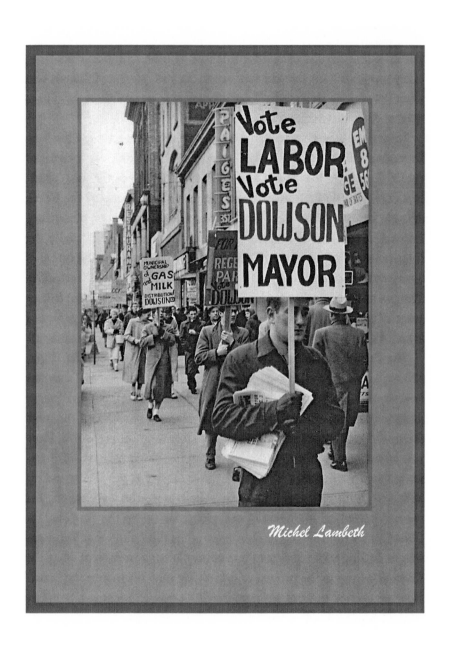

Michel Lambeth

The 1956 SEL campaign: Pat Mitchell (Schulz) at the back, me in the middle, and Jerry Houle in front

Chapter 1

Arrival in Toronto

*I*T'S OFTEN SAID THAT BECOMING A SOCIALIST CAN BE A CONTINGENCY— it depends upon whom you meet first—and certainly that was the case with me. An immigrant from Northern Ireland, I had arrived in Toronto in the spring of 1955. On a warm summer Sunday evening, as I wandered down Yonge Street with nothing much to do, looking in shop windows, I noticed a few interesting looking books in a shop just north of Wellesley, at number 569. The large sign above the window read: "Toronto Labour Bookstore." The store was closed. I made a point of returning a few days later, and this would be my first exposure to socialist ideas and the beginning of a life-long commitment to radical politics I have never regretted.

One of the first conversations I remember having with Ross Dowson, the person who ran the store and who would later have a large influence on my life, was about a novel that questioned Christianity's origins, by Robert Graves, the then well known English writer and poet that I had been trying to track down. His novel, "King Jesus," had been recommended to me for giving an alternative explanation to the Jesus myth.

Later Ross told me he had been at first curious that someone "just off the boat" from Ireland, so to speak, and who didn't seem to have much of an education, would be interested in a Graves' novel, and he thought this might possibly be "an expression of the higher cultural level" of British workers compared to Canadian workers. I wasn't so sure—his generalization seemed somewhat sweeping at the time—but I was happy to take the compliment anyway. He was always on the look-out for people sympathetic to his views. He suggested other titles, including Karl Kautsky's "Foundations of Christianity." I had never heard of it, or Kautsky. He didn't have the Graves book in stock, he said, but he would order it for me if I wished. That was a special feature of the store: he would order any book the customer wanted, a service not offered by many bookstores in those days.

It's true I didn't have much of an education. It was easy then for the British to get into Canada because its immigration policy privileged them and not much formal education was required. I had left school before my fourteenth birthday, the legal age at that time for school leaving in Northern Ireland. Most of the young people in the area where I grew up—Protestant working class Shankill Road—terminated their formal education at that age, or earlier if they could. In the whole time I lived in Belfast, I had never known or met anyone who had gone to a secondary school, never mind university. My family was the poorest of the poor. There was a common joke around my neighbourhood that had a lot of truth to it: "If anyone around here paid their rent two weeks in a row, the police would be visiting to see where the money came from."

Violence and drunkenness were part of popular culture and daily life as I grew up. Fist-fights could arise from even the slightest of disagreements. Near where I lived there were pubs on most of the street corners. I remember, as a young person, often witnessing on a Saturday night grown men fighting toe-to-toe on the street, usually with a crowd of onlookers around them. It was a kind of popular entertainment. Boxing was a very popular sport in Belfast and big-name boxers were big heroes to me and my friends. Most of my school-mates at one time or other became members of boxing clubs but it was a pastime I quickly abandoned when I found myself on the receiving end of a few hard punches.

I got my first full-time paying job in Greeves Linen Mills on Cooper Street when I was just fourteen. I became friends with a young Peter Sharpe, one of Northern Ireland's top amateur boxers who worked alongside me. My family lived across the street from Tommy Armour, an Irish welterweight professional champion and a hero of the neighbourhood.

The Belfast I had left to go to Canada was a gloomy and grey place, bigoted and impoverished, with the highest unemployment rate in Britain. Hostile to the South and to even the mere possibility of a "United Ireland," the Ulster Government was ruled by the iron hand of the Orange Order through the Ulster Unionist Party, whose MPs at Westminster were integrated into the extreme right-wing of the British Tory Party. Shamefully, these MPs, who were elected from some of the poorest working class areas of Western Europe, voted consistently against badly needed social reforms, such as the National Health Plan and the educational reforms that were brought in by the Labour Party in the years following World War II. Political representation for the Catholic one-third of the population had been reduced in Stormont, the seat of the government, by gerrymandering, and further reduced municipally by a voting system based upon property ownership, giving wealthier voters multiple votes, an arrangement that would later lead to a social explosion and the birth of the civil rights movement in the late Sixties. Aside from those features, Belfast in many respects resembled a typical English smoke-belt industrial city such as Birmingham or Coventry. And like those cities, it had expanded rapidly during the Industrial Revolution and with the spread of British colonialism. The Belfast ruling class from the beginning of England's occupation had been granted a favoured status in trade throughout the empire, with a monopoly in the linen industry alongside of which grew up a highly developed engineering industry for the servicing and manufacture of textile machines. Under British colonialism, most of Ireland's industry was concentrated in the north and the south's economy remained largely agrarian. One of the main centres in Britain for the manufacture of armaments and air-craft, the city was the home of one of the largest ship-building yards in the world, Harland and Wolff, out of which came the Titanic and many other large ocean liners.

The Great Depression had hit Belfast very hard and the years during the war were one of the few periods many workers ever had had a job, before or after. With the war's end, high unemployment returned anew. Problems of housing and slum conditions were common across both communities, Protestant or Catholic. But in comparison to the Catholics, the Protestants retained a privileged position that continues to this day. The Catholics were and are a persecuted religious minority. Prior to the First World War and in the interwar years—in a series of what we would term today "ethnic cleansing" campaigns organized by the Orange Order— Catholics were systematically driven out of skilled jobs in engineering and ship-building. In bloody rampages, Catholic families were "cleansed" from mixed communities and their homes frequently burned to the ground. My chums and I often played soccer in the large area of wasteland at Argyle and Cooper streets, where many of their houses once stood. Today, there is a large wall nearby separating the two communities, built after similar "religious cleansing" in the 1970s.[1]

During the Second World War, Harland and Wolff at its height employed more than 51,000 people. Of these, less than a thousand were Catholic and this mostly consisted of unskilled labourers. Jobs were handed out on the basis of whom you or your family knew. Foremen, openly members of the Orange Order, determined who was hired and who was promoted. And for a young couple getting married, it was commonly known—and without any sense of embarrassment—membership in the political arm of the Orange Order, the Unionist Party, which controlled City council, gave them the privileged position of getting to the top of the list for municipal housing.

I didn't have the good fortune of knowing anyone in the shipyards or in engineering who could help me land a decent job, so when I left school at the age of fourteen (actually thirteen: I simply did not show-up for classes the last few months and no one seemed to care), I started work at Greeves' Spinning Mill near the Falls Road. A large plant with over a thousand workers, it had an approximate equal mix from both communities. I still remember the call of the mill sirens in the mornings six days a week as I trudged the dreary streets along with hundreds of other workers streaming towards the factory gates. There were no unions in the mills then, and even though Catholics and Protestants worked alongside each other every hour of the day, little social mixing took place. I remember once when I was invited by a Catholic workmate to his home in the Lower Falls Road area, his mother became very agitated upon learning that I "came from the Shankill"; she warned me it wasn't a good idea for me to be in that part of town. At my young age, I was obviously naïve to the depths of the hatreds. Dating between the sexes across the two religions, needless to say, was intensely discouraged. Someone who crossed that line would soon become a victim of gossip and shunning, and could readily suffer violence, even from within their own family. Mixed marriages were indeed rare and during times of unrest, such hapless couples could be targeted for special treatment by Protestant thugs and could have their homes set ablaze. I worked at Greeves' spinning mill for two years, wheeling containers of combed flax from one section of the mill to the other for further processing, a dull, boring, and physically demanding job, especially for a young teenager. Finally, an uncle who was secretary of the Belfast Trades' Council got me a job at Andrew's Flour Mill on Townsend Street—using the traditional Protestant connections. That's where I served my apprenticeship as a miller, five years, which I completed in 1955, the year I left for Canada. The religious divide in the flour mill—with proportionally fewer Catholics, I recollect—was much sharper than in Greeves. I don't remember any social mixing or going for drinks together, which one would expect in a normal factory setting anywhere else in the world. I recall that whenever prominent members of the British royal family visited the city on their occasional official tours, the plant would be abuzz with speculation when the police would unexpectedly show up at the plant and pick up a few Catholic workers to hold until the visit was over. In 1953 during the time of the Queen's coronation, a couple of workers in my department did not show up for work one day because the police had raided their homes in the middle of the night and held them for three days. None of the other Protestant workers said anything about this and when the missing Catholics showed up after their release, it was as if nothing had happened and there was a wall between us and them about certain topics which couldn't be crossed or talked about. One of the workers who had been picked up by the police happened to be on the same work crew I was on and I got to know him better than most because we ate lunch together every day. He was an older man, in his forties, who I still remember after all this time. His name was Brian Gormley and from hints I heard from others, he was or had been a rank and file Republican activist. I was surprised at how readily he accepted the harassment, as if half expecting it in some kind of fatalistic way. He was one of the few people in those days who tried to explain to me how the division between Catholics and Protestants had kept the bulk of the population poor, and how the arch-reactionary Winston Churchill had intervened prior to the war to break up a growing unity in Belfast across the religious divide. Until then, it was probably my heaviest political discussion and it challenged some of my set beliefs about religion and class. Much later, when I became active in socialist politics, I took his name as a pseudonym out of respect for his memory.

I've always been intrigued about how a radical idea can enter one's thinking, even when only a child, and can often come from sometimes the strangest places. In my case, I can remember in school when I was twelve or thirteen years old, when we were being taught by a young "teacher in training"—it couldn't have been very long after the war because one day he talked to us about the intense cold of the Canadian prairies where he had trained in the air-force—and he told us about how the row housing lining the dreary streets which made up the slums of Belfast and where most of the young people who were listening to him lived, had been built by the wealthy linen mill-owners for their workforce. Despite accumulating great wealth, he told us with a tone of anger in his voice, they had not provided even the most basic necessities—no green space, no hot water, no indoor toilets, and no thought for the social or recreational needs of the people who lived in them. We, his young listeners, did not think they were slums, nor did we think they were such bad places to live. It was all we had ever known. It was only many years later when I was in Canada that I recognized what he was talking about had in reality come from Frederick Engels', "Condition of the Working Class in England." And I still remember very clearly another experience from a little bit earlier, that had an influence upon me and began to change my thinking when I was around ten or eleven and when I played with my cousin who lived across the street from me. One day I was talking to my aunt about religion, when out of the blue she asked me, "If God made the world, who made God?" I was startled by her question, and of course had no answer. She wasn't a sophisticated woman by any means, and probably only had a minimum of education, but she was totally irreverent with an outspoken opinion on just about everything. She laughed at my confusion, in a sort of triumph, and even though I had no alternate explanation, it was a question that rattled around in my young brain for a very long time.

From early on I read just about anything I could get my hands on, probably a form of escape from the awful material and intellectual poverty of my life. I read everything—from women's magazines, newspapers, to any kind of pulp fiction. The local public library was my main source for books and at least once a week I would visit it. Through reading I became vaguely conscious of my lack of education, and while working at the flour mill I began to think that getting a trade as a miller would be insufficient if I was to escape the fate of my peers and find a better life for myself. I had entered an apprenticeship programme and had completed a series of evening courses about the technology of grain milling, but as anyone who has done it knows, taking evening courses and working at a full time job at the same time, especially if one is on shift-work, will test the endurance of even the most dedicated. I was always wondering how it would be possible to get a fuller education when I got the idea I might be able to achieve it through athletics. Athletics, like everything else in Northern Ireland, was divided along religious lines in those days and I belonged to North Belfast Harriers, a cross-country running club in Ligoniel, near Cavehill and overlooking West Belfast. I had won a few club meets and had placed well in regular competition. The club was in a race every second week throughout the winter and, as a result, my time over distance was steadily improving. My ears pricked up one day when I heard about several Belfast runners who had won scholarships to American universities because of their ability to run a four minute, thirty-five second mile. That's all they needed, I heard. I'm sure there were other requirements, but my ignorance was such I didn't know enough to ask. By my twentieth birthday I found I was easily able to break five minutes and the idea began to germinate in my brain that if I got to Toronto, I could maybe train and do better and it would be my gateway into higher education.

By the time I arrived in Toronto, I wasn't totally apolitical. By my late teens I had already begun exploring ideas and was searching out weightier reading material that gave some explanation of the world and current events. Most of it I've now forgotten, but I remember being impressed with Paul Blanshard's books about Catholics in the U.S., oblivious to his Protestant biases. I also read the work of the American journalist John Gunther,[2] in order to try and understand America. I had even gone the route of attending the rallies of one of the evangelical crusades—usually organized by American preachers—that seemed to sweep through Belfast on a regular basis in those days, but I found them boring and always suspected they were something of a scam. This is how I progressed from a doubt about a God to ambivalence and then criticism and rejection. It was no big issue for me, I remember, no "moral crises" or great self-examination and I suppose it's the path taken by many who come to eventually reject religion. By the time I had arrived in Canada, even though I was looking to getting myself involved in athletics, I considered myself an atheist and communist, not truly understanding what these terms meant. But I knew enough to be aware that those in authority in our society hated the Soviet Union and the Communists, and seemed deathly afraid of them. If that was the case, I thought to myself, I was on the side of the Communists, more a form of iconoclasm on my part than anything else.

Such was my political formation when I first came across the Toronto Labour Bookstore in 1955. The store was run by Ross Dowson, then in his early thirties, slightly balding, slim and of medium height with much of the appearance of a small business man. Very conscious of his appearance, he exercised regularly and was very careful about his diet. He lived in the rear of store, in an area separated off, like a tiny apartment, with small kitchen, a toilet and a basin, but no shower or bath. He was between apartments at the time, he told me, but I later found out he was in this arrangement because of a lack of money and it was the only way he could live so that he could function as a professional revolutionary. It was his way of helping pay the rent for the store. "I am compelled to live behind the store so we can handle the rent..." he wrote to Joe Hansen, a leader of the American Socialist Workers Party.[3]

At the rear of the bookstore, stairs led down to a basement. A few times that summer as I was in the store browsing among the books, I would notice a person wandering casually through, saying hello to Ross and then heading to the rear and down into the basement—somewhat furtively, I thought to myself. I was curious as to where they were going and eventually I got to meet them. They were part of the rotation to help staff the store: Ruth and Jerry Houle, Pat and Jimmy Mitchell and sometimes Verne and Ann Olson—all, I would later learn, were leaders of the political group that owned the store. They were there usually on Friday evening and Saturdays—but Ross was the person who was there most of the time and with whom customers visiting the store would have the most discussions. And when things were not too busy—which was quite often—it was common to see him sitting at his desk beside the cash register, intently hammering away on an old Underwood typewriter getting out his correspondence, the noise clattering throughout the store. Not having learned to touch-type, he poked incredibly fast at the machine with his two fore-fingers and he was very proud that he could push out as many as ten onion-skin copies with each letter.

It turned out the Toronto Labour Bookstore was a kind of political centre, run in a very business-like manner, with a notice of fixed hours posted on the door, open every day, except Sunday. Political debate—sometimes argument—would often dominate the discussions. The bookstore, not very large, about twenty feet deep, carried a wide and intelligent selection of books, on every topic that might be of interest to anyone who was critically minded, but if a customer was interested in a book on a particular question, Ross would quickly order it. He selected the bookstore stock, which included a lot of radical monthly periodicals from around the world, but alongside them was an ample display of "skin" magazines, ranging from those about nudism to others verging on pornography. When challenged about carrying this kind of literature in "a socialist" bookstore, he would rebuff the criticism stressing the importance of socialists having a liberated attitude towards sexuality and being hostile to the hypocritical "Puritan" ethos of capitalist society which sought to censor such literature. Beside, he said, the high-markup helped subsidize the sale of the socialist books, which sort of settled the argument for many of us. I don't recall discussing in those days pornography as an aspect of women's oppression. That would come later, but I remember Pat Mitchell and Ruth Houle, two leading women in the group, complaining bitterly about the matter, saying it brought some creepy characters into the place, who came for the skin books and nothing else. But I suspect Ross' resistance to changing the store's policy may have been motivated, not only by his libertarian beliefs, but possibly because of his own sexual orientation. In the fifties, homosexuality was illegal in Canada and gays could suffer severe legal sanctions; Ross, who was gay, I was to discover, concealed his sexual orientation under a personal declaration that he was "celibate," often the refuge of gay men in those oppressive times to explain their apparent lack of interest in the opposite sex. Probably because of his influence—and unlike in the broader society—there was a much more tolerant attitude towards sexuality and gays in the group than existed for example in our sister organization, the American Socialist Workers Party. Although formally unrecognized as such, gays were active in the Toronto group. There were no barriers. Indeed, there was a strict code in the group that members' personal relations were topics outside the bounds of politics and their own business. I don't remember us talking formally about the matter or there being a formal discussion about the issue, but there was a severe prohibition about gossiping about a respective member's sexuality.

Aside from this, it's impossible to forget Ross' imperious declarations on this or that subject, a characteristic he maintained throughout his life. For him, it wasn't sufficient that someone who claimed to be a socialist be skilled in class struggle politics, they also had to have an opinion on such matters as art, architecture, anthropology or music. For many of us, being virtual blank slates on these issues—especially me with my low level of education—we often had the spaces in our brains filled with his powerful and strongly argued opinions. But I later came to realize that his forceful way of arguing his views concealed an important blind spot that probably limited his development as a thinker. As he would announce from time to time, it was his opinion that Marxism had resolved the major theoretical problems confronting socialists. "The more I read," he wrote to one correspondent, "... the more I have had to conclude that the main problems, the theoretical problems, have been resolved by the socialist movement—the task is to popularize and make known our ideas."[4] Not that I thought any differently at the time, but this tended to see Marxism as an immutable set of ideas rather than a body of work and a methodology that continually enriched itself from many diverse sources of intellectual work, and even from others outside the Marxist movement and from the living experience of the class struggle itself.

It wasn't long after I began visiting the bookstore that I was invited to the group's regular public monthly forums. These were usually held Sunday evenings at the Mineworkers' Hall on Isabella Street in downtown Toronto. My lasting memory of those forums—usually on a political topic of the day—was that they were often very poorly attended, sometimes by only a handful of people and at other times by around thirty. It became obvious there was some unhappiness with this state of affairs. One meeting I remember very well, even though I don't remember the topic, that had only a few people in attendance and with Paddy Stanton, a prominent member of the group, the speaker. You could plainly see the annoyance on his face, as he—to Ross' horror—looking at the empty seats in front of him, denounced all those "who had not shown up" and for not having the wit to know their own interests!

Sometimes the forum would be turned over to a visiting speaker. I remember one well attended forum where a platform was provided for Helen Sobell, the wife of Morton Sobell, who had been convicted in the United States in 1951 alongside the Rosenbergs on charges of spying for the Soviet Union and had received a thirty years sentence. Helen's visit to Toronto was part of her North American tour to talk about the case, part of her tireless campaign to get her husband out of jail. Her argument was that Sobell had been framed and was innocent, a position with which we all agreed. Whether he was guilty or not wouldn't have mattered much to the audience, most of whom supported the Soviet Union. Ross was the secretary of a small Sobell defense committee in Toronto that included a few members of the Labour Progressive Party, another name for the Communist Party. I remember participating in a picket line about Sobell outside the U.S. Consulate, mostly made up of the group's members and a few others. Over the years, I always wondered what eventually happened to Morton Sobell, until I read in the *New York Times* in 2008 that he had in fact been working for the Russians all along. He just didn't think he had done anything wrong.

When I first walked through the doors of the Toronto Labour Bookstore that summer in those horrible years of hysterical anti-communism, a political neophyte with no experience in any kind of political organization, I nevertheless considered myself a supporter of the Soviet Union. This sentiment might have come from a natural youthful rebelliousness on my part, but I'm sure it was also influenced by some the experiences I had had while on my first time out of Ireland, hitch-hiking with a couple of workmates in France during the previous summer. We had arrived in Paris on Bastille Day, the 14th of July, a couple of months after the French garrison at Bien Dien Phu had fallen, the final defeat of the French colonialists by the Vietnamese, led by General Vo Nguyen Giap. The French, in their arrogance, had thought they were invincible. But with the material help of Russia and China, the Vietnamese captured the French base after a historic fifty-seven day battle. This was all news to me and my workmates. We couldn't have found Vietnam on the map. The Paris papers were full of the news, but serendipitously at the time, we were staying at a large youth hostel, Stad Molotov in the south of Paris, which was run by a French Communist Party youth organization and the people running the hostel explained to us what was going on. We had booked in there solely because of its reputation as one of the least expensive hostels in Paris.

It was startling to see the effect of the Vietnam catastrophe on Paris. One evening as we walked along a main boulevard, we saw a massive flow of people heading towards the city centre. At first, we didn't know what to make of it. None of us spoke French. It was the largest gathering on the streets any of us had ever seen in our lives. It made the annual Twelfth of July Orange Order parades in Belfast look tiny. Thousands were coming and going and the streets were packed with automobiles racing around, horns blasting, flags and banners sticking out of the windows and flowing in the wind. Some were patriotic with the French tri-colour, and others red, with the hammer and sickle. Most people were very friendly and wanted to talk and there were discussions going on everywhere. It was like a gigantic festival. I was amazed by it all and as we continued our travels around France I began to think over the evils of colonialism and within a few months I began to look sympathetically at Communism.

When I first met the socialists at the Toronto Labour Bookstore, in my naiveté I initially suspected that they possibly might be members of the Communist Party who were hiding their real views because of the severity of anti-communist feelings in North America in that period. And that would have been perfectly understandable in those days. Toronto seemed very unlike Europe to me, or even good old reactionary Orange Belfast, where it was quite common to discuss ideas—no matter how outrageous—with people one met in everyday life. In 1955, "socialism" was a dirty word in Canada, as was "communism." It was still the height of the Cold War. The Korean War had ended a couple of years before with a Communist victory and every day it was common to see articles in the press about the possibility of nuclear war. For example, air raid shelters had been constructed in New York and it was quite normal to hear public warnings and see notices for air raid exercises organized by the authorities on a regular basis to prepare for the coming Armageddon.

I soon found out I was wrong in my suspicions about the people around the Toronto Labour Bookstore. It turned out they were extremely critical of Stalin, and they identified themselves to me as being "supporters of the Cooperative Commonwealth Federation (CCF)"; they referred to themselves sometimes as "the club." Most of their activities seemed to revolve around the bookstore. They were not a public organization and had no official title. I soon discovered they lived a kind of semi-clandestine existence. In fact, they had existed in Canada as a small revolutionary socialist organization since the 1930s and which had its origins in the Communist Party, under the leadership of Jack MacDonald and Maurice Spector, two founding leaders of that Party who had been expelled by the Stalinists after they had aligned themselves with Leon Trotsky. During the war, the group was declared illegal by the Canadian government and was forced into an underground existence, losing many of its members during the difficult conditions of the war years. At the war's end, the group reconstituted itself publicly as the Revolutionary Workers Party (RWP) and began publishing a journal, *Labour Challenge*. "In 1945," Ross Dowson would later write in evaluating this experience, "we had hoped the post-war revolutionary upsurge would result in the advanced workers deserting the CCF, bypassing the reformist stages in their development of political consciousness and move directly to the recognition of the need for a revolutionary vanguard party."[5] Behind this perspective also, was a conviction in the inability of capitalism to revive itself in the post-war period.

By the time I met up with the group, they had given up any existence as an independent or public political organization and were "entered" in the CCF, a tactic they were having some difficulty maintaining because in 1954 most of its members had been expelled, the news of which had been reported in newspapers around the world. Shortly after I met the group in 1955, it dawned on me that this was the same group I had first read about in the newspapers in Belfast when I was preparing to emigrate and when I was paying attention to any news coming from Canada. In red scare type articles, common in those witch-hunting times, it had been reported that a group of "communists" had been expelled from the CCF. During the expulsions, Paddy Stanton, a member of the CCF since 1934, was a spokesperson for the expellees and had put up a spirited defense against the leadership, arguing for the right of all socialists to be in the party because of its federated and working class character. The group managed to get some support from the ranks and a few prominent individuals in the party, including Colin Cameron, a popular left-wing Member of Parliament from Nanaimo, B.C. but not enough to reverse the expulsions. Fourteen were purged, eight of them "entered" members of the group, plus one from the CCF Youth. It would be but one of many expulsions the group would suffer during the course of its life, including from the CCF's successor, the NDP.

When I first came around, "the Club" still had a few remaining members in the Ontario CCF, but that was no longer its major area of activity. It was trying to recruit directly to itself, mainly through the Toronto Labour Bookstore and its public forums. I had been one of the group's first contacts in months, and they worked hard to recruit me and I remember becoming somewhat apprehensive when all of a sudden I received many invitations to visit various members' homes for supper. In Belfast, it was very unusual for people to invite relative strangers to their homes. "What do they want?" I thought to myself, suspecting an ulterior motive of some kind. I had never been around organized politics before and didn't realize this was part of the process of recruitment and how groups got new members. Because of the "entry" tactic, the process of recruitment was intensive and the "the Club" was compelled to balance the need to grow with the necessity of not revealing too much about its existence as a defined organization out of fear of other members being expelled from the CCF, and possible outright proscription.

The task of recruiting me had been given to Verne and Ann Olson, I soon discovered. One evening, out of the blue, Verne and Ann invited me for supper to their home in Swansea in the west end of Toronto.

Verne, who got around on crutches as a result of polio he had contracted as a child, was one of the main leaders of the group and he and Ann had the distinction of being the only couple in the group who owned a home. Later they would play an important role in defense of the Cuban Revolution and become leaders of the very successful Fair Play for Cuba Committee (FPCC). After a few visits to their home, they finally explained to me that "the Club" was in reality "a revolutionary party," and proposed that I become a member. I readily agreed. Soon I was attending "branch" meetings, a branch being a local unit of the organization. There were only two "branches" in the entire country—one in Vancouver where members met in each others' homes, and one in Toronto, that met every Wednesday evening in the basement of the bookstore, surroundings that gave a kind of clandestine atmosphere to the proceedings. Very quickly I realized I had taken on a whole set of ideas, some of which I barely understood, as I began my participation in the life of the organization. It was a momentous step for me and everyone made a point of warmly welcoming me into their ranks, which were not many. There were about ten people at my first meeting, out of a total membership of about fifteen in the Toronto area.

In my new country, the anti-Communist witch-hunt still set the political tone for discourse in much of the working class and had subsided little from the time of the media hysteria surrounding the Igor Gouzenko affair and the jailing of Communist Party MPs Sam Carr and Fred Rose just after the end of the Second World War. Right up into the fifties, Communists were still being expelled from many trade union Local's executives, and the word "socialism," as I've mentioned, was an anathema to many. Outside radical circles, socialism couldn't even be mentioned in casual conversation, such was the feeling of hostility towards radical ideas. My first overwhelming sense of the organization I had just joined was its small size and isolation but everyone seemed very conscious that the witch-hunt hysteria might succeed in distancing the group from any meaningful connection to the working class, causing it to become sectarian, and eventually destroying it, or at least making it more difficult for working class militants to be won over to its views. The members aspired to be "normal" and eschewed any style of dress or behaviour that might further isolate them, but on becoming part of the group, one unavoidably became part of society's "bohemia" and "Avant garde." We were very much out of step with the times. For my part, it was the beginning of a conscious commitment to socialism that would change my thinking in fundamental ways, something I would not have even dreamt about when I first looked in the window of the Toronto Labour Bookstore shortly after I had gotten off the boat from Ireland.

Michel Lambeth

Top Jimmy Mitchell, Max Armstrong (among the founding leaders of the early Socialist Party of Canada), Jerry Houle and Ross Dowson

Bottom Clockwise around the table, with back to the camera, Max Armstrong, Jerry Houle, a person unknown and Peter Metheus (Joe Johnson)

Chapter 2

The World Party of Socialism

*I*WASN'T IN THE "CLUB" VERY LONG BEFORE I LEARNED FROM MY NEW comrades that aside from being "a revolutionary party," they considered themselves to be "the Canadian section of the Fourth International (F.I.)" I had no idea what this meant. It was the first I had ever heard of it. They told me it had been formed in 1938 under the leadership of Leon Trotsky, the leader alongside Lenin of the Russian Revolution. After Lenin's death, the rest of the world's Communist Parties had fallen under Stalin's sway and had become mainly foreign policy instruments of the Union of Soviet Socialist Republics (USSR). It was the beginning of my education about Russia, the attitude to which was a fundamental feature of the group's politics.

The Fourth International was tiny compared to those Internationals that had preceded it. The First International was founded by Karl Marx and Friedrich Engels in 1864 and lasted until its dissolution after the 1871 Paris Commune. With the rise of the workers' movement in Europe, especially in Germany, Marx and Engels founded the Second International in 1888. With the failure of the Second International on the outbreak of the First World War— its parties supported their respective governments' war efforts—the Bolsheviks under Lenin and Trotsky organized the Third International, which they envisioned would provide the general staff for what they believed was an impending world revolution. All these early Internationals were based upon mass organizations in various countries around the world. Trotsky, when he was preparing to launch the Fourth International, was aware that it would be by no means a mass organization and would be mainly comprised of small groupings in several countries around the world. His initial hope was that the Soviet bureaucracy would be overthrown in a political revolution and a resurgent working class in the USSR would provide a base for the new organization. When that turned out to be very unlikely, he came to believe that the coming horrors of the Second World War would lead to a powerful revolutionary upsurge and the new International would win a mass influence and possibly lead the working class to socialist revolution, a continuation of the world revolution which had begun in Russia in 1917. Trotsky was assassinated in 1940 in Mexico by an agent of Stalin, just as the war was beginning to unfold, and, by the war's end, most of the organizations supporting his views were decimated.

Despite Trotsky's optimism and hopes, except for a scattering of countries such as Bolivia and Ceylon—now Sri Lanka—the new International remained comprised of relatively small organizations. In the advanced capitalist countries of Western Europe, at the end of the war and in the immediate post-war period during a rapid rise of working-class militancy, it was the Communist, Social Democratic and Labour parties that saw their ranks swell. At its Third World Congress in 1951, the Fourth International set out to chart a new course to deal with this reality. The previous Congress had been in France shortly after the end of the war when it expected a revolutionary upsurge to sweep Europe and cast the traditional workers' parties aside. The 1951 Congress set about trying to deal with the new conditions facing the movement, especially the growth in influence of the Communist parties. For example, in Yugoslavia the Communist Party, led by Josip Broz Tito, had taken power and was implementing a planned economy, after defeating fascism in a guerrilla struggle. The Communists in Yugoslavia were in a battle with Stalin so their country could chart its own course domestically and in international relations. In Eastern Europe in the years immediately after the war, the countries bordering the Soviet Union, whose pro-fascist regimes had collapsed in the course of the defeat of the German army, had been maintained for a while as "buffer countries," with their capitalist economies and governing coalitions intact (although pillaged by Russia under the guise of "war preparations") but with the onset of the Cold War they had their economies nationalized and brought under state control. In China the Communist Party took power in 1949 after a long peasant war against the American backed dictator, Chiang Kai-Shek, whose Koumintang regime had fled to the island of Taiwan. In many countries such as Italy and France, the Communist Parties, that had led the resistance to the fascist occupations, had increased their influence as mass working class parties, even in some cases by-passing the social democrats in political and social influence, but wherever they could they had entered into coalition governments with the capitalist parties. War was raging in Korea with the intervention of the Americans to prevent the unification of the country under the control of the Korean Communist Party. Use of the hydrogen bomb against China was being pushed by sections of the American ruling class. It was universally anticipated that nuclear war would break out at any time.

So real was the fear of war, that some of the European leaders of the Fourth International were pointing to the month of June 1953, as the date when this catastrophe would occur.[1] If this were to happen, they asked, what would be its effect upon the Communist and Social Democratic parties? The 1951 F.I. Congress had speculated that they would go into crises under such pressures and that left-wing forces would then emerge to challenge the policies of their leaderships, leading to possible splits and a re-alignment of all those who considered themselves to be revolutionary. The delegates feared that the organizations of the F.I. would be rendered irrelevant in this eventuality if they did not take special measures to link up with such possible new forces. Michel Pablo, who was the main leader in Europe, looked to a tactic that had first been proposed by Trotsky in the 1930s to the French section, that is, a short-term "entry" into the French Socialist Party to link up with a left opposition that was evolving revolutionary positions and breaking from the right-wing. The American Socialist Workers Party had utilized a similar tactic in 1936 by "entering" Norman Thomas' Socialist Party for eighteen months—they suspended publication of *The Militant*, their weekly—to build what eventually became the Socialist Workers Party.[2] Jack MacDonald and Maurice Spector, in the Socialist Workers' League in Canada, had been expelled before the war from the CCF, having "entered" that party.

The "entry tactic" deployed in those earlier instances was seen as a short-term measure only, designed to take advantage of developing political opportunities in those parties and to help lead the opposition forces, whoever they might be, in a revolutionary direction. The "entry tactic" proposed by the Third World Congress in 1951 however, was very different in that it was seen as a "long term tactic," an "entry tactic sui generis" as its originators characterized it, with all independent work of the organization subordinated to it. In Argentina, it meant "entry" into the Peronist movement and in Bolivia an orientation to the bourgeois nationalist, Movimiento Nacionalista Revolucionario (MNR). In France and Italy, this meant "entry" into the Communist Party, in Britain, "entry" into the Labour Party, and in Canada, "entry" into the CCF with the virtual disappearance in those countries of any public face of the F.I. It became the basic tactical orientation in Europe right up until the end of the Sixties.

The resolutions of the 1951 Congress containing the analysis and the new political perspectives, including the "entry tactic sui generis," received the overwhelming endorsement of the delegates, including the leadership of the SWP who had attended the Congress as observers (a condition forced upon them because of the punitive requirement of the Voorhis Act that legally prevented them from belonging to any international organization). However, it wasn't long after the 1951 Congress, that tensions flared up over how the new tactic was being interpreted and the SWP became very alarmed when an opposition developed in New York led by Bert Cochran, Mike Bartell and Harry Frankel (later better known as Harry Braverman, a major intellectual who later wrote for *Monthly Review*), an opposition that claimed for itself a special understanding of the 1951 Congress' line. This was a worrisome development for the SWP, as Joe Hansen many years later told Isaac Deutscher, because "it involved the first rift in our basic cadre" since 1939–40.[3] Moreover, they were, according to James P. Cannon, encouraged in their activities by Michel Pablo, the then International Secretary in Paris, whom the Americans accused of setting up a secret personal faction, loyal to him. Cannon accused Pablo of inappropriately intervening in some sections—namely the British and the French—to try and overturn majorities in the sections who had developed differences with the new international line, a way of functioning that Cannon termed "Cominternism," likening it to the practice of Stalin in transforming the parties of the Third International (the Comintern), into subservient vehicles for the policies of the Soviet bureaucracy, a process by which they became foreign policy instruments for the USSR. The upshot was that the SWP issued an "Open Letter," calling for the formation of "an anti-Pabloite faction" to resist the Paris centre, leading to a factional struggle that resulted in a "cold split," lasting from 1953 to 1964. The majority of the French section led by Pierre Lambert, the British led by Gerry Healy, the Swiss, the Canadians led by Ross Dowson, the Chinese, led by Peng Shu-Tse, among others from around the world, declared their support for the SWP-led faction.

The Canadian group, when I met it, had gone through this faction fight the previous year and had lost almost half the Toronto branch when the pro-Pablo people, who were termed "the Rose group"—the name of its leader, Joe Rosenthal, Ross' brother-in-law, who used the pseudonym "Rose" for security reasons—walked out in 1954. I remember Ross telling me with some glee how, not trusting the other side he had swiftly changed the locks on the doors of the group's small bookstore and office when he received a hint from his sister that a split was in the offing. He was afraid, he said, they might abscond with the files and records. This, of course, resulted in an avalanche of bitter denunciations against Ross for his "undemocratic" behaviour, but that didn't seem to bother him one bit, when he talked about it later. In fact, I remember him being proud of it. But there were losses on the majority side too, from people who had simply grown tired of the struggle and who wanted to get on with their personal lives. Barry Brent, a young leader in Toronto, was one. He had been in Vancouver working with the branch there and had returned to Toronto before the faction fight. After I joined, I met him on a few occasions whenever he dropped into the bookstore on Yonge Street. He was then working on Bay Street making his living in a brokerage company. A very capable writer, he had supported Ross in the dispute with the Rose group.

In many respects, the disagreement in Canada took on all the appearances of a family dispute because Joe Rosenthal was married to Ross' sister, Joyce. (Joe later became a very successful artist and illustrator in Toronto). Murray Dowson, one of the founders of the group and Ross' brother, the editor of the group's paper immediately after the war, also supported Pablo and Rosenthal. Hugh Dowson, another brother, supported Ross. A tool and die maker by trade, Hugh worked for many years in Douglas Aircraft where he was active in the UAW and represented the local on the Toronto and District Labour Council. The Dowson family gatherings, Hugh once told me, especially at Thanksgiving and Christmas, were often very uncomfortable affairs, as they all tried to keep up a fake cordiality, just for their mother's sake. The hostility was very intense. At one point in the dispute, Ross accused the Rose people of voting with the right-wing of the CCF against Ross' supporters when they were being expelled in 1954.[4]

Chapter 3

The Club

WHEN I ENCOUNTERED IT IN THE SUMMER OF 1955, THE "CLUB" WAS still in the recovery stage from the previous year's split. It had picked up a few people during the course of the expulsions from the CCF, among them Harry Paine, Pat Mitchell, George Bryant and Joe Rosenblatt. (George had been in the group a couple of years before me and was working at renovating homes to make a living, but his real passion was photography and documentary film making, having worked with John Grierson on documentary films at the National Film Board.) Another person with a passion for photography who was around our group in those years, and who stands out in my recollection of them, is Michel Lambeth, not so much for his engagement with our politics, but for what he would later become. I don't recall if he was ever a member, but he attended our branch meetings from time to time—sometimes close sympathizers would be invited to sit in—and our monthly forums. It's when he took up photography full time. Because I left for Vancouver a few years later, I don't remember how long he was around, but many of the photos in the early *Workers Vanguard* are his. In poverty most of his career, he committed suicide in 1977, a terrible loss.[1] I have included in this volume some of his early work covering the SEL's 1956 mayoralty campaign, not only because of its high quality, but also because his images reveal the faces of some of the men and women who appear in this memoir, especially in the early years.

A long-time friend of Ross'—who also was interested in photography —and of Ross' generation, I remember Michel having a reticence about him that bordered on shyness. Looking at him, you wouldn't have figured he had been a tank-gunner in WWII. Exceptionally talented and inspired by Andre Breton, the great French photographer, his work reminds me of Dorothea Lange's, the great American photographer famous for her work in the Depression. A giant in the history of Canadian image making and unrecognized by the cultural establishment during most of his lifetime, it has only been in recent years that the importance of his work, a treasure trove of which is in Library Archives Canada (LAC),[2] has come to be appreciated by serious students of the medium.

Most of the above people would play an important role in the future of the group over its life. But the "Club" was tiny. By November it had a grand total of eighteen members on the books.[3] Alan Harris, a recent immigrant from England, and I were its first recruits that year. I was later to learn that there had been other splits prior to the Rose dispute. With the decline of radicalization after the end of the Second World War a few people had walked away at that time, some because of the Fourth International's opposition to Zionism and the formation of the State of Israel. But in my youthful enthusiasm in 1955, I was surprised it was so small. At my first meeting in the basement of 569 Yonge Street, about a dozen people were present. This must be but one branch among many, I thought to myself, but I couldn't have been more wrong. It was small and isolated, with another branch in Vancouver, slightly smaller and a few individual supporters here and there across the country.

I was uneducated, true, but I am sure I had a primitive class consciousness, that I think may have been the beginning of a political awareness on my part and which is why I found the group so attractive. It was obviously small and limited in its activities. Yet for me as a young person, joining a socialist organization, no matter how small, was like at last awakening from a long sleep. Vague ideas and feelings I had about society that I had come to by myself, now began to be integrated into a systematic historical and political outlook, a new understanding about the world and how society is organized and a conviction about the grim future of humanity if fundamental change did not take place. Above all, it gave a coherent expression to what had been a sense of injustice, that I had until then been unable to articulate. Questions about why the working people whom I had grown up amongst should have their lives materially impoverished and their development as human beings intellectually stunted in the linen mills and factories of Belfast in order that a few owners could become even wealthier than before. The idea that God and religion is a product of man, and not the other way around, that the economic system of capitalism is not humanity's normal existence, to paraphrase Trotsky, but only a stage in the historical development of society, was intoxicating. For a young person, these new insights, compensated for all the problems that might confront a small socialist organization as it made its way in the world. This is the true power of Marxism, I discovered: it provides a powerful tool for even the most illiterate to understand the economic relationship of capitalist exploitation, the extraction of surplus value from workers' labour, about knowing how society functions for the benefit of the capitalists who rule through their political parties. It also enables workers to grasp their own history—"all history is a history of class struggle"—and that they carry on their shoulders the future of humanity. To this day I have always separated those two phases of my adult life: the period before and after joining the group, which is not to deny the truth that a person's attachment to a political grouping is often accidental, as I say at the beginning of these "recollections," the luck of the draw, so to speak, contingent upon whom one meet first.

I remember that the "Club's" business meetings, although small, were exceptionally well organized. "How can we organize a revolution, if we can't organize our own meetings properly?" they would ask themselves. Workers expect us to be business-like, and not waste time, my new comrades would say. Elections took place annually in the group for a Branch Organizer and a branch Executive Committee, from which several sub-committees were formed to lead such work as CCF and trade-union activity and any campaigns in which the branch might be involved. A chairperson was elected at each meeting, which usually lasted about two to two and a half hours and was held weekly. The chair's function was to make sure the business of the meeting was conducted efficiently and democratically and a dim view was taken of any chairperson who utilized their position to speak at length or used the position to project their own views. Possible recruits—known as "contacts"—were discussed regularly and individual members were assigned to speak to them. Absences were reported to the meeting with explanations, and recorded. And there was great annoyance if a meeting started late; "Why are we wasting time?" members would ask. The agenda was always the same and comprised of a list of items beginning with a reading by the secretary of the minutes of the previous meeting followed by a vote to accept them. Business arising out of the previous minutes would be reported on by the branch organizer and incorporated into the agenda. Reports from the various sub-committees of the branch were always presented with time allocated for discussion, such as a trade union report or a report from the executive or educational committee. A financial report was given by the Financial Secretary at least once a month and the books were always balanced. At every meeting, dues, a nominal amount set by the constitution, were collected. Members, however, in addition to contributing to an annual fund drive, were expected to make a regular monthly financial "pledge" over and above the dues, based upon what they thought they could afford. This was usually set after a discussion between the new recruit and the treasurer and was considered to be the most democratic way to finance the organization, which could not survive on dues alone. Those who earned the most gave the most, and whatever they gave was seen as an important expression of that member's commitment to the organization. If a member was stingy in this regard, it would be doubtful if they would be elected to anything in the organization. A short educational discussion was scheduled for each meeting, lasting about half an hour, usually in the middle of the agenda. It was often where new members would learn to speak publicly for the first time, usually around a prepared topic, either a current political question or a Marxist classic. I remember soon after I joined being persuaded to prepare some introductory comments on

Engels' "Socialism, Utopian and Scientific," which I remember I inarticulately mumbled my way through. I think I got more out of the presentation than the branch members, but this was seen as a crucial way to raise the political understanding of new recruits. In addition, study sessions were organized on special texts such as Trotsky's *History of the Russian Revolution,* Marx's *Capital* and the *Communist Manifesto.*

The first job I got soon after arriving in Toronto was at a department store, Eaton's, one of the largest in the country. All the money I had saved in Belfast for my trip to Canada was about exhausted. The guy at the Unemployment Insurance Office wasn't very reassuring when I went to see him and wondered out loud why I had come at such a bleak economic time. My heart sank. Unemployment is high, he said. Unfortunately I had the misfortune to arrive when the post-war boom had been interrupted by a recession, and lay-offs were taking place everywhere. Around a million were unemployed across the country. He suggested I try Eaton's. I'd never heard of the place. "They hire a lot of Irish there. I've sent them quite a few people from Northern Ireland," he said, "and they always do well." Timothy Eaton was originally from Belfast. And sure enough, I got a job in the Fur Department, in the College Street store at Yonge Street, but I left after two weeks when I received my first paycheque of $60.00. I had at first figured they had made a mistake and went over to the accounting department, thinking they had only paid me for one week instead of two. But I was wrong. I later discovered Eaton's—like most non-union places—was notorious for its low pay. I knew other people who worked there and I found out that the only way many of them could survive on the low wages was by stealing inventory from the store, such as cameras and other items, sometimes to order, to supplement their income. "Shrinkage" at Eaton's must have been huge.

After my brief stay at Eaton's, I was pretty confident that, if necessary, I could get a job in a flour mill somewhere because of my training in Belfast. I had been avoiding that route because it would have meant a life of steady shift-work. Flour milling is a 24/7, continuous process. In Belfast I had found shift-work very disruptive of my social life and I wasn't keen to see the same thing happen again. After a few days of looking for work, however, the need for money finally overcame my feelings about the unpleasantness of shift-work. I headed out to Maple Leaf Milling in the Junction district in Toronto's west end, a large mill now no longer there, which employed approximately 300 workers. I was hired on the spot and the pay was pretty good for those days, $1. 50 and hour making the $60 a week—about twice what I was getting at Eaton's and a lot more than I had ever earned in Belfast. By my calculation, simply taking the boat to Canada had about doubled my standard of living. I could now afford to buy an automobile, and eat in restaurants, which would have been impossible in Belfast.

I soon discovered that the flour-milling industry in Canada was very different from that in Britain and that it did not require the same level of skills I had acquired with my apprenticeship. In Britain most of the wheat for breadmaking was imported, impacting the country's balance of payments difficulties, a lingering problem from the war. Out of economic necessity, to produce white flour, the wheat, by government regulation, had to be milled to very high efficiencies, as much as 85%, with the remainder of the kernel, the bran, going to animal feed. This demanded higher skills and training on the part of the mill operators, along with heavy bleaching by chlorine to produce the white product beloved by mass-production bakeries. By contrast, in North America, where hard wheat, Manitoba Red, was abundant and inexpensive, it was milled to only 40% efficiency, or even less. This meant, for example, that the high speed rolling mills which crack and grind the kernels of wheat in the milling process, the heart of the operation, required very few skills to adjust and maintain. Maple Leaf's milling's machines were adjusted at the beginning of the shift and the wheat blasted through them with hardly anyone paying attention for many hours. Even though I was paid more, I didn't see much of a future for myself in that industry, but it is where I had my first experience of being in a union.

Maple Leaf Milling was organized by the United Packinghouse Workers of America (UPWA), a predecessor of the Commercial and Food-workers union, one of the more militant unions in the Ontario Federation of Labour (OFL) in those years and had been an early proponent of the CCF. It was my first experience of working in Canada and I was immediately appalled at the level of prejudice against immigrants, often expressed in the daily banter between the workers. Not against English speaking workers such as myself, but there were crude epithets and name-calling against Italians and Ukrainians, referred to commonly as "wops" and "DPers."[4] Belfast was almost totally white when I left it for Canada. Only a handful of Jews and Blacks lived there. They were virtually invisible as minorities, and while there was anti-Semitism and racism, it was never much of an issue that I remember. I had never personally met any Jews or Blacks until I came to Canada. The only naked prejudice I had ever witnessed in Belfast was against Catholics, even though I probably would never have recognized it as such. As I've discovered since, it's common for members of an oppressing majority not to recognize their own prejudices. The prejudice in the flour mill in my adopted country was new to me and shocking, and with my newfound burgeoning political awareness about the need for worker solidarity, irrespective of creed, race or nationality, I finally talked it over with my new comrades. They suggested I approach the local's executive about writing an article on the subject for the local's monthly bulletin and when I mentioned the idea to the local's president, he happily agreed and Ross helped me write a short piece. In truth, it was mainly Ross' effort with my name on it, and it impressed the hell out of the local's leadership so much, very soon they proposed that I become Recording Secretary, to which, after discussing it in our trade union fraction, I agreed. I was soon elected and became active in the local and got to meet other militants in locals of the UPWA, such as in the large Canada Packers plant nearby. These connections would prove very valuable in the CCF Youth, but more about that later.

I was only in the mill a year before I managed to get myself fired. I would like to say this was the result of militant union activity, but it wasn't. I had no one to blame but myself, because I had become so intensely active—attending meetings both in the CCF and the group's activities, as well as socializing with my new comrades—I would often get to bed so late at night I would have difficulty getting up in the mornings and would get into work late. Besides I was getting fed-up with shift work. After a few warnings from my foreman, they showed me the door.

"The Club" didn't have a newspaper when I first made contact with it, but it was expert at getting leaflets and brochures out quickly on the political issues it deemed important, on an as needed basis. One issue was racism. Toronto was much more of a white-bread kind of city than it is now, and the Black population was very small, concentrated mainly in the Spadina and Dundas area and suffering, as it did in the rest of Canada, from deep prejudice. This was on full view one evening at the Palais Royale, a large ballroom on Lakeshore Boulevard, when staff intervened to prevent a black man from dancing with a white woman, humiliating them and ejecting them onto the street. The couple had openly breached Toronto's unofficial form of segregation under which very little social mixing took place between blacks and whites. The Palais Royale was well known for its racist policies. In response, some activists in the black community organized a picket line to protest the incident the following weekend. "The Club" was very active in getting support for the picket line, collaborating with Danny Braithwaite, a young black activist who worked in the United Rubber plant in Toronto and who was one of the leaders of the protest, helping him publish leaflets on the issue and circulating them throughout the unions. After a lot of publicity in the press and a series of picket lines outside their premises, the management of Palais Royale finally relented and changed their policies. This was a couple of few years before the civil-rights movement burst onto the scene in the U.S. so it was seen in those difficult times as an important victory for the local black community in Toronto. Even though "The Club" did not have its own newspaper, its ability to quickly produce and circulate leaflets about the evils of racism, allowed it to have an important influence upon this event and it won the respect of many black activists because of it.

And when Paddy Stanton, a welder in the construction trades, had charges preferred against him in the International Iron Workers Union by the bureaucracy for being "a Trotskyist Communist" and "disrupting the local," he was expelled and had his union card lifted. One of the older members of "The Club," he had been a leader of the group on the West Coast. He had come out of the One Big Union and the Wobblies (the International Workers of the World) that had been strong in British Columbia in the thirties, and for several years, he had been chairman of the Labor Council in Prince Rupert where "The Club" had a small grouping of supporters. He had apparently "disrupted the local" in Toronto by having it protest a visit to the city by the notorious anti-Communist witch-hunter, Senator Joe McCarthy and by urging other Iron Worker locals to do likewise. Paddy's expulsion meant he was immediately deprived of making a living. Like most unions in construction, the Iron Workers had a "hiring hall" clause in their contract that meant only members holding valid union cards could get work. At Paddy's "trial," information about his "Trotskyist-Communism" was provided to the witch-hunters by the CCF, from which he had recently been expelled. In response, "The Club" hired a lawyer and launched a vigourous campaign to have him reinstated, publishing several leaflets under his signature, criticizing the leadership of his union, which were then circulated in the Toronto Labour Council and throughout the labour movement. Because of this pressure, he finally managed to have his union card in the Ironworkers returned to him and was able to work again at his trade, but he was banned from ever attending union meetings, a ban that would last the remainder of his life.

Michel Lambeth

From left: Harry Paine (partly obscured), Alan Harris, 'Peter', whose surname I can't remember, and Jimmy Mitchell.

Chapter 4

The Socialist Educational League

TOWARDS THE END OF 1955, MY NEW COMRADES CEASED BEING THE anonymous sounding "The Club," and took the name, Socialist Educational League (SEL), a name artfully conceived to make it slightly more difficult for the CCF leadership to expel members they had not yet discovered. It began publishing a monthly journal, *The Workers Vanguard*, the same title as a paper put out by Jack MacDonald and Maurice Spector when they had been expelled from the Communist Party in the thirties. Paddy Stanton became the National Chairman and Ross its National Secretary. Jim Mitchell became editor of the paper but in actual practice, Ross was very much in control because he was the only one in the group with the capability to carry out that function. He had been the editor of *Labour Challenge*, the Revolutionary Workers Party's paper, published in 1946. The American SWP, to help the Canadians take advantage of the radical upsurge that swept the country immediately after the war, had assigned one of its leading cadres, whose name I can't remember, a skilled journalist, to re-locate to Toronto for more than six months, including financially supporting her. She trained Ross and the people around him in basic journalism. That paper lasted until 1951. The new paper's name, *Workers Vanguard*, was more of a promise to the future than a reality, but it expressed very accurately how the group viewed itself as a "vanguard" party of the working class—if not in physical reality, then in the realm of ideas and programme, as Ross expressed it a couple of years later. "(W)e are a party in that we have a distinct programme and tradition, and not only in numbers," he wrote. I remember we would explain to ourselves and our sympathizers once we got to know them, that "the SEL was the form the Fourth International in Canada took at that time."[1] A lot of the group's energy went into the paper's writing, production and circulation. Each day, Ross would faithfully mark Toronto's *Globe and Mail* with a dark, soft pencil, eventually to be clipped by any member or supporter who happened to drop into the office, even on their lunch hours, for the use of those of us writing articles for the paper or for someone preparing to give a talk at a coming forum. Then they would be sorted in preparation for the editorial meeting. There was always a large pile of these waiting to be clipped, piled on a large ping-pong table in the basement of what we called our "headquarters."

It was assumed everyone would write for the paper and most of us tried our hand at it at one time or another. For me, it was always a painful process. I had little formal education and had not written anything for publication—ever. That I would ever write for anything had never ever entered my head. Back in Belfast among my friends there were absolutely no literary aspirations of any kind. Unlike other members of the SEL, who had had some high school or other training, I was virtually illiterate. I often felt ashamed of how little I knew. When an article would eventually be produced under my name after much sweat and tears and encouragement from my comrades, there would be much re-writing and editing of the text and sometimes arguments about cutting this or that to make it fit the paper. The *Workers Vanguard*'s circulation jumped in the summer and dropped dramatically in the winter, with a base of around a thousand paid subscriptions. Every summer the SEL would organize a subscription campaign—an introductory offer of fifty cents for six months—in working class areas of the city, especially in those areas where the CCF received a high vote.

Without having looked at the paper recently, my impression of those early issues of the paper was that they looked awfully "heavy," a word we would use to describe written material that wasn't very accessible to the average reader. The paper was very much marked by Ross' writing style and sometimes he would laugh about his articles being criticized "for looking as though they had been written by someone whose first language was Russian." The abbreviations and acronyms in the headlines of the new paper were sometimes strange looking; to get more words in, the titles would occasionally be incomprehensible to anyone who was not on the left. Looking at a bound volume from those years, and considering our limited resources, I now realize it was pretty good. It could have been better, of course, but considering the lack of experience of most of us it holds up very well. It looks well written and lively with a laser sharp focus on the working class politics of the period.

Elections, when the opportunity arose, were an important part of the SEL's activities. During the Second World War, having been forced underground, the Trotskyists had no public expression, but immediately after the war, in 1946, amidst the radical upsurge in Canada that followed it, they had formed themselves as the Revolutionary Workers Party (RWP) and contested the municipal elections, the results of which gave the Toronto establishment a bit of a fright. In 1946, Murray Dowson, Ross' brother, got 11% of the votes for Mayor. The following year, Ross headed the ticket and got 24,000, or 17% of the total votes cast. It was a large vote for a small revolutionary organization and it received a lot of media attention, a high point in the RWP's existence. Ross told me that it was a remarkable time. People were just about lining up at the door to join, some of them returning ex-servicemen. The group grew very quickly in that short period. After that, however, as the long post-war expansion of capitalism began and the radicalization dissipated, many of the new members drifted away and in the subsequent municipal elections, votes for the group declined to insignificantly small numbers.

The first issue of *Workers Vanguard* in the late Fall of 1955 was essentially an election brochure for the group's intervention in the municipal elections that year, with Ross again running for mayor and Paddy Stanton for Board of Control. The paper also announced the birth of the SEL, the first open and public organization of the group since the dissolution of the RWL when it "entered" the CCF in 1951. I remember being in awe of how the group functioned in that election. They were very disciplined.

Even though the group was very small, it approached the campaign very professionally and tried to get a hearing in the all-candidates meetings—some of them attended by a couple of hundred people, large crowds in those days—where the paper would be distributed, while Ross and Paddy from the platform would use the opportunity to challenge the views of capitalist candidates and put forward a socialist perspective. The vote that year was nowhere like in 1946 and 1947 and I was a little shocked that it was so low—around 2,400 for Ross and 4,000 for Paddy, a very small percentage of the total votes cast. I had a hard time reconciling the very low vote with the enormous effort the group had put into the campaign. I suppose I was naïve in thinking we would get a fair hearing. It was the first election campaign I had ever participated in, and I had spent most of my time knocking on doors talking to people and giving out the paper and I suppose I expected a lot more. Press, radio and television all but ignored us. In my naiveté, I had entertained the possibility of getting at least one of our people elected. The rest of the group had a more realistic outlook, however: they saw that even in a period of declining political interest, the elections would, at a minimum, provide an opportunity for popularizing socialist ideas that would allow us to reach a much broader audience than normal and to give us some practice in how to explain socialist ideas to ordinary workers, or at least to its "advanced layers," meaning those who had some level of class consciousness. The group saw it as an opportunity to get free advertising for its ideas and we ran in the city elections every year in that period.

The results of the 1956 and 1958 elections were about the same as for other years. 1958, however, stands out in my memory for two reasons. For one, the SEL slate was much larger, reflecting the fact that we had recruited a few more people and were growing a little bit. And, secondly, it resulted in an important member of the Toronto group being forced to leave the country, ending up in jail in the United States. Ross headed the ticket to run for Board of Control. (Ford Brand, a CCF member backed by the Toronto Labour Council, was running for mayor that year.) For aldermanic positions, we put forward Hugh Dowson, Ross' brother;

Joe Rosenblatt, today a major Canadian poet and writer living on Vancouver Island; Ken Sutherland, a long-time member of the group and union activist in General Steelwares (who also happened to be a well-regarded chess master in the Canada); and Peter Metheus, a new recruit. Sadly, Peter Metheus, out of a mistaken sense of responsibility, had made a grave mistake that had drastic personal consequences for him in allowing us to place his name on the ticket. Peter, whom we thought was from Winnipeg and a Canadian, was in reality an American citizen named Joseph Johnson. He had been recruited into the SEL the previous year and had quickly become one of its leaders. It turned out he was from Minneapolis and had fled to Canada to avoid the draft and the Korean War and had found work in Winnipeg under the assumed name of "Peter Metheus." This was all revealed to us when he told us that, a few weeks after the municipal campaign was over, the RCMP had paid him a visit to "check his papers." Apparently "someone in the public," they told him, had fingered him as a result of the election campaign and had "informed the FBI." Although we all tended to believe this at the time, looking back at it now, I have my doubts. Since then, we have had a long experience in Canada of the RCMP's undemocratic methods in intervening in political groups to try and disrupt or destroy them. I think a more likely explanation is that someone in our organization or close to it may have been working for them and checking the personal backgrounds of recruits, looking for "illegalities." No matter, it was a personal tragedy for Joe and a big loss for us. When he heard that his draft number had been called and that he was being charged with draft evasion, we advised him to immediately return to Minneapolis where he was sentenced to two years in prison and a $500 fine, a lot of money at that time. But that wasn't the end of it. I saw him at a SWP convention shortly after and I remember him telling me how hard the experience of being in prison had been for him and how he had been able to carry out political activity among his fellow inmates. He had joined the SWP after his release and had become the organizer of the Minneapolis SWP but this did not go unnoticed by the U.S. government. It continued to pursue him. Not long after having served the sentence of two years for having, as an American citizen, evaded the draft, in a truly Orwellian turn of events he was brought before the courts again under a clause (which was later declared invalid) in the anti-Communist Smith Act, to face deportation because they deemed him to be a "stateless person" for having taken the oath of allegiance to the Queen in the 1958 Toronto elections.[2] Following a vigourous campaign by the Committee to Oppose the Deportation of Joe Johnson, initiated by the SWP, Joe finally won his case.

Pat Mitchell (behind) and me during SEL's 1956 Toronto Mayoralty campaign.

Chapter 5

Our American Co-Thinkers

THE SEL'S RELATIONSHIP WITH THE AMERICAN SWP WAS VERY important to it. They are "our American co-thinkers," we would proudly boast. Collaboration with them had helped sustain the group during the difficult days of the witch-hunt, and especially after the debilitating split with the Rose grouping. The SWP's weekly, *The Militant*, and their theoretical journal, *International Socialist Review*, were important sources of information and analysis. Very valuable assets, they were looked upon as a guide to what was happening in the U.S. and around the world. James P. Cannon's *History of American Trotskyism and Struggle for A Proletarian Party*[1] were considered essential reading. The SWP, although at a low point in those years with only a couple of hundred members, was many times larger than us. They had been crucial to the rebuilding of the F.I. in the post-war period and were very experienced in the American class struggle. Their leadership went back to the twenties when James P. Cannon was a leader of the American CP. Cannon, Farrell Dobbs, Tom Kerry, George Novack, Joe Hansen, Murry and Myra Tanner Weiss always took a keen interest in how the Toronto group was getting along. Compared to most of us, who were young and recent recruits, all of them were much older than us with obviously more political maturity. We were always treated with great warmth and respect by them, and they were never overbearing or intimidating. We had a very close relationship, although I'm not too sure how high Canadian politics were on their agenda. Canada gets very little mention in the American press, or in the press anywhere outside Canada, so I would not be surprised that they were not that well informed about the country's political life. They were usually cautious in expressing their views on Canadian issues generally, keeping a hands-off approach to our internal problems and being careful about criticizing our activities. But it was as if we were part of a common organization and we looked up to the SWP as a model we wished to emulate. We helped them in their campaigns and they helped us with ours. When they were active in campaigning for Morton Sobell's release from prison, we were also. During elections, for example, when they ran Farrell Dobbs for President and Myra Tanner Weiss for Vice President, their campaign team would always include Toronto in their schedule of meetings and we would always organize well in advance to get a good audience out for them.

In those years, the SWP made a special effort to help the SEL solve a problem we had great difficulty in dealing with by ourselves: cadre development. Many of our "cadre" were new to politics and had very little experience in the class struggle, barely what you would call "cadre." To help us raise our political level, on a kind of "forced march" basis, the SWP would make a special effort to allow us to participate in an intense cadre development programme they ran each winter at Mountain Spring Camp. Amongst us, the camp had a legendary reputation as a place to visit. Most of the members of our Canadian group had visited it at one time or another. A rural property of around fifty acres near the Pocono foothills in New Jersey, with a natural pond some distance from the main buildings, it could accommodate over two hundred people for special conferences and meetings. At its centre was an old stone farmhouse where the party members who ran the camp full-time lived. For city dwellers, it was a beautiful place for a vacation and at nominal cost, and every summer the SWP would organize a range of educational sessions there. When I visited it one summer, Alan Hansen—Joe Hansen's brother— and his wife Bea ran the operation. A lot of work had gone into improving the facility, and party members—a few of them architects and many of them skilled carpenters—had constructed residential "cabanas" throughout the grounds. A large dining room and kitchen, sitting at the top of a hill, overlooked the main buildings of the camp. The SWP had purchased it in the early forties with the financial help of George and Connie Weissman, longtime members in New York who came from a wealthy family.

Meetings of the SWP's National Committee took place there, but in the winter it became the site of a "cadre" school, where around ten leading pre-selected members of the organization gathered for an intensive study of Marxism. The school had been organized in the depth of the McCarthy period to provide a place where a handful of the leadership cadre of the party, who were normally very busy with party assignments and with very little time to read, would be rotated through it to have an opportunity for study, free from the pressures of party life. During the first few years of its existence, the school's participants were made up exclusively of the party's top leadership, but by the time the Canadians were sending people there, it was comprised mainly of leading activists from the party's branches across the country. Bunny Batten was one of the first of our group to go there and in other years Alan Harris and Cliff Orchard had participated. I had the good fortune to be there for the winter of 1961-62.

In many respects our SEL group operated very much like a branch of the SWP, not involved in that party's life as participants, but more voyeur-like than anything else. We regularly received their internal bulletins during their pre-convention periods and we even scheduled time in our own meetings to discuss them. We had no representation on the SWP's National Committee, although members of our leadership bodies would sometimes attend its meetings, neither did we write anything for their pre-convention discussions that were a feature of SWP internal life in my time; despite this, no major policy decision or organizational change was ever made by the Canadians without first getting the approval of the SWP. The proposal, for example, in 1955 to modify the "entry tactic" by setting up a new public formation, which would not publicly be "formally affiliated with the F.I." was first run past the SWP leadership for their approval at a NC meeting, with James P. Cannon suggesting the name, "Socialist Educational League."[2]

The branch of the SWP with which we had the closest relationship was, naturally enough, the one in Buffalo. However, that cooled a little after they developed differences with New York about the nature of Stalinism and the 1956 workers' uprising in Hungary, during which they sided with the Russians, characterizing the revolution as an attempt at "capitalist restoration." And in Vancouver, we worked closely with the Seattle branch led by Clara Kaye and Richard Fraser until that also cooled after Seattle became critical of the SWP's support for Malcolm X and black nationalism. And during U.S. Presidential elections, a couple of car loads of us would often drive down to Buffalo to help the branch collect signatures to get Farrell Dobbs on the ballot. In the U.S., to get on the ballot, a minority party is forced to collect many signatures, sometimes thousands, in every electoral district in the country, and they have to be signatures of people who are not registered Democrats or Republicans. Often the validity of the thousands of signatures is challenged by lawyers for the main parties, in order to keep alternative parties off the ballot. When we were helping the SWP, we Canadians often stood on the street corners or went door to door, frequently in the black communities of Buffalo asking people to sign our registration sheets. Aware of the effects of McCarthyism, I was always impressed by the friendly reception we would receive from the average person, even though we would sometimes be greeted with hostility and have a door occasionally slammed in our faces. It was daunting work and the Buffalo people were appreciative of our help. A young Deirdre Griswold, who later would be one of the founders of the Workers' World Party (WWP), would give me lodgings and that's when I first met Sam Marcy, their main leader, and Vince Copeland, another prominent leader of the group and Deirdre's father. We also got to meet some of their trade union activists at that time. Some of them had been arrested and imprisoned in 1954 for defying an injunction during a major strike at Bethlehem Steel. When I was there, most of their activists were no longer in the Steelworkers. The support we gave them was always warmly reciprocated because they often came up to Toronto to our forums and public events. This mutual solidarity was important because it tended to counter our feelings of isolation from the mass movement and gave us comfort in realizing our small group was part of a much larger movement that existed way beyond our borders. By the time I got to know them, the Buffalo people were politically isolated, maybe more so than us, and it was noticeable they were making a special effort to hold onto every single member. They were very close to each other personally and very much involved in each other's lives and had developed a strong social programme and we noticed they would regularly be in each other's homes for supper. Personal relations within the branch seemed at times to become even more important than politics.

Close personal relations also characterized the SEL. Inevitably, I suppose, in that difficult political period it was also a way for us to hold onto members. We had a very active social committee which every month sponsored a social in Verne and Ann Olson's home, put on special events at New Year's Eve, and in the summer organized picnics on Centre Island. In contrast to Buffalo, however, although suffering similar difficulties because of the low level of political and class consciousness in the country and our political isolation, we in Toronto were always involved, indirectly, in politics at the level of the state, whether it was municipal, provincial or federal, a benefit I now realize that flowed from our orientation to the CCF, the "entry tactic." Even though we were a small group, because of our "entry tactic" into the CCF, we were compelled to always pay close attention to the bigger political issues facing the country and even think in a practical way about what should be done if socialists ever took office and not just repeat abstract demands derived from Marxist texts. Of necessity, we could not ignore the bigger political questions and we were often forced to think about issues confronting the working class as a whole, in the immediate sense, even in the municipal arena, which helped us hold sectarianism at bay and minimize the internal effects of small group politics. That tended to make our discussions in Toronto more down to earth, more political and contemporary. Being active in a small organization where one's views are seldom challenged is very different from being in an organization where one might be a delegate to a CCF convention, for example, and be forced to debate supporters of the leadership. That was the case for the SEL.

We couldn't just repeat dogma that can be an easy way out when confronted with difficult questions. We had to grapple seriously with social democracy's ideas on a one-to-one basis and provide a meaningful alternative. That was always our big challenge and sometimes we would have the occasional victory by defeating them on a specific resolution on a convention floor. We lived our political lives in our own organization, but we were always looking at what was going on in the big picture, at the level of the state. In the constituencies, where we still had a few members or supporters, when conventions rolled around every second year, we made a special effort to have resolutions submitted pushing socialist ideas and trying to take advantage of any contradictions in the party as the leadership came in conflict with the membership over their adaptation to capitalism. One example of this in those years was the question of German rearmament. As part of its war drive against the Soviet Union, the Americans were driving hard to incorporate Germany into the western war machine in the process of setting up NATO. The issue was posed of how the CCF should respond, and that created a crisis in the party when M. J. Coldwell, the leader of the federal party and three of his MPs voted for German rearmament, defying National Council and National Convention decisions on the matter. The left in the CCF opposed this betrayal and we did our best to give voice to it. The Buffalo SWP, in contrast, always seemed to me less concerned about broader political issues such as this and more interested in the internal debates in the SWP and the more general theoretical questions, such as what attitude to take towards China and Eastern Europe.

Chapter 6

Problems on the 1956 Cross-Country Tour

*I*N THE SUMMER OF 1956, THE GROUP, UNDER ITS NEW NAME, SEL, resumed its tradition of organizing "national tours." Previously, these tours had involved a couple of the group's leaders heading out by automobile to contact members across the country, attempting to establish the "skeletal forms upon which to build the movement," with the word "movement" a synonym for "party."[1] Mostly sleeping in their car, in the early fifties they would cross the country and end up on the West Coast to meet with supporters where a "national convention" would take place in Vancouver. Airline travel cost a lot in those days, so this kind of trip was an inexpensive way to organize a national get-together. The tours had been suspended during the faction fight with the Rose grouping and now the intention was to get them going again, but on a more ambitious scale and much better organized, to renew contacts with supporters across the country and the left of the CCF that had significant presence in many communities across the Prairies.

The 1956 tour, which was scheduled to last for two months, ran into difficulties in the West. It had been led by two very experienced leaders of the group, Paddy Stanton and Jim Mitchell, both on its "Political Committee," the main leadership body of the organization. A recent recruit from England, Alan Harris, who had joined the group around the same time as me, was the third member of the team. Unfortunately, right from the start, Jim and Paddy did not get along with each other. Jim, a stationary engineer by trade, was active in the International Union of Operating Engineers (IUOE) and had quit his job to participate in the trip across the country. He and his wife Kit had been members of the group in Montreal before it had dissolved—its leader, Jean-Marie Bedard had supported Rose—and they and their two small children had relocated to Toronto. By the time of the 1956 tour, Jim's relationship with Kit was on the rocks and they had split up. In his late twenties, I remember him as tall, blond and good-looking. He was a very good guitar player with a large repertoire of folk songs and a better than average voice, tremendous attributes in a small group such as ours. He was always on call to perform at our monthly socials and was much admired by the few young women in the group. Also an expert at home renovations, he was extremely generous with his time for members who needed assistance. I remember him helping me renovate an old apartment and totally ignoring the building code—if he hadn't it would have been too expensive for my limited budget.

From the beginning of the 1956 tour, Paddy had personal difficulties with Jim, and at first I couldn't figure out why. Jim on the other hand, had great respect for Paddy, but the feeling, it seemed to me, was never really reciprocated. Paddy, born in Dublin, in his late fifties at that time, physically imposing, was very overweight with a large stomach—"a large corporation," as we would say in Belfast—and with a tremendous baritone voice that could dominate any meeting hall. He had a long history of involvement in labour struggles on the West Coast, both in the unions and in the CCF where he was known for a sharp wit, his oratory and his wizardry at producing clever sound-bites news journalists loved. I remember once when he spoke at a large meeting organized by the Toronto Labour Council to protest high unemployment in the city, being quoted in the *Globe and Mail* talking about how "the workers live in wage slavery and the reformists want to put velvet on their chains." He was the product of the much earlier radical period in Canada marked by the 1929 Great Depression when there was a wave of mass protests around the issue of unemployment and when the CCF came into being. When I got to know him he seemed to be out of step with the times and the reality of the situation we were in then as we tried to break out of the stultifying period of anti-communism. Unlike on the West Coast where most of our group was made up of people closer in age to Paddy, in the East during the Rose crises many of the people of his generation had seen that as an occasion to drift away into inactivity.

When I met him, he was very much set in his ways, verging on the dogmatic and impatient with the slow progress the group seemed to be making, but in any case I liked him a lot and we got along very well together. The fact I was Irish of course helped, but he was very much at ease around young people. Very patient when it came to educating new recruits about socialist ideas, he was one of the first to explain to me the concept of surplus value—the amount of value created by the worker at the point of production over and above his wages which is appropriated by the capitalist. Hence the exploitation of workers under capitalism, he would say. Paddy, it turned out, was an avid fly fisherman, and every summer, much to Ross' chagrin, he would head up to Lake Eugenia near Owen Sound, Ontario, where he rented a cabin for the entire fishing season. I remember making a trip up to visit him one year and almost being eaten alive by the mosquitoes as we searched for brook trout along an out-of-the way stream that fed the lake. We had to struggle with great effort through dense bush to get to it. The black flies were vicious and the mosquitoes enormous but that didn't deter Paddy from trying to catch fish. Others in the group—if they were lucky enough—would occasionally be invited to visit him. We considered it a high honour. My friend Joe Rosenblatt went many times and on Paddy's death wrote a commemorative poem.[2] It was a remarkable achievement for Ross to have persuaded Paddy to take a couple of months off from catching trout, which he looked forward to all year, to instead cross the country making socialist propaganda.

I was too inexperienced at the time to recognize it, but it had been clearly a mistake for Ross to have paired Paddy and Jim together to do anything, never mind go on a national tour and expect that their feeling of mutual responsibility to the group would somehow see them through their differences. But I had the distinct impression Ross was setting Jim some kind of test to see if he was "a real leader." To get things underway,

Jim was tasked with searching for a vehicle for the tour which could be modified so that Paddy, Alan and he could sleep in it and prepare meals, a sort of camper van before there was any such thing commercially available. There wasn't much money for this, but the vehicle had to be capacious enough to carry their food, clothes and personal effects plus a good supply of literature to be sold to the group's political contacts. Staying at hotels or motels was out of the question because of the expense.

Jim soon located a second-hand panelled delivery van which seemed to be in good condition—low miles on the odometer—and, at a reasonable price, suitable for the purpose at hand. The vehicle, it turned out, had previously been owned by a processing plant for the delivery of poultry to retailers. An unpleasant odour of dead chickens permeated it. Despite this, Jim and Paddy thought it would be suitable for the trip and Jim got the go-ahead to purchase it. Washing it with soap and bleach only somewhat lessened the disagreeable odour, but Jim and Paddy thought this would not be a problem and that it would eventually go away by itself. I don't know what Alan Harris, the other member of the tour, was thinking about all this; having recently come into the group, he probably thought these folks knew what they were doing so he went along without complaining.

The organizing of the "tour" and its progress was a major event in the life of our small group, an activity that would continue for many years. Early that summer, many of us gathered to give it a big send-off from the parking space at the back of the bookstore on Yonge Street. Alan, Jim and Paddy had good success in the early part of the trip, selling dozens of subscriptions and lots of literature in Sault Ste. Marie in northern Ontario, but when they reached Sudbury they encountered a situation that made it difficult for them to carry out their work, and a problem that would bedevil us there for the next several years. "The fact that we call for CCF governments in Ottawa and the provinces," they wrote, "proved to be a barrier between us and the Sudbury miners. The miners equate the CCF with the Steelworkers union which, in an orgy of red-baiting over the past several years, has been raiding their union. We had to explain over and over again that the leadership is not the CCF, how the SEL is fighting for a socialist, anti-red-baiting CCF policy…"[3] As a result, they didn't stay long in Sudbury and headed north. One of their goals was to get to Winnipeg in good time to attend the CCF National Convention that year to appeal Jim and Paddy's expulsions from the party the previous year. The Winnipeg Convention—one of the smallest in recent years with approximately two hundred delegates—became notorious in the history of Canadian social democracy because it's where the Regina Manifesto was dumped and the new Winnipeg Declaration was adopted, shifting the party more programmatically to the right in an attempt to make it more palatable to the ruling class. Jim and Paddy's reports do not say whether they made any headway on the expulsion issue—I suspect they didn't—but they wrote that they were able to renew contacts among the two hundred-odd delegates with a small socialist opposition and sell a few subscriptions.[4]

The usual practice for our "tours" was to utilize campsites at Provincial and National parks across the country, sometimes staying at a location for several nights at a time. In the close proximity to each other in the difficult conditions of living and sleeping in the truck, it was essential that everyone get along and habits such as snoring could be extremely irritating. Jim later told me that Paddy's snoring had kept him awake most nights and by the time they reached the Prairies it was driving him nuts, so much so that tension over it led to a break-down in their working relations. Personally they couldn't tolerate each other and by the middle of August Jim left the tour and had headed home by bus. Ross figured things were not going well when one day he received a cryptic request from Paddy—"Send $50"—with no details about what it was for. A few days later, much to Ross' surprise, Jim strolled, all by himself, into the store. Aside from the discomfort of Paddy's snoring, they also had had the problem of the aroma of dead poultry that permeated the truck that was intensified by the heat and from which they could not escape. But they had other disagreements from the get-go about the day-to-day functioning of the team, Jim would later tell me, over matters such as where to go when they arrived in a town and who to see first, down to the food they were cooking and when to do their laundry. Alan was a bystander to all this. A key idea behind the tour was that it was supposed to be self-financing through the sale of literature, so a lot of people had to be visited to make this happen. Jim said Paddy was not sufficiently fit for such activity and they were running out of money very fast, requiring many phone calls to Toronto for help. I later learned about what may have been a further complicating factor in their relationship. The gossip in the group was that Paddy, the previous year, may have been attracted to Jim's ex-wife, Kit. Kit told me that Paddy had invited her out for supper one evening not long after she and Jim had broken up. That relationship did not go anywhere, she told me, but I can't help but think this may have played a role in the feelings of personal antipathy between Paddy and Jim.

It was a big crisis for us, with a lot of personal drama surrounding it. Ross quickly persuaded Jerry Houle, one of the leaders in Toronto who was part of the cohort that had been expelled from the CCF in 1954, to quit his job in a Toronto rubber plant to take over the running of the store full-time, much to his wife Ruth's annoyance, I might add, because it was agreed to, she told me, without consulting her. Ross immediately headed out by train—a thirty-six hour journey—to take Jim's place in Saskatoon. After the completion of that tour, there was no way Ross would forgive Jim for his "failure." Even I, with limited experience in those things, could see that his future in the group was bleak. It was only many years later that I came to understand how this "all or nothing" aspect of Ross' personality could have a negative effect on a small group such as ours. Later Ross developed personal differences with Jerry, leading to Jerry leaving the leadership. This was also the case with Pat Mitchell who became the branch organizer. It wasn't long before Ross was also her severest critic. And it was also true of how he treated two very capable intellectuals in our ranks then, Bruce and Bunny Batten. It was as if no one could meet the standard Ross had set for what constitutes a revolutionary leader. In Jim's case, after the fiasco of the 1956 tour, no matter what he said or did, Ross always seemed to be his worst critic. By the end of the year he was no longer editor of the paper and Ross had taken his place.

In my immaturity then, I must admit, I didn't fully grasp the significance of what was taking place, but I've now come to see it as an example of the negative effect of a very strong leader's personality if it remains unchecked in a small group, especially if most of its membership is new to politics and not too politically experienced and especially when there is a low ebb in the class struggle. Looking back at it from this distance in time, I now see it also as a manifestation of a kind of sectarianism, a political pathology that can affect any small organization, especially in a long drawn out conservative period like the situation in the 1950s. With many supporters drifting away due to simple tiredness or just plain demoralization, the very existence of the organization began to seem in question. Such was our desperation, for example, to find new recruits, that a few of our members would even occasionally rent out rooms in their homes or apartments in the hope of getting a lodger who could be won over to the organization. Verne and Ann Olson did this several times.

The few people we were recruiting were generally of a low political sophistication and with no independent experience in the class struggle, yet the organization tended to expect that they should somehow quickly attain an immediate grasp of some of the key aspects of Marxism. Many of us were unable to have a critical understanding of the array of ideas to which the group subscribed so we tended to adopt them at face value. The most experienced person in the group, of course, was Ross, who was critical to its functioning and even its existence. Working full time at a salary not much above the minimum wage, he had recruited most of its members. In his intellectual and political development, he stood head and shoulders above everyone else but while playing an absolutely pivotal role in the development of the group and helping save it from extinction, he was also a liability in that his personality and the peculiarities that flowed from it could be extremely damaging. The inevitable personality differences that can occur in the functioning of any organization, can be especially damaging in a small group, and sometimes take on a political character and are mixed up in the general teacher-student relationship, an old problem I think of being unable to shake off the intellectual domination of a mentor.

Not long after Ross and Alan returned to Toronto at the conclusion of the trip out west, Ross proposed that Jim Mitchell and Pat, his wife, re-locate to Vancouver to work with the group there and to "open a branch office of the Vanguard Publishing Association," a preliminary step towards setting up a bookstore. They both agreed to this, of course, being loyal comrades, though I'm sure reluctantly. Jim's heart, it turned out, was not really into this new assignment, because it wasn't long before he backed out and a few months later he had resigned from the Political Committee. He left the group not too long after that, having decided to pursue a career in music. Despite what happened to him, he always remained politically close and loyal, often working full time where his skills were needed on the group's many projects. I always regarded his departure as a sad loss.

Within a few months, Jim had enrolled in the University of Toronto's Conservatory of Music. He became a professional musician with the Halifax Symphony. A member of the musicians' union, he had a passion for jazz and soon organized a small ensemble comprised of some very talented musicians which toured on weekends working gigs throughout southern Ontario and our group's functions. When we had moved the headquarters from Yonge Street to an old building on Queen Street West—a storefront just a few doors from a burlesque theatre, where the Sheraton Hotel now sits, long before the new City Hall existed—Jim often utilized the space for practices on Sundays, and paid rent to our group for the privilege.

I remember him once pointing out to me one of his band's musicians, someone who would later become a towering figure in Canadian music, Paul Hoffert, a skinny kid at the time of around fourteen or younger, whose songs and music would subsequently rise to the top of the charts in North America. He was one of the original members of Jim's jazz group, playing piano and xylophone. Jim had met Hoffert at the music faculty at the University of Toronto. Whether Hoffert was any good then,

I had no idea, but he sounded alright to me. I remember Jim saying he thought the guy was a musical prodigy. Jim, in his late twenties, came from a very poor working class family in Montreal. When I first met him, sometimes over a drink he and I would compare notes to see who came from the poorest background, something that would annoy Pat no end. Her family was of Dutch working class background and she had become a public school teacher and she found that kind of banter totally uninteresting. She was one of the few women leaders of the group and was among those who had been expelled from the CCF in 1953.[5] She later became a leader in the seventies of the feminist movement in Canada and a key figure in the campaign for abortion rights and a dedicated advocate for a federally funded day-care system. Pat was one of the main organizers of the first International Woman's Day demonstrations in Toronto. A very capable speaker and a popular leader of the feminist movement, tragically, her life was cut short by breast cancer in 1984 while still in her prime at the age of fifty. The Pat Schulz Child Care Centre in Toronto is named in her honour.

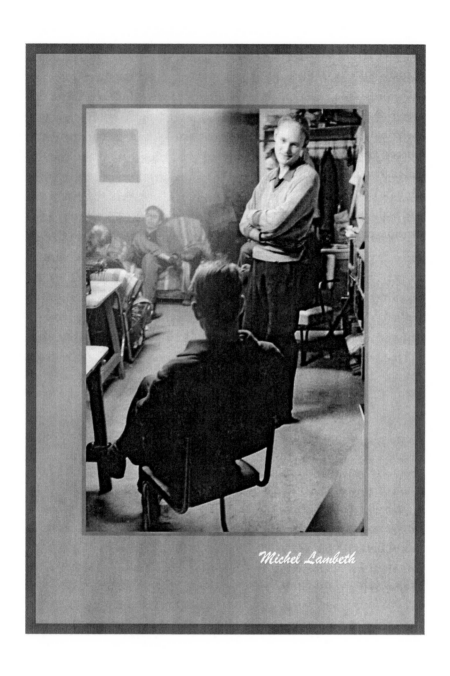

Michel Lambeth

From left clockwise: seated on couch, Joe Rosenblatt, Harry Paine (obscured), Jimmy Mitchell (standing), and seated with back to camera, Jerry Houle.

Chapter 7

Activity in the Unions

*A*CTIVITY IN THE TRADE UNION MOVEMENT WAS OF CENTRAL importance to the SEL. Believing that a fundamental transformation of capitalist society could only take place when the working class succeeded in overthrowing the state and had implemented a planned economy, we looked upon trade unions as an elementary line of defence of the workers against the capitalists in the daily class struggle until such a change took place. Therefore it was critical, we believed, that any organization that aspired to change society should have the bulk of its membership in them. Many of our activities were directed to that end, even if we had little influence in the unions. This was a few years before the student and youth radicalization that would characterize the latter part of the following decade, but in those years whenever we discussed possibilities for growth, we always thought solely in terms of the working class and the unions and new members of our group if they happened to be out of work, were encouraged to get jobs in plants that had been successfully organized.

Hugh Dowson, a tool and die maker in de Havilland's Air-craft, organized by the United Auto Workers (UAW), was probably our most experienced trade unionist. A skilled trades' steward, he was for many years his Local's delegate to the Toronto and District Labour Council, often winning that position despite opposition from the official UAW slate. Also active in a union was Meyer Shapiro, who had a background in Jewish left organizations, such as Hashomer Hatzair and the Workmen's Circle, and had been a member of our group since 1951. He worked in the Post Office and would later become a Toronto leader in the series of strikes that led to the formation of the present Canadian Union of Postal Workers (CUPW). Verne Olson had been a leader of a Local of the United Electrical Workers (UE) in Phillips Electronics and had played an important part in resisting the raid of the International Union of Electrical Workers (IUE) on UE that resulted in him, along with many other workers, losing their jobs.

Maintaining a functioning trade union fraction—a term we used to describe our caucus of union members—was a normal part of regular branch life, even though the fraction would only meet from time to time, its functioning depending on what was happening in specific unions. It was not seen as a special project but arose out of the normal existence of those members who happened to be in unions. It was not as if we told our members, "You must go and work in a factory"; it was a normal fact of political life in the group. Members who worked in plants tended to have a higher moral status in the organization—part of our "proletarian orientation," also seen in the informal understanding that no one could be on the SEL's "national committee," its highest body, if they hadn't spent some time working in a factory.[1] Unlike today where a high proportion of the population attends university and many workers even attain degrees, in those years only a tiny percentage had attended post secondary educational institutions. We had, what I must confess, was a prejudice against university students as being generally "petit bourgeois" and "supporters of the system," aloof from the concerns of people in the factories with the universities being training institutions for the ruling class. Our rigid approach to leadership became considerably modified in later years, however, during the youth radicalization of the Sixties when we all understood that the primary need of a small organization such as ours was the "primitive accumulation of cadres," and that you must recruit members from wherever you can. In those days, while our recruits were mainly working class, it was only an individual here and there.

The McCarthy witch-hunt and the anti-Communist crusade, which had reached its zenith during the Korean War, had a dramatic impact in Canada, making it difficult for socialists to be active at a time when the social democratic leadership of the unions and the CCF collaborated actively with the RCMP to have Mine Mill and UE excluded from National and Provincial federations. Communist Party militants and independent radicals were systematically purged from leadership bodies at a local level. To try and preserve our connection to the CCF and sometimes to protect members who had sensitive jobs, our members were usually forced to utilize pseudonyms for our records, and for when they wrote for the paper and internal bulletins. An unfortunate connotation of this measure, however, was that it tended to leave the impression we were engaged in some kind of "illicit" activity. It was sometimes difficult to explain this to new people who were first coming in contact with us, but it was almost impossible to function politically without this kind of security measure. If one of our members was seen to be publicly connected to the organization, the leaders of the CCF, with the cooperation of the trade-union bureaucracy, would target them for expulsion. And there was also the problem of the continuing pressure from the state. On cross-country *Workers Vanguard* tours, the RCMP would often follow us and harass us, trying to make our lives as difficult as possible. And while the anti-Communist hysteria was a factor in our activities in Canada, we at the time considered ourselves lucky compared to the SWP in the U.S., where the House Un-American Activities Committee (HUAC) ran rampant in "democratic" America and tens of thousands of people had been driven out of their jobs, especially teachers. I remember Murry Weiss, a leader of the SWP telling me one time how in New York City the FBI agents would regularly, on garbage day, drive up to the front doors of party members' homes, in their large black automobiles and jump out—in full public view with all the neighbours watching through their curtains—to take away the members' garbage cans, and return them a few hours later, a form of harassment to put excruciating personal pressure on the member and to isolate them from their community. After such incidents, neighbours were usually more reluctant than ever to be seen talking to them.

A radical left in the unions in Canada was only something to dream about in those years; nevertheless, we were always on the lookout for any kind of opportunity to increase our influence or to give us even a small breakthrough to get us out of our isolation. I was involved in one of these in the spring of 1956, after I was fired from Maple Leaf Milling. It all began out of a conversation Alan Harris and I had at the bookstore one day. Like me, he had recently arrived in Canada. He was from Norfolk, England, a recent immigrant who had recently joined the SEL. The topic came up of an organizing drive the UE had begun to bring the Radio Valve Corporation of America's main plant in Toronto into the union. UE was under the influence of the Labour Progressive Party (LPP), the name of Communist Party in Canada, and had been purged from the Ontario Federation of Labour (OFL) during the witch-hunt. Radio Valve was a major manufacturer of cathode ray tubes for television sets. In the midst of the discussion at the bookstore, Ross suggested to us that we should perhaps go and check them out. Soon we each had jobs in the Rexdale plant in the suburbs of Toronto. I worked as a "quality control technician," a fancy name for lifting tubes off the assembly line and plugging them into a test panel to check for defects, and Alan, if I remember correctly, was a forklift operator. It wasn't long before we had become involved with the UE in an intense organizing drive. A recently constructed, massive assembly plant, I remember it had a very long conveyor chain snaking around the inside of it, something I had never seen before, carrying hundreds of large cathode ray tubes (picture tubes) upon which workers performed designated operations, completing the tubes' assembly. A major difficulty in organizing the plant turned out to be, ironically, the company's policy of paying better than average wages, close to those in the unionized plants, to prevent any union getting a toehold. Most of the workforce, we soon discovered, about five hundred or so, were recent hires, many from Newfoundland and the East Coast, and a few university students working for the summer to pay their way through school.

One of the students I remember very well from that experience was a young black man from Trinidad, Lyle Williams, who was a few years older than me. He was in the process of completing a degree at the University of Toronto (U of T) and worked alongside me doing the same job during the summer. We often had many long conversations on the afternoon shift about colonialism and politics, just to relieve the boredom of working on an assembly line. As a consequence he and I became friendly with each other. He had brought his wife and child with him to Toronto and was living in residence at U of T. His family was from the administrative elite in Trinidad and he and his friends were intensely interested in the possibility of a united federation of the Caribbean. From time to time, I would give him our paper, *Workers Vanguard and the Militant* and the odd pamphlet, such as James P. Cannon's *Socialism on Trial*,[2] a record of the trial of the SWP leader under the Smith Act during World War II in the U.S. He also attended some of our forums and had met Ross. A few times he invited me to his apartment for supper where for the first time I tasted Trinidadian cooking. He was a lot more sophisticated than me, and I tried very hard to recruit him to our group, but without any success. Very often, I had difficulty dealing with his questions. I was very enthusiastic about my new ideas. I remember once he listened to me, with a quizzical look on his face, as I explained at length how sure I was we would soon have a working class government in Canada that would establish socialism. He wanted to know when, and I said, without much hesitation, "within five years." "Are you sure?" he replied, in a very skeptical tone. I assured him I was totally convinced. "Yes," I went on, "there's no way capitalism can overcome its contradictions. The workers will surely soon overthrow it." I was in the midst of reading some of James P. Cannon's work, especially his 1946 speech, "The Coming American Revolution," that had been produced as a pamphlet and which, even though ten years had passed, I was convinced was still a valid perspective. "Would you like to place a bet on that?" Lyle shot back, "how about $20 that it will come in five years?" I started to think that perhaps I should be a little bit more cautious; that was a lot of money for me then. "How about ten years?" I asked. It's a bet, Lyle replied with a laugh. I often wondered where his career took him, because if I ever met him again I would pay him his $20. But what I was saying to Lyle as we worked on that assembly line wasn't that much out of sync with how our group viewed the world and how we sustained ourselves in the hostile political world we lived in. We saw ourselves as part of the world socialist revolution that had begun in Russia in 1917 and which had been interrupted by the Second World War but began again after the war with the upsurge in the colonial revolution and the expansion of the planned economy into Eastern Europe and the victory of the Chinese in 1949. Our hope was that revolution would sweep Canada once the working class finally came to its senses to take the power away from the ruling class. What we didn't appreciate fully was the hardy resilience of capitalism after the war and the inherent ability of the system to reinvent itself and learn from each crisis, the beginning of the long economic expansion that is now regarded by economists, even Marxist ones, as "the golden age of capitalism."

Before I got through my probation at the Radio Valve Corporation, however, I was shown the front door of the plant, ending my discussions with Lyle; he came to a few of our forums after that but eventually returned to Trinidad with his family and I lost contact with him, though I was once told he had entered the diplomatic service of his newly independent country. I had been careless in my union organizing. A supervisor had scurried to the front office to report that he had overheard me talking about the union. Over the years, the company had been very successful in keeping the union out of its plants by maintaining a rigourous anti-union policy; inside the plant we couldn't allow any impression to exist that we were signing anyone up. We didn't have the labour protection legislation then that we have today, and anyone seen signing someone up could be instantly dismissed. The way we worked around this problem was that the pro-union people in the plant would quietly seek out those who looked like good candidates for a union card and we would then obtain their addresses so that we could visit them in the evening or week-ends in order that a longer conversation could take place, a common practice when organizing in an anti-union environment. Often the union would book off activists in their other organized plants to work full time on the drive. Union supporters from the targeted plant met on a regular basis with these organizers—sometimes once a week—to plan their work.

When I was fired, the union suggested—and I readily agreed—that because we had reached a point of having signed up sufficient numbers to apply for a certification hearing in front of the Labour Board, fighting the company over a single firing would be a diversion, so we let it drop. One of the UE staffers then suggested I apply for work at Amalgamated Electric, a large electrical manufacturing plant, a subsidiary of a large British company, English Electric in Toronto's east end on Carlaw Street, where UE was the certified bargaining agent. I was hired immediately.

Getting fired from Radio Valve turned out to be a lucky break for our group, because it led to us recruiting a few more people. Even though UE was outside the "official union" movement, it was a lot better than not being in any union whatsoever. In addition, because of the influence of the CP in the union, unlike unions that were under social-democratic control, it tended to have a few radical activists in the local leadership to whom Marxism was not a foreign concept. Moreover, the SEL had a supporter there, a Trotskyist of Ukrainian background from the Prairies who had been a member during the war, but who in the following years had drifted away. I only remember that his first name was Peter and, although born in Canada, he spoke with a strong Ukrainian accent. Occasionally he visited the bookstore and sometimes he would attend our public forums. I later learned from him that he had been an active union militant, but that the CP had isolated him during the war when they were promoting their "no-strike pledge" and had even recommended that the company fire him because of his opposition to their policies. He had been glad to see me when I showed up in the plant.

I started work on the loading dock getting large industrial electrical switches ready for shipping across the country. That's where I learned how to effectively hammer in nails, along with a little bit of elementary carpentry, a skill I've found useful during the course of my life. The switches, sometime weighing several tons, were mounted on large wooden pallets and boxed with lumber to get them ready for customers. I worked hard and kept my head down to make sure I got through my three months' probation, a determination reinforced by our group's attitude to work discipline that insisted if you couldn't hold down a job, how could you possibly help lead workers in their daily struggles against the boss.

I had learned my lesson very well from Radio Valve, but I was still on the lookout for other militants. On the first or second day on the job, I met an Irish immigrant like myself, but from County Cork, Ireland. Brian Clarke was a few years older than me. It was the beginning of a small "breakthrough" for us. He quickly let me know how much he hated the capitalist system and sometimes the tears would well up in his eyes as we talked about its injustices, but swiftly he could change mood and start to joke around and make fun of our supervisor, just to pass the time it often seemed. He had a wicked sense of humour, but applied it in such a clever way that his victims did not realize he was playing with them. He and his sister—who worked as a secretary somewhere in the city and had a very good voice and was trying to develop a career as a singer— had recently arrived in the city. Brian, who would booze and party most weekends and arrive on the job on Monday mornings with a colossal hangover, looking "like death warmed over," as the saying goes, was always broke and borrowing money to see him through until his next pay cheque. Very soon, I invited him down to our bookstore where he met Ross and Paddy and a few other people from the group. In no time at all he began attending our forums and had soon joined our group. He was great fun and became active in the union, but we couldn't hold him in the group and he soon drifted off. After borrowing money from Ross to finance his trip, he headed out to Chicago and never returned. It's where he intended to go all along. Toronto was only a temporary stop on the way there. He told me that while he had much admiration for the SEL and was in total sympathy with its aims, we were just too busy for him, with far too many meetings for him to attend. Around us he didn't seem to have time to do anything else, he told me. And when I look back on it, he had a point, but more on that later.

It's also where we met Pat Brain. He had recently come over from Birmingham, England, and had such strong accent I at first had a difficult time understanding him. He became very active in the union and soon took a keen interest in our group, joining immediately and becoming one of its leading activists and was part of our youth organization a year or so later. In the Sixties, he returned to England where he was active in the Vietnam Solidarity Campaign and in the International Marxist Group.

Another important recruit from Amalgamated Electric was Carl Duerst, in his fifties, a truly remarkable man and physically imposing, so tall he towered over me and he needed to bend over to hear me speak because of the noise in the plant. Active in the union in an earlier period, he had helped get UE into the plant and he may have even been in the CP at one time, but I don't remember now. He was married with a family. A highly skilled assembler and wiring technician, he worked on the large switches I was preparing for shipping. Taking advantage of the seniority system, I had "bumped" into the better paying and more skilled job and I was fortunate to become his helper. Slowly but surely as we worked on the switches, and discussing politics of course, he began to express some interest in our ideas, and began, like Brian and Pat, coming to our activities, and he became active again in the Local.

Participation in UE Local 514 was of fundamental importance to us. We considered it essential to take responsible positions in it, such as becoming stewards at a shop-floor level and even going on the Executive Board, if we could manage it. And every time a UE National Convention rolled around, we always made a point of trying to get ourselves elected as delegates and occasionally we would have a good resolution submitted by the Local, sometimes over the opposition of the CP's supporters in the Local who would mobilize to defeat us. We always resented their dogma of "union patriotism" that the national leaders persistently promoted, along the lines that UE was the "best union in the country" with the "best contracts" and the suggestion that all other unions in the OFL were inferior to them, a rationalization that we figured allowed them to justify their isolation after having been purged from the OFL. Among the issues we consistently criticized the national leadership about, aside from their tendency to sign weak contracts, was the question of their position on "independent political action." The national union supported the LPP's line of building "anti-monopoly coalitions," which meant supporting the Liberals every time Provincial or Federal elections rolled around. Naturally, our SEL caucus prepared very well for the union's various gatherings. I enjoyed making "interventions," doing the best I could to argue against the national union's election policy and trying to persuade it to change it, and to support the CCF. Sometimes we were lucky enough to succeed in forcing the matter onto the floor of a convention and we would have good debate about it. I remember us challenging C. S. Jackson, UE's national leader on their opposition to the Canadian Labour Congress (CLC) and the CCF's move to build a "new party."

Pat Brain took him on from a floor microphone when Jackson refused to accept an amendment from Local 514 that called for support for the CLC's move, saying that aside from being the correct thing to do politically, it would also help to mitigate the union's isolation from the CLC and maybe even could open the door for the union again joining it.[3] Jackson's position carried, of course, but in the run-up to the founding of the NDP, the UE, despite being barred from representation in it because of the red-baiting stance of the CLC and the CCF, much to our surprise reversed its position and came out in support of the NDP. Obviously, we had been but one voice in the union calling for this policy.

Over time, we got to know the main leaders of Local 514 quite well. They had really worked very hard to hold it together and build it ever since it was organized. Rod Lockhart and his wife, both of them either in the CP or sympathetic to it, were its main leaders. They turned out to be a very decent couple, totally dedicated to the cause of the working class. What made our relations easier with them was that in personal conversations, we could discuss with them as Marxists, lifting our discussions to a much better level than what you would normally experience in an OFL union. We finally ended up on good terms with Rod and his wife because I believe they came to respect us for our work in building the local, but that was as close as it got. They appreciated that we were always prominent in the Local's various campaigns, but in their relations with us, all they could see in front of them was that we had the potential of making their lives extremely difficult by pressuring them to take a more radical path. These good relations eventually extended to the Local's business agent, who had at one time been active in the CP. We had an active fraction there until finally the plant closed in the early sixties.

From left: Pat Mitchell, me (with pencilled in mustache for security reasons) and Jerry Houle.

Chapter 8

The Teamsters

NOT LONG AFTER OUR LITTLE BREAKTHROUGH IN AMALGAMATED Electric, the SEL was soon faced with a much bigger opportunity to engage in more impressive trade union work, in a totally unexpected union, the Teamsters. According to Ross, it was "the biggest thing that I remember having happened to our Canadian movement."[1] All told, in the late fifties as I remember it, and ironically for a self-professed working class organization, we still didn't have that many of our members in unions and certainly had no concentration of members in any particular local of a union. In addition to our few people in Amalgamated Electric, Hugh Dowson was in de Havilland Aircraft, and we also had a few people from time to time in General Steelwares, a large plant south of Gerard Street near the Don River in Toronto's East End. Ken Sutherland and a couple of our members had gotten jobs there, but the plant was organized by the Steelworkers' Union and under the firm control of a clique of right-wing social democrats. Ken reported that its monthly membership meetings would very often barely have a quorum of members in attendance.

Once we stood a good chance of getting a couple of militants onto the Executive Board, but we unfortunately suffered an embarrassing set-back when one of our members who was running for the Executive was arrested by a plain-clothed cop on the street just outside the plant. He had taken a *Globe and Mail* newspaper from its box without paying for it, and was fired when the company heard about it. It was a petty and quite dumb thing to do, something he had done many times before, he later told us. As a result, our opponents very happily spread the gossip about this incident throughout the plant, helping to torpedo our efforts to get on the Local's Executive. I remember how we were acutely embarrassed by it and of course it set us back quite a bit. Getting our members established in the plant in the first place hadn't been easy, by any means. In those depressed times, even when we would finally manage to get someone into a targetted plant, there would often be layoffs and they would be quickly out on the street again, the result of the policy of "last hired, first fired." We also had a couple of people—Joe Rosenblatt comes to mind—working at Canadian Pacific Railway on the loading dock in Toronto, but none of this compared to what happened in the Teamsters as the decade came to an end. It was one of the few times in those years when our group made a focused effort to get as many members as possible into a specific union local of a specific industry.

As the decade came to a close, Toronto became the focal point for a series of wildcat strikes in the trucking industry throughout Ontario. It was a time of great turmoil in the International Brotherhood of Teamsters which was undergoing a deep crisis, its membership in a state of revolt, especially in Ontario where many of its locals were under trusteeship, the most egregious case being that of a large Windsor local of some 5,800 members that had been in trusteeship for an amazing fourteen years and another large local in Toronto, with over 5,500 members, that had been in trusteeship for more than a year. The union's head office in Washington had been under investigation by the Labour Department for corruption and as a result, in February 1958, under a court order, Jimmy Hoffa was forced out of office and replaced by a government appointed "board of monitors" that promptly began an anti-union campaign that lasted twenty-seven months, carried out under the guise of "getting Hoffa," all the while delaying a convention that ostensibly it had been put in place to organize. In the meantime, the Hoffa machine was still in control, with many of its locals in Ontario suffering under his trusteeships.

Our initial involvement in the Teamsters came about, not as a result of some grand strategy on our part but out of the simple, economic necessity of one of our members who happened to be desperate for a job.

Wally Mitchell, Jim's younger brother, was very broke and needed money in a hurry. He had come up to Toronto from Montreal to look for work. I remember it very well because in order to help make ends meet, Ken Sutherland, Alan Harris and I had shared a large apartment at the corner of Glenholme Avenue and St. Clair Avenue West—the building is still there—and Wally was staying with us for a while until he could find work and have his own place. He got a job almost immediately as a driver for a bottling plant, delivering Coca-Cola to convenience stores around the city and he quickly let Harry Paine, who happened to be looking for work at the same time, know there were job openings. By July 1959, Harry found himself in Smith Transport, a subsidiary of the Canadian Pacific Railways and one of the largest trucking companies in the country. As luck would have it, this happened to be one the main sites of Teamster anti-administration activity in the city. Confusion seemed to reign throughout the union, Harry and Wally told us. We soon found out that there were at least three opposition factions in the locals, the eponymous Davidson, McTaggert and Nealan caucuses, plus a grouping of supporters of the Canadian Brotherhood of Railway, Transportation and General Workers union, (CBRT), who were calling for affiliation instead to their union, all of these groupings arrayed to various degrees against a pro-Jimmy Hoffa machine that was in control of the central union apparatus.

Strikes seemed to be happening every other week, often against the companies and even occasionally against the Locals' administrators, mainly over the trusteeships Hoffa had imposed and the resulting feeble contracts that had been signed with the companies with virtually no input from the membership. As the turmoil spread, Wally and Harry kept bringing back first-hand accounts of what was going on. Right away, the SEL's trade union committee—mainly pressured by Ross Dowson—began to look for others in our group who could try their luck at finding jobs as drivers so that they could become active in what for us was a promising situation, or as we would commonly say to ourselves, "play a role and try and give some leadership in the struggle." Alan Harris and George Bryant soon got jobs there. Both had the driver's license requirement that allowed them to drive large trucks and soon they were followed by others who got jobs working in the trucking barns, with the common sense advice that all of them refrain from union activity until they were through their probation, which was usually three months. One thing we quickly noted about the Teamster membership was that while there would be great militancy on the job, because the barns were scattered across the city, they were very difficult for the union to service, and as a consequence had a small measure of independence from the bureaucracy. In addition, most of the workers had a very tenuous connection to the union, quite unlike in a factory setting where the workers would usually all be in one location. One of the advantages of this situation was that support for the leadership in the membership was often very thin.

By the spring of 1960, Ken McTaggert, the Business Agent for Teamster Local 514, had succeeded in rallying the local's members to oppose the trusteeship and had persuaded the Ontario government to intervene and force new elections, all of which provided a marvellous opening for our few members. The emergence from trusteeship allowed us to participate in the election as an organized force as we joined with other militants to challenge the Local's old leadership. It was a small and promising beginning foray into the union, but in that election the votes were never ever counted. A former Local president appealed to the courts and successfully challenged the proceedings. He had been unjustly disqualified from running by a Hoffa-appointed trustee.[2]

Around this time we met up for the first time with Joe Hendsbee, a socialist activist, an American who had recently come from Boston and who had gained a very good reputation in the membership for his militancy. It was unusual for our group to meet an individual such as him, because in those days radical socialists in the labour movement were few and far between. Politically he considered himself a Marxist and had been on the periphery of the LPP for a while. At first he was a little leery of the SEL but because of our class struggle approach to the union's problems, there was soon a meeting of minds. He would shortly go on to join the SEL, playing a pivotal role over the next few years in helping us build a radical opposition to the Hoffa machine. Later he would be thrown out of his job and black-listed from the trucking industry in Ontario and forced to move to Vancouver where he pitched in to help build the SEL, before eventually parting company with us. Meeting up with Hendsbee had made it easier for us to make contact with many other militants and very quickly we were able to set up a small, but tightly organized opposition caucus, called the "Forward With Democracy" (FWD) caucus. Soon it had about fifty rank and file members attending its meetings—that were open to everyone—that and its very existence began to change everything. Not only was it arguing for democracy and better wages and membership control and criticizing how the union was being run, but it was also contesting for leadership with the other three competing opposition groupings, all of whom seemed to be struggling with each other to see who could get control in a typical case of the "outs" fighting the "ins."

When the election finally rolled around, it took place in the midst of an orgy of red-baiting initiated by Ken McDougall, Washington's candidate to take over, against the FWD's slate of candidates, headed up by Bill Davidson. Since the earlier aborted election, he had thrown his lot in with the FWD to challenge the Hoffa machine. It was a hard fight during which we began to produce the first of a four-page, monthly tabloid, named *FWD*, edited by Hendsbee, which just about discombobulated the McDougall gang. Despite a virulent red-baiting offensive against us, however, we came very close to defeating him. McDougall won by a margin of only 43 votes in a field of seven candidates and it was by no means a clean sweep for him. FWD managed to achieve a toehold on the union's Executive Board by having several members of its slate elected to it, including that of trustee.[3] But most importantly, the election had brought to an end the Hoffa enforced trusteeship and had opened the Local up to the possibility—for the first time in many years—of a more vigourous internal life that would see the membership challenge the leadership's policies time and time again, and sometimes defeat them.

By February 1962, we had produced another issue of *FWD* in an attempt to break the union brass' monopoly of news about an impending contract fight. Not many Locals in those days had their own union paper so this was a bit of a novelty, a first step we always argued if the rank and file was to get control of their union. It was clear, the paper had filled a vacuum and as a result, the caucus quickly increased its influence across the union.

One of the largest wildcat strikes in which we had a significant role in those years happened in the summer of 1962 when eight thousand Ontario truckers spontaneously shut down their company barns to immediately link up with thousands of Quebec truckers who had walked out a few days earlier. Trucking in Ontario was paralyzed for six weeks. The key demand was a $2. 50 hourly wage with a contract for two years. The wild-cat had begun on May 27th when the 2,000 member Teamster local, 938, walked out in defiance of McDougall who had been in negotiations with the trucking companies since the previous October and was manoeuvring to get the membership to accept a contract that it had earlier rejected.

It all began at a mass meeting in Toronto's Scarborough Arena, where McDougall failed to get his angry membership to accept a government appointed conciliator's report. FWD supporters were in the forefront in opposing the negotiating committee's capitulation and during the course of the stormy mass gathering—punctuated by many fist-fights provoked by goons brought in to Toronto by Hoffa's people for the occasion. Supporters of FWD were accused from the platform by McDougall of being "splitters," among other heinous crimes. Eventually, when the vote was finally taken on a Labour Department conciliator's report, McDougall refused to allow the ballots to be counted, telling his angry members they would be counted the following day. At which point, the members, deeply suspicious, and having none of it, stormed out of the hall and immediately launched a wildcat strike.[4] Not that long after, on June 5th, in the Palace Pier, a large dance hall on Toronto's lakeshore, another attempt was made by the brass to get the rank and file to end their wild-cat strike and accept another conciliator's report that turned out to be much the same as the old one, but again it was soundly rejected. With that rebuff, McDougall turned to the assembled members to inform then that in future, the negotiating committee would have the final say on contract terms, without their input. "Days of big wage increases have gone," he had informed everyone.[5]

That 1962 strike was led entirely by the Strike Committee, which was in the hands of the militants. It had immediately organized flying squads made up of rank and file members to keep the trucking barns shutdown and the trucks off the road. But the companies refused to budge and were encouraged to do so by the union's Washington head office, which we believed was in cahoots with the employers' association in opposing the strike. The strike lasted six weeks but finally the 8,500 workers were forced back to work and accepted a contract not that much different from the original conciliator's report they had overwhelmingly rejected before the strike had begun. Union staff had done everything in their power to sabotage it, even to the extent of encouraging the companies to keep their barns open. Strike pay was cut off for the members and the strike was declared illegal by Washington, by which time McDougall had effectively dissolved the Strike Committee by the simple method of not calling any more meetings. He immediately put an end to the strike bulletins he had been pressured into issuing and proceeded to break the long standing unity of the Toronto Locals by unilaterally signing contracts with individual companies and without even a membership vote, to end the strike.[6] It was a bitter defeat for the membership.

By 1966, as the much criticized four-year contract with the trucking employers came to an end, a new mood of militancy among workers could be seen throughout Ontario in a wave of strikes in the auto, steel and other industries. It also found its expression, as was to be expected, throughout the Teamsters' union, but especially in Local 938, where many League for Socialist Action (LSA) members were active. The central issue in the negotiations as the old contract came to an end was a demand for the scrapping of the forty-eight hour week and its replacement with the forty-hour week. When Ken McDougall, who chaired the joint negotiating committee for the five Ontario locals, reached an agreement with the employers that fell far short of that demand, and instead was proposing the acceptance of a forty-three and a half hour work week to come into effect three years hence, an angry Teamsters' membership revolted when it heard about it. Within twenty-four hours, as in 1962, spontaneous strikes had spread throughout Ontario, paralyzing the shipment of goods in Hamilton, Oshawa and Toronto. But after a couple of days, when the workers returned to work, they were met with a vicious campaign of reprisals that saw the firing of ten of their leaders and a demand by the employers that the Provincial Labour Department fine the Hamilton local $2,000,000, and that two hundred members be prosecuted for taking strike action, all of which only succeeded in making the workers even more angry.[7]

As in the 1962 strike, Local 938 in Toronto again became a centre of the rapidly growing opposition to the Hoffa machine. At an angry membership meeting following the wildcats, a motion of non-confidence in Ken McDougall was passed and his power to fire business agents was removed and the negotiating committee was re-organized to include two leaders of the wildcat strikes to provide it some backbone, one of them, Ken Thibideau a leader of the Hamilton Local. When the augmented negotiating committee met with management, it demanded that all reprisals be dropped—otherwise negotiations would cease. But just as the next membership meeting was about to take place, on December 10th, and to save McDougall's bacon, Hoffa intervened to slap another trusteeship on the Local and keep McDougall and his cronies in power.[8]

By then the FWD caucus had outlived its usefulness. According to George Bryant, after the defeat of the 1962 strike and under the difficult conditions of the trusteeship, it had become increasingly difficult for our people in the union to sustain.[9] With its support declining and some of its supporters becoming increasingly undisciplined and unwilling to adhere to previously agreed to decisions, the LSA's[10] George Bryant, Jimmy Howel and Harry Paine initiated its dissolution. In the new and rising mood of militancy at the end of 1965, they had reached out to new opposition forces in the other four Locals in southern Ontario to help set up a new rank and file caucus that would provide leadership in the struggle for a new contract. A focal point for resistance to management became the "No Reprisals Defense Fund" that our LSA members had helped set up to defend and to financially support the fired strikers. We were also instrumental in producing the Teamsters Information Bulletin to publicize recommendations about a work-to-rule campaign and a proposal for refusal of overtime to pressure the bosses to come to an agreement. Our prestige had grown to such an extent that Harry Paine was elected Chairman of the union's all-powerful Strike Committee. For a short period, under the regime of the trusteeship, the strike committee in effect displaced the Executive Committee and took control of the Local.[11] And similar to 1962, the rank and file caucus was again instrumental in persuading the membership to turn down the companies' offer.

Not wanting the ascendant opposition to get its bearings, the bosses went on the offensive. Taking advantage of the divisions in the union about the trusteeship issue and the absence of a structure to organize an effective resistance to them, they seized the moment to lock out over 21,000 workers.[12] It turned out to be a long and grueling fourteen-week strike, with several of the Locals finally forced into submission and acceptance of the employers' proposals, with even the weary militant Local 938 voting for the rotten contract. And Hoffa again intervened to force an end, at the same time firing all those on staff who hadn't been sufficiently quick in responding to his demands.

Naturally, as an outgrowth of our activity in the Teamsters, many of the people with whom we had been collaborating began to participate more and more in the LSA's activities. That's how we got to know, of course, Jimmy Howel, who I have mentioned already, and his wife Mary, both of whom would later became important in the life of the Toronto branch and who, aside from his work in the Teamsters, helped us establish a summer camp, Camp Poundmaker, to carry out educational work. Jimmy had won wide respect among the Teamster rank and file not only because of his debating skills but also due to his fearlessness in physically confronting the goons the Teamster's brass would utilize to shutdown the militants' voices at monthly meetings. Alan Harris once told us of an occasion at the first mass meeting of the 1962 strike when he had finally been able to get himself recognized by the chair and that as he stood up to speak, several goons lunged at him to drag him to the floor but Jimmy jumped in to block their way, smashing one of them to the floor, with sharp blows to their heads and allowing Alan to finish his remarks. Driving transport in Toronto was a tough job in those days and violence was never far away. Fights would often break out on the city streets between drivers, sometimes with non-union operators over such things as parking and getting access to a building to deliver goods. Jimmy was well known for being very fast with his fists.

Quite a few Teamsters joined us at that time, sometimes even in groups of five, I remember, a startling number for a small group such as ours and we grew very quickly. In my estimation, very early on we had recruited around thirty-five or forty of them to the League for Socialist Action (LSA) which by that time had succeeded the SEL. But it turned out it was much easier to recruit them than to hold them. I'm sure it would have been very different if there had been a general rise in society of class consciousness among workers and while there had been an outburst of union militancy here and there, this was still not the case. Those were still politically conservative times and we were but a small organization. Despite our best efforts to hold on to the new recruits, the turnover was rapid. Many had joined the group with high expectations that we could not meet and obviously some of them had illusions about our real strength. Most were mature workers and had been in the workforce for considerable time, older than most of us, but attracted to our group, mainly because of our effectiveness in the union. They slowly drifted away, however. The burden of family commitments along with participation in the union and involvement in a political group just became too much for many of them. I remember one of them whom I had gotten to know very well. It was his first involvement in any kind of socialist activity, he told me over a beer. Married, in his forties and with a couple of children, he owned his own house, something unusual because most of us lived in apartments or shared accommodations in those days. He was a driver for a long-haul trucking company and would often be away from Toronto for a couple of weeks at a time driving down to the American South and as far west as Vancouver. Shortly after he came into the group, I remember him one evening sitting next to me at a branch meeting. I was startled when he turned to me and enquired, in all seriousness, "Ernie, when are we going to get the guns and go for it?" He didn't have the time to wait for revolution. He had to have it now. Not that he was "adventurist" or some kind of ultra leftist; he was only lacking in political understanding.

The Teamster experience was but one example of our always being on the lookout for a "breakthrough" in the class struggle where our ideas might be taken up by an important segment of the working class. I cite the foregoing, not to suggest there was a big radicalisation taking place, but to show how we as a small revolutionary group functioned and what was possible if you got a break and were seriously organized. During the course of the fight in the Local, at one point we made a bloc with Ken McTaggert's caucus—he had been a business agent who had found himself on Hoffa's wrong side—getting him to agree to a very radical statement as a basis of unity, for winning a majority on the Executive Board of the Local but it wasn't very long before he had broken that agreement and made his peace with Hoffa.

Our involvement in the Teamsters turned out to be an exceptional experience for us, but it happened not by any grand plan or design on our part, as I've mentioned, but rather because of our belief that the working class would eventually take the path to social revolution and our total commitment to its emancipation. We were only doing what comes naturally if you have such ideas. We had seen an opportunity to help a group of workers in their struggles with their employers and against the union bureaucracy and had grabbed it. It was primarily a trade union struggle and we were involved in it in one form or other well into the decade. If someone had stated then that "we needed a working class orientation," as sometimes happens today when socialists talk amongst themselves, we would have been very puzzled because it would have been like telling a fish it should swim in water.

Top Left to right: Ross Dowson, Virginia (Bunny) Batten and a person whose name I
don't remember

Bottom Left to right: Ross Dowson, Virginia (Bunny) Batten and Bruce Batton

Chapter 9

The Cooperative Commonwealth Federation

*T*OWARDS THE END OF THE FIFTIES, THE DARK CLOUDS OF THE WITCH-hunt in Canada, although beginning to lift, were still very much present. The radical left in the country was small and isolated. But it was not something that we were prepared to accept as a given fact. We were always on the lookout for political openings whereby we could widen our contacts with other socialists or left moving workers. For example, the CCF had been in decline towards the end of the decade but still there remained a scattering of socialists throughout the party, working valiantly trying to push it to the left. Although most of our political energy was focused on our own independent activities in building our group, we still maintained a policy of encouraging those of our members who could do so to join and become active in the CCF.

The CCF, founded in 1932 and morphing into the NDP in 1961, had been in reality a coalition of reform socialists, Christian socialists of various stripes, labour activists and farmers' organizations, primarily an agrarian response to the terrible conditions of the Great Depression of the 1930s. It had been endorsed in 1943 by the CCL, the main federation of the industrial unions in Canada as "the political arm of labour." The CCF's founding document, the Regina Manifesto, which today would be considered a very radical statement—almost revolutionary—called for the social ownership of the means of production. Under Tommy Douglas' leadership in 1944, the Party had won office in Saskatchewan and one year earlier, under Ted Joliffe, it became the official opposition in Ontario. Most of the industrial unions in Canada supported the party in one form or another, their main motivation to avoid the gains won at the bargaining table being taken away in the legislatures. It's the main reason today the Canadian Labour Congress (CLC) still supports the NDP. In practical terms, aside from asking for their members to support the party, this meant giving the party financial support and assigning staff to work for it during election campaigns. Not all unions supported this policy, however, notably the craft unions in the Trades and Labour Congress that were noted for a more conservative viewpoint, that of "rewarding our friends and punishing our enemies," what we termed "Gomperism," after the political strategy of Samuel Gompers when he was head of the American Federation of Labour (AFL). In practical terms, this policy led to support for the Liberal Party at election time and going cap in hand to them if they were elected, seeking favours.

The issue of "independent labour political action" was never really settled in the labour movement during the life of the CCF and was debated late into the decade and was usually on the agenda of most union conventions. In those unions that supported this policy, many locals set up Political Action Committees, "PACs" as they were commonly known, especially at election time to help win support for the party. Where they did not exist, we in the SEL would use our influence to have PACs established and encourage others to do likewise. The CP, the craft unions and Tory and Liberal supporters in all the unions, on the other hand, were the sharpest critics of this political orientation. From early on, however, the Trotskyists gave the CCF "critical support," seeing it as representing a means by which working people in their majority might break from the big capitalist parties electorally on their way to creating a working class political alternative in Canada, similar to the Labour Parties in Britain and Australia. The CCF, the SEL believed, was the form "the Labour Party was taking in Canada."[1]

The question of whether the Canadian labour movement *as a whole* would have its own party would remain unresolved until the founding of the NDP. For our part, we regarded ourselves as being part of a broad politically progressive current within the labour movement fighting to get the unions to break from both capitalist parties. We maintained that the CCF in a limited way was a political expression of that class independence. The issue would frequently confront us in a very practical way, such as when the CCF would be under attack from right-wing elements in the unions, often card-carrying Liberals and Tories, and especially from craft unions. Our group would usually ally with left-wing social democrats to fend them off. For the left it was always a big issue during election time when the question of who workers should vote for would be on the agenda. Since its founding, the CCF had steadily increased its support in Ontario where an important body of trade unionists led by the Steelworkers and Packinghouse workers had helped get it established but the labour movement's support for the party was by no means unanimous. Right up to the founding of the NDP, party activists were still trying to broaden the labour movement's support for CCF and would sometimes be defeated by a combination of Liberals and supporters of the Communist Party.

Over their history, Canadian Trotskyists always had some kind of "orientation" to the CCF, whether it was trying to link up with its left wing or simply calling for a vote for it at election time. They firmly believed that the next "historical step" for the working class, after having formed its mass industrial unions, was for it to form its own political party, most likely a labour party based on the unions, the path workers in Britain and Australia had taken at the beginning of the 20th century. Jack MacDonald, for example—as I have already mentioned, he was one of the early leaders of the group in Canada—was expelled from the CCF after "entering" it in 1937. When the group re-established itself after the Second World War, its newspaper, *Labour Challenge*, carried the slogan on its masthead, "For affiliation of the unions to the CCF." In contrast to this, the CP, still carried its "popular front" line of the war period, of building a cross-class anti-monopoly coalition and was hostile over the years to any position that supported the CCF. This is not to say that there were not considerable modifications to our group's attitude to the CCF over time. Probably the most dramatic was in its approach immediately after the Second World War when it organized itself as the Revolutionary Workers Party (RWP) and published *Labour Challenge* with the perspective that it could directly appeal to the working class and win mass support to itself. "In 1945 we had hoped the post war revolutionary upsurge," Ross Dowson would later write, "would result in the advanced workers deserting the CCF, bypassing the reformist stages in their development of political consciousness and move directly to the recognition of the need for a revolutionary vanguard party."[2] This tactic was based on an estimation of the deep crises of capitalism continuing after the war but with the expansion of the economy during the post war reconstruction, militancy in the working class decreased and the group was forced to dissolve itself as a political party in 1951 and function, at least until 1955, "entered" in the CCF as "a nameless semi-underground faction ..."[3]

Not long after I came into the group, it was suggested to me I should join the High Park CCF, a constituency near where I lived in those days, so I went along to a meetings one evening and signed up as a member, becoming active in its youth group. After the purging of its left-wing in 1954, the CCF Youth was then in a sad state of decline and many of its constituency organizations rarely met. That's probably why at an annual city-wide meeting in 1956 it was so easy for us to get control of the entire Toronto organization by getting a majority on its City Executive. I unexpectedly managed to get myself elected city organizer and Alan Harris became chairman. However, we weren't city-wide leaders very long. Soon after getting elected, the Suez crisis broke out—the invasion of Egypt by Britain, France and Israel in July, 1956, a clear case of imperialist aggression over Egypt's nationalization of the Suez Canal. In response to the invasion, our majority on the Executive organized the CCF Youth to publicly protest the aggression against Egypt by means of a protest rally outside the British Consular offices in downtown Toronto, and in true ecumenical spirit that ran counter to the anti-Communist mood of the adult party leadership, we invited the Young Communist League (YCL) to come along. Very surprised to get the invite, they were very pleased to participate. Because of the prevailing mood, I imagine, such invitations were few and far between. A couple of hundred people showed up. Everyone was of the opinion it was a delightful success and a way of making the CCF Youth a more militant and relevant organization, we thought, but the week was hardly out before we were summarily expelled because we had "allowed Communists to participate." But suddenly we were in touch with more CP youth than ever, an unexpected and positive consequence of getting kicked out of the CCF Youth.

Alan Harris carrying a picket sign during our 1956 election campaign

Chapter 10

Crisis in the Communist Party

*T*HE LATE FIFTIES ALSO HAPPENED TO BE A PERIOD WHEN THE LABOUR Progressive Party (LPP), the official name of the Communist Party in Canada, was going through a major internal crisis, from which it would never recover. In addition to the shock of the Khrushchev revelations, by November 1956 LPP members were seeing on their televisions every day Russian tanks smashing through barricades on the streets of Budapest, Hungary, crushing the workers who after one of the most successful strikes in Europe, had seized power and overthrown the old Stalinist regime. We in the SEL supported the workers and we quickly redoubled our efforts to become a factor in the LPP's internal debate, by reaching out to as many of its members and supporters as we could find to see what they were thinking—this was one of the reasons why our engagement with them during the CCF Youth anti-Suez protest was so important. Our hope was that at least a few of them would come to re-evaluate the Stalin legacy and perhaps we would win them to our ranks. We also tried to take advantage of their crisis by selling our literature outside LPP events, especially a recently published booklet by Peter Fryer who had been the British CP's correspondent in Budapest during the revolution.[1]

Even though the confidence of the LPP seemed to be collapsing like a pricked balloon, they were still a substantial force, with approximately 1,300 attending their May Day meeting in Toronto that year. Most of our group stood outside that event distributing a special leaflet we had prepared for the occasion and selling our literature. I found it something of a weird experience standing on the pavement outside the Ukrainian

Hall on Bathurst Street in Toronto with people rushing past us to get in, avoiding eye contact and refusing to talk. Of course, their people at the door refused to let us in, but a few weeks later we were able to quietly slip in to a special meeting on the 20th Congress of the Soviet party and the Khrushchev Speech, that had about 450 people in the hall. We were even allowed to ask a few questions from the floor and for the first time it seemed the mood was changing because people seemed to listen to us respectful and "there was no Trotsky baiting."[2] Still, the prejudice against us was very strong. It was hard to overcome the years of cultivated hostility towards us—and a few of their hard-liners accused us of being "fascists" and or "capitalist agents." We didn't win any of them to our ranks, as far as I can recall, even though droves of them tore up their membership cards. But later in the Sixties, many of their sons and daughters, "red diaper" babies, became active in our group, many of them taking up leadership positions.

The CP in the U.S. was in a similar crisis. An opposition group had emerged there, comprised mainly of Afro-Americans and concentrated in New Jersey, in what later became the Progressive Labour Party (PLP). The political climate for the left in the country was beginning to change for the better. The hard factional lines between the various socialist organizations had begun to soften appreciably as people began to search for explanations about what had happened in the Soviet Union. To help this process along, the SWP began to advance what became known as, "a regroupment policy" towards the socialist left. They immediately received support for this from A. J. Muste, an early leader of the Workers Party, and Vincent Hallinan, an important civil rights lawyer, and jointly they sponsored a series of large public forums in New York to deal with some of the issues that such a "regroupment" of the left might confront in the future. The SWP's overall concept was—like ours in Canada— that the building of a mass revolutionary party would not happen by the simple accretion of individuals, but that under the pressure of events— a rise in the class struggle—leftists and militants would of necessity have to come together on the basis of a militant programme to create such a party. The SWP believed that a first step in this process would be for socialists, wherever possible, to begin talking to each other and cooperating on common projects. The discussion with the PLP culminated with the SWP and the PLP that year supporting each other's candidates in the New York state elections.

Michel Lambeth

A view of the interior of the SEL's 1956 municipal election campaign headquarters. From left: an activist whose name I don't remember, Ken Sutherland, Peter Metheus, (from the U.S. and whose real name was Joe Johnson), Virginia "Bunny" Batten, and Ruth Houle.

Chapter 11

Marriage and the Founding of the YSA

*I*was working at Amalgamated Electric in the early summer of 1957 when Cliff Orchard and I decided we would like to spend a week's vacation at the SWP's Mountain Spring Camp in the Pocono Hills of Pennsylvania to attend their summer educational session. It was our first time there. Cliff was not a member of our group at that time but I was hoping I could recruit him. Later he became a leader of the LSA. At the camp, there was lots of discussion on the fringes of the seminars about the possibility of future close relations between the PLP and the SWP, but the hot news everyone was talking about was the emergence of a left wing in the Young Socialist League (YSL),[1] the youth organization of Max Shachtman's Independent Socialist League (ISL), both of which claimed to be "Marxist." There was a certain irony to this turn of events, however, a sort of second kick at the can for the SWP that they seemed to be relishing. Well known in American radical circles, Shachtman had been an early leader in the SWP alongside Cannon during the time of Trotsky and had been one of the founding leaders of the Fourth International. He later split on the question of what attitude socialists should have towards the Soviet Union, well documented in Cannon's *The Struggle for a Proletarian Party*[2] and in Trotsky's *In Defense of Marxism.*[3] Until this period, Shachtman had been able to represent himself as a "Trotskyist," even a "revolutionary," but by that summer he was moving rapidly towards social democracy and had given up the idea of building any kind of revolutionary organization and was on his way into the Democratic Party. Many of the following details come from a report I sent to Toronto that summer.[4]

The ISL, I was told, was much smaller than the SWP, with only a few members in New York, but the YSL by everyone's estimate had about 200 members nation-wide. Shachtman, the previous year, had proposed dissolving it into the Socialist Party-Social Democratic Federation (SP-SDF) that was led by Norman Thomas, probably one of the US's best known social democrats. In preparation for such a move, the ISL and YSL had moved to the right by mirroring the SP-SDF's electoral policies as much as possible, which meant a policy of passivity in response to the AFL-CIO supporting candidates of the Democratic Party, a tactic generally seen by everyone on the left as the ISL's deep desire to wash itself of the "commie" label to gain bourgeois acceptance and respectability. All of which precipitated an internal crisis in the organization. The left-wing countered this support for the Democrats by demanding that, instead, all socialist candidates should be supported—that would, naturally enough, include the SWP. This move to the right raised such a storm of protest that Bogdan Denitch and Michael Harrington, the two main leaders of the organizations, were compelled to acquiesce to a referendum of the membership, which the opposition won by a large margin, a small detail they managed to keep hidden from the membership until two months after the YSL went on public record supporting Democratic Party candidates in the election. The left-wing of YSL—notably Jim Robertson, Tim Wohlforth and Shane Mage—challenged this rightward orientation. Shachtman, Denitch and Harrington's response was to threaten expulsion, calling their critics "Cannonite agents," and "sectarians" for not being "realistic and practical" and "not being conscious of the American working class' hatred of Stalinism." In the course of their struggle, the left in the YSL found they were beginning to gain a new appreciation of the SWP which was giving them full support and helping to print some of their bulletins.

The SWP's pointman in this work was Murry Weiss, who was fixated on winning a new layer of young militants to the views of the SWP. He and his wife, Myra were members of the party's Political Committee and she had been the vice-presidential candidate alongside Dobbs in the previous SWP Presidential campaign. When I met Murry that summer, he was obviously on the look-out for young people who could help him with this work. Not about to let this opportunity slip out of their grasp, the SWP had begun to quickly set up their own youth organization, American Youth for Socialism (AYS) to begin to collaborate with left in the YSL and to help them in their faction fight. Already joint meetings were being held in some parts of the country. Because of the long period of slow growth, there were not many around the SWP in those days who could be classified as youth, and those few were mostly the sons and daughters of party members. In any case, the SWP pushed ahead quickly to get a youth organization off the ground under the leadership of Bert Deck and his wife, René. Calling Bert a youth was a bit of an exaggeration, I remember thinking; with his balding head, to me he looked to be in his early forties, but the SWP was not about to let such formalities stand in its way.

It wasn't long after Cliff Orchard and I got back from Mountain Spring Camp that Ross got a call from Murry Weiss asking if it would be possible for me to go down to New York for a while to help the SWP "with their youth work," and to lend a hand to the Wohlforth-Robertson-Mage grouping—really a faction—in YSL and to help prepare the ground for its approaching convention that had every appearance of heading towards a split. The SWP was scouring its ranks to see who would classify as youth and urging anyone—and there weren't many who met that criterion—to come to New York to help it augment the numbers of its newly minted youth organization, the AYS.

I felt honoured by Murry's call and I raised it with our small Amalgamated Electric fraction. I remember they were initially unhappy with the idea of me pulling out, until Ross had a discussion with them to turn them around. Before Murry's invitation, I had been to New York for only a few days at a time to sit in on meetings of the National Committee and other such special events, so I hardly knew anything about the city. While I was growing up in Belfast, like most of my generation, American culture loomed large for me, especially Hollywood movies and popular music.

To me, everything brilliant seemed to come from America. Just the thought of being in New York, one of the greatest cities in the world for a few months left me dazzled. After Murry's call, I left immediately to hitchhike down there.

When I got to 116 University Place, the headquarters of the SWP, it seemed to be a hive of activity, with many people coming and going, an appearance that seemed to belie its small membership. A low-rise building of about four storeys, the SWP rented everything above the second. Someone called for Murry from one of the offices upstairs to come and meet me. He then introduced me to Bert Deck, who after a short and friendly conversation suggested I stay with him and his wife René for a week or so until a more permanent place could be found for me. I was immediately cast into the thick of things, attending what seemed like an endless round of caucus meetings and my head literally spun from looking over past issues of the ISL's journal, *Labor Action* and reading Internal Bulletins to get caught up with the dispute. The AYS people with whom I worked were Jim Lambrecht, Arthur Felberbaum and a very young Nora Roberts—she was about fifteen at the time and the daughter of long time editor of *The Militant*, Dan Roberts. All were in the leadership of the new youth group, but I had the distinct feeling it was in a rather feeble state and only in the process of coming into being. They told me their main priority was to try and help the opposition in the YSL get as much support as possible and asked if I would work with Tim Wohlforth and his wife Martha on this. I met Tim and Martha soon after. They lived on the fourth floor of a "walk-up" in downtown Manhattan. Their son Karl was only a few weeks old and Tim, a very speedy writer, scratched out a living, editing house organs for various commercial companies.

One of my first assignments was to visit everyone I could in the YSL. Every day Tim and Martha fed me lists of addresses of members and delegates who had to be visited within the next few weeks. Before this, when I had imagined New York, I had an impression it would be a very wealthy and modern city, but I soon came to see, as I knocked on the doors of the contacts on the list that had been provided to me, social conditions seemed just as bad as some areas of Belfast, with the divide between the obscenely wealthy and the working class much greater. This was long before gentrification swept North America and many of the old brownstone buildings that looked alright from the outside were comprised entirely of run-down "walk-up," cold-water flats—which means, no hot water—and no elevators. All my time, day and evening, was spent hunting for YSL members. Most of them were people who had attended the previous conventions and Tim wanted to get the left's material into their hands to see if they could be recruited. I don't remember having any "breakthrough" moments. I recall that a lot of them would look at me with a questioning expression on their face. I'm sure they were trying to make sense of my heavy Belfast accent and many wouldn't even open their doors to me. The few I did meet who were open to talking seemed more fed up with the factionalism than anything else, but we learned through the grapevine that the YSL's National office was a little rattled by what we were doing and had launched their own campaign to counter us.

Robertson, who was living in California and who along with Wohlforth and Shane Mage a few years later would split from the SWP on the issue of Cuba, was not in New York at that time, but I met him a month or so later in the opposition caucus as we got close to the convention. I remember how he took great delight in the factionalism and seemed to be having a great time of it. He was in his element in the fight and I was very impressed by how well he had prepared for it. In his briefcase, all marked up with notations, were all the previous documents of the organization, including the written submissions to the discussion from around the country. In our packed meetings at Wohlforth's home as we prepared for the convention, I saw him periodically diving, with some relish, into his "personal faction fighters kit" as he liked to call it—to drag out some reference or other to back up a point he was making in the discussion. The left was not sure what its support at the convention would be.

Despite the charges and counter charges, the convention itself seemed to me fairly open and democratic compared to what I had experienced in the labour movement in Canada. I don't remember any complaints about a lack of democracy or delegates not getting recognized from the floor or long procedural wrangles, as often happened in the CCF in Canada. Of course, it was a much smaller affair, with approximately twenty-five voting delegates, but with the alternates, fraternal delegates and observers present, the hall was packed. Harrington was the majority's reporter on their "Perspective for Unity" document. He was very up front about what they were doing, stating it was of vital necessity for them to break out of their isolation and that the only road to this was to the right. In his view, social democracy was in the "third camp" and a labour party would evolve out of it. He stressed that all issues for the working class were subservient to the building of a labour party and that the lack of a labour party in the United States was a reflection of its low level of political consciousness. In his opinion, both organized labour and the bureaucracy were to the left of the workers. He lauded the SP-SDF in that it was not in any way connected to Russia and had a tradition of being known as "socialist" to many workers. He rejected completely the possibility of recruiting anyone to the left of the social democrats and saw no hope, for example, in recruiting CP youth or getting anything from the crisis that was then shaking the CP.

Wohlforth presented the minority position. He argued that Harrington's position was based upon a conception that capitalism in America had a long-term perspective, a conception which many Marxist scholars rejected, he said. He was scornful of the YSL's leaders for presenting their orientation to social democracy as a clever "entry tactic" and exaggerating the strength of the SP-SDF when the reality was that that organization was very inactive. He said that Harrington and company were ignoring what was happening to their left and were overly concerned with how they appeared in the eyes of the SD-SDF and attacking their notion of how a labour party would eventually develop in America. He argued that they ignored the example how the CIO had been built, which had come out of a militant working class upsurge, and which might be the way a labour party in the U.S. could be formed in the future.

This was followed by a hard and vigourous floor debate and it even seemed at times that Harrington and Denitch would be defeated. We were holding our breath, hoping some of the centrists would swing over to us, but the eventual vote gave the leadership a clear majority: their resolution carried 18 to 5. I was surprised our vote was so low because we seemed to have many speakers supporting our positions from the floor. Apparently an arrangement had been made before the convention by the YSL leadership to include a few delegates from the centre on the incoming leadership slate, after they had agreed to shut up of course. Next morning it could be seen a split was all but assured when discussion took place about the guarantees the SP-SDF would provide the YSL regarding the "entry." Harrington and Denitch did not want any, and finally a resolution was moved to exclude the left from the whole process. This provoked something of an uproar and it was voted down, only receiving two votes, Denitch's and the person who had moved it. Later it was introduced again in another form and was about to be voted down once more, when a large balding man, looking overweight and not quite a youth, incredulously walked onto the platform demanding that he be allowed to speak, as was his right as a "delegate," he said, albeit "fraternal." It was an incongruous sight, seeing him standing there among the youth demanding they listen to him. Max Shachtman was then in his early fifties.

I was intrigued at seeing and hearing this major personality from the history of American Trotskyism because I had only known about him by reputation and from Trotsky and Cannon's struggle with him in the late thirties. He clearly had not lost his oratorical skills and I remember he made a few jokes at the expense of his critics that even made me smile, but I remember above all thinking how cynical he sounded. "I'm not crossing the river Styx into the Underworld," he said, refusing to concede that his end destination was the Democratic Party.[5] Tipping his hat to his Trotskyist origins, he reached into the history of the Fourth International to compare his opponents to those who had opposed Trotsky's "turn" toward the French Socialist Party in the thirties. Then his manner changed abruptly. Apparently he and the right wing had gotten hold of some internal correspondence between Murry Weiss and Cannon wherein Murry spoke of "smashing Shachtmanism," so Shachtman then launched into a bitter tirade against his critics, the tone of which appalled even some of his own supporters, telling the delegates the resolution before them was his and that it was one of "my people" who had moved it, arrogantly, literally bullying, demanding the delegates support it and exposing the true nature of the YSL's relationship to the ISL: it didn't have much independence, if any. Nevertheless, the motion carried.

The other major discussion at the convention was on the Hungarian Revolution, which showed the degree of ideological preparation the YSL was undergoing to become more palatable to the SD-SDF. Shane Mage showed that even on this question, the YSL's so called "Marxist" leadership's rightward drift when it called for support for Hungary's small-holders' party and in reality was supporting some kind of capitalist democracy, dumping its traditional "third camp" position. At the end of the convention, the minority walked out, about twenty-five in all, to eventually form their own youth organization. But that evening we had a small victory that was totally unexpected and in which I had a part. As I wrote to Ross shortly after, "There was one worker at the convention! Only one, a trade unionist from Steel in Pittsburg. He supported the right wing because they had contacted him first and he didn't know much except that he was against the union bureaucrats and capitalism. I went to their after-convention social and got into a conversation with the guy and went to a bar to shoot the bull. It ended with him being recruited to the left-wing caucus. It's now a standard joke of how we stole the proletarian base of the YSL."[6]

A few weeks after the convention, the AYS and the new grouping merged to become the Young Socialist Alliance (YSA), a youth organization politically in agreement with the SWP, but organizationally independent of it. A monthly journal, *Young Socialist,* was launched, with me on the editorial board as the Toronto representative, which, I have to admit, was more for decoration than anything else, because I seldom wrote for it and never played any part in its editorial deliberations. As for Shachtman and the ISL, they continued to shift to the right, even acting as a right-wing pressure on the SP-SDF to dissolve into the Democratic Party, and infamously supporting American imperialism's Bay of Pigs invasion of Cuba and later its war in Vietnam; the YSA went in a diametrically opposite direction, expanding across the country with branches on many campuses and becoming one of the main forces in the American left defending the Cuban Revolution and leading the struggle against the Vietnam War.

At about the time the ISL and the YSL were getting rid of their left wings, the American CP was entering a state of disintegration under the impact of the Khrushchev revelations and the events in Hungary. Hoping that a few of their youth might be attracted to the YSL-AYS joint organization, we made a special effort to get in touch with as many of them as possible. As I would experience later in Toronto, it turned out to be a very difficult task. Many had had their fill of radical politics and were in a state of deep disillusionment, or had dropped out of political activity entirely. But we managed to meet a few of them in any case—mainly on the periphery of the CP—who were looking for explanations of what had happened in the USSR and who were interested in a new realignment on the left. That's how I came to meet Hannah Lerner who would eventually become my wife. She and a few of her friends had been involved in the discussions with Bert and René Deck about setting up the new youth organization. Although they were only a handful, they were regarded as representatives of a new layer of young people on the fringes of the CP who were now being shaken loose from it and were looking for another political alternative. After a meeting one evening, she and I went for coffee and from there on we started seeing each other. An excellent folk singer and guitarist with training as an artist at Bard College, she was always asked to bring her guitar along and perform at the new youth organization's social events. She and her parents, middle class Jews, lived in Brooklyn and shared their house with her grandparents who had come from Russia to the U.S. before the war and worked in the garment industry.

Hannah's parents had been around the CP and in the thirties they were engaged in helping the CP organize the unorganized for the CIO, but they had long withdrawn from the CP and had only a loose informal connection to its cultural milieu. Her father, Abe Lerner, worked in publishing and was a nationally acclaimed book designer for Random House, but unofficially he still helped design books and pamphlets for International Publishers, the CP's publishing house. I later learned that he had been the designer of many of their most scurrilous pamphlets that denounced the Trotskyists as "fascists"; I imagined he must have been more than perturbed when he learned about his daughter's close relationship with one of them. If this was so, he hid it very well because he always treated me with the greatest courtesy. A new edition of Trotsky's *Literature and Revolution* had just been published by a commercial printer and I gave him a copy. I think it was the first time he had read Trotsky through un-prejudiced eyes and had seen a critique of "socialist realism" from the left. He told me he liked the work. Being in publishing, he could often get books for next to nothing and one day, to my surprise, he gave me a copy of Trotsky's monumental *History of the Russian Revolution,* which Random House had just published. A very expensive book, it had been out of print for a long time and I was glad to get it. It was also a sign to me that his prejudices about Trotsky were beginning to break down. He was thoroughly disillusioned with the CP by this time because of what Khrushchev had said about Stalin and the later revelations about anti-Semitism in the USSR, and he had encouraged Hannah's support for John Gates, leader of an opposition in the CP. Like many of the Gates people, however, he was using the crisis to increase the distance between the CP and him, and was on his way out of politics altogether.

When Hannah introduced me to her family, the atmosphere was at the beginning a little strained, to say the least, but eventually they warmed up a bit and made me very welcome. Aside from the politics, it must have been a very difficult situation for them. In their eyes, I was an uncultured young man—which was true—who belonged to a political grouping that was hostile to many things they had believed for a long time, and on top of that I was taking away their daughter. Hannah was strong willed and they knew they would be unable to change her mind so they resigned themselves to letting her go. I was in love with their daughter, so I guess they figured they should make the best of the situation.

And then I ran into money problems. It had been my understanding before I had left Toronto for New York that the SWP would help finance my stay there. I had some savings, but certainly not enough to cover all my expenses. Even though Bert and René Deck arranged for me to billet with various comrades, I still needed money for food and incidental expenses. Murry Weiss, while always apologetic, seemed to be unable to get me any help from the party. Although I was totally unaware of it at the time, I'm sure I was seen by Farrell Dobbs and Tom Kerry, as part of Murry and Myra Tanner Weiss' "coterie," an informal grouping that seemed to be made up of Jim Lambrecht, Arthur Felberbaum and Nora Roberts, leaders of the new youth organization, AYS and some other members of the New York branch, who had high hopes for increasing the membership through the "regroupment" experience and more from the crisis in the American CP. I later learned they had criticisms of the SWP leadership about how it had handled this experience. I was never able to find out what all of their complaints were and it seemed to me to be something nebulous mainly about Farrell and Tom Kerry's "inflexibility" in dealing with the "regroupment" process. The way this affected me was that during the whole time I was in New York that summer, I was always scrimping around for money just to get by, an old story in my life it would turn out and one that would be repeated when I was on other assignments for our group. For my part, I was oblivious to any differences Murry and Myra might have had with the leadership. Hannah and I had supper with them many times in their apartment and never did I hear any expressions of criticism of Farrell, or maybe I was just too much of a neophyte to pick up the signals. Myra and Murry left the SWP in the early Sixties. It was a sad loss for me; I had gotten to like them very much.

Michel Lambeth

Top *Toronto Labour Bookstore discussing an election campaign. Standing on the left of the photo is Ross Dowson. Clockwise from him: Paddy Stanton and Joe Rosenblatt, seated. Jerry Houle, standing, Harry Paine, with hand holding his leg. Someone I only remember as "Peter", on chair. Jim Mitchell, standing with his hand on face.*

Bottom *Jimmy Mitchell and Ros Dowson*

Chapter 12

Regroupment

*A*FTER MY SIX-MONTH STAY IN NEW YORK, HANNAH RETURNED WITH me to Toronto. A seaman in the SWP who was scheduled to ship out to Europe kindly loaned us his car and we loaded it up with Hannah's stuff, including her guitar, and headed north, after giving her parents the assurance we would marry as soon as possible. Despite having a radical background, they couldn't throw off the bourgeois morality of the times: the practice of couples living together unwed, was frowned upon, even in "progressive" New York. But Hannah and I were excited and happy. Helping build a new youth organization had been an exhilarating experience for us and we were looking forward to seeing if the same thing could happen north of the border.

After a few days back in Toronto, we gave a report to the SEL about what had transpired at the YSL conference. Not long after that, the SEL decided to initiate its own "regroupment" process to take advantage of the crisis in the LPP that hadn't abated much since I had left for New York. We were hoping we could find a few people to work with us outside our own milieu and Joe Salsberg, a long time leader of the LPP—the name of the CP in Canada—seemed a possible candidate. He was probably the LPP's most important public figure at the time and very influential in the Jewish community. He, along with a few other leaders such as Harry Binder, Smith Sims, Norman Penner, (whose son would later become a leader of the Canadian Trotskyists and who was at the time a leader of their youth organization), and Guy Caron and Henri Gagnon in Montreal, were in open revolt, eventually leading to their departure from the Party.

In earlier years, Salsberg had been on Toronto's City Council and had sat in the Ontario Provincial Legislature for the Spadina riding until his defeat in 1955. He was in the news when we arrived in Toronto, because he had publicly criticized Tim Buck, the party leader, for remaining silent about the Khrushchev speech and about Buck's appalling silence on discrimination against Jews and the suppression of their culture in the Soviet Union. I remember getting a first-hand look at the LPP crisis one time when I sneaked into the hall of the United Jewish People's Order (UJPO) one evening during a closed meeting of CP supporters to hear Salsberg speak after he had returned from a trip to Eastern Europe. He reported on his investigations and observations about the persecution of Jews, especially at the time of the so-called "doctor's plot" in 1953 when a group of medical people, mainly Jewish, were falsely accused by the infamous Laventia Beria of trying to poison Stalin. The packed hall was deathly silent except for the occasional gasps of horror from the audience as it sat quietly listening to Salsberg's damning account. He did not mince his words much in condemning the failure of the LPP leadership to take a stand. His articles in UJPO's *Vochenblott* were reproduced around the world and especially in Eastern Europe, and I'm sure they became an important element contributing to the international discrediting of Stalinism. In Canada, it seemed to be the final straw for many supporters who left the Party in droves and even the UJPO eventually broke away. Support for the LPP in the Jewish community fell through the floor, especially in Montreal where it had had a very active base, but the fact that Salsberg said he had known about the persecution of Jews in the USSR since 1939 and had said nothing didn't in any way help his credibility.[1]

After a short struggle, Buck pushed Salsberg out of the Party. There was some speculation in our circles that he might head up a new left force and so Ross went to see him a couple of times to sound him out on the possibility that the thousands who were walking away from the CCF and those leaving the LPP might be interested in some kind of "regroupment" process, in which he, Salsberg, could have an important influence. Salsberg was obviously looking all the non-LPP groups over, because he told Ross he had been touch with the Labour Forum, a loose grouping set up by Murray Dowson, Ross' brother, and Joe Rosenthal of the "Rose" group. Leo Huberman of *Monthly Review* had spoken there, as had Scott Nearing, but our estimation was that this would not go anywhere because the Rosenthal grouping was running out of steam and seemed to be barely functioning. (An important source of Ross' intelligence about this came from his sister Joyce, who was Joe's wife.) More importantly, we were hoping Salsberg was watching what was going on in New York where there was talk about a "united ticket" of the left in the forthcoming New York state elections and which might have encouraged him to work with us. We had also learned through the grapevine, that he was in touch with the Gagnon people in Montreal and was trying to work out some kind of formal relationship with them, so we began to think a "regroupment" policy might have some basis in reality in Canada. This idea rapidly moved up on our agenda, however, when we heard that hundreds were walking away from the LPP in Quebec and that Henri Gagnon, an electrician and popular working class militant, along with its main leaders Jacques Rouleau and Guy Caron, had begun to organize a new political formation, the Council of Socialist Clubs, comprised of seven LPP clubs that had been expelled from the Party. They were openly talking about "regroupment" and were organizing a series of public forums to publicly promote that idea. In Toronto, we immediately organized a car load from our group to go to Montreal to meet with them, the first of several discussions that reached a stage where Ross was invited to be on a panel of one of their forums. That forum turned out to have a very long speakers' list and was attended by a hundred and sixty people, a large meeting for Montreal. I remember it going on for a long time. Gagnon was the main speaker. There were other ex-leaders of the LPP there, and Ross. Also on the platform was our own Paddy Stanton and me, along with Gabriel Glazer, an independent socialist we had been in contact with, and Danny Daniels, the Canadian correspondent for the U.S. weekly *National Guardian*. My purpose for being there was to give a report about our Youth Socialist Forums in Toronto, which had only been in existence a few months, and which I will describe more fully later in this chapter. In my comments I tried to cast it as the first steps in a kind of spontaneous socialist regroupment among young people, not mentioning my membership in the SEL, saying that "ten or eleven of us had got it off the ground" to get it going.[2] I don't think I fooled anyone.

It proved to be very difficult to move our relations with the Gagnon group beyond that of making the occasional visit to them, to more formal and regular cooperation. Although they were friendly and very open to us every time we visited Montreal, for some reason or other, we never seemed to be able get any of them to come to Toronto for discussions or participate in our activities, our forums, for example. I don't remember any of them ever speaking there. Another complication may have resulted from a delayed effect in Montreal of the dispute with the Rosenthal group. Jean-Marie Bedard, who had been married to Ross' sister, Lois, and who, in his better days, had been the leader of the Montreal group, had sided with Rosenthal and had reappeared in the Council of Socialist Clubs and had very good relations, it seemed, with Gagnon. Bedard may not have been very interested in making our lives any easier. But aside from that, our main problem, of course, was that none of us spoke French. This greatly limited our contact with them, even though most of them were bilingual and we had yet to work out our position on the question of Quebec "separation." In the end we dismissed them as moving in a "nationalist" direction and, even a few years later in 1963, we still regarded the separatist forces in Quebec as being "petty bourgeois" that could "weaken the left in Quebec by cutting it off from the mainstream of the working class, the best organized, the most politically conscious working class."[3]

What we failed to recognize was that we were at the beginning of a rise of a new national consciousness in Quebec that would eventually give birth to a mass independence movement against English Canada. Who knows what role Gagnon could have played in that? In the early Sixties, we saw the main difficulty as being primarily organizational rather than national in that we did not have a branch of our group there that could have had a more continuous relationship with them. To that end, we persuaded Bruce Batten and his wife Virginia, known to us as "Bunny," (she was at the SWP's cadre school that winter), to relocate and begin the process of our "colonizing" Montreal, an unfortunate word to describe the SEL's efforts to establish a Montreal branch. Bruce and Virginia did not last long in Montreal, however, and soon began to develop differences with Ross about the orientation of the group, the substance of which I don't remember now. The next thing I knew they were on their way to Vancouver, and by 1959 they were out of the organization with Ross denouncing a statement they wrote as "... a pitiful thing. A classic emanation from a couple of petit bourgeois..." It didn't help much either that when Michel Pablo published their statement in his internal bulletin, which circulated internationally, it was picked up by some of our critics in Vancouver who quickly circulated it around the left.[4] Bruce and Bunny's fall from grace was always a puzzling development for me because I had known them ever since I had joined the group and I don't remember any doubt ever being expressed about their loyalty and commitment to our ideas. Bunny later became a professor at York University.

It was only after Richard Fidler, Bob Horne and Mike Mill, later known as "Michel" Mill, relocated to Montreal—in a new "colonization" effort—that we were able to establish a functioning branch and begin to come to terms with the Quebec question. By 1970 we had moved from a position of supporting self-determination to advocating total independence, all the while refusing to recognize that our grouping there should be independent from Toronto, if we were to be consistent.

It was through that early Montreal experience we met Milton Acorn, who was then in the LPP and who would eventually become known throughout Canada as a "worker poet." Milton, originally from Prince Edward Island, was even then well known in radical circles for his poetry, but we had never met him before going to Montreal. I remember Ross telling me that on first contact with Milton he had half expected to meet some kind of "effete petit-bourgeois" type and that he was completely surprised when Milton turned out to be a callous-handed carpenter who, aside from trying to establish himself as a poet, was expressing some interest in our ideas.

During our efforts to connect in a meaningful way with Gagnon and his supporters in Montreal, Joe Salsberg in Toronto showed no interest whatsoever in working with the SEL. Our hopes in this regard were raised, however, when he came out publicly "for a realignment of socialist forces in Canada for a new Party of Canadian Marxism." We also learned that Murray Dowson and Joe Rosenthal had been in touch with him to get him to speak at one of their Labour Forums. Murray and Joe had achieved some success in bringing in speakers for their forums from *Monthly Review* in New York, and we were fearful they might poison Salsberg against us—though I suspect he had a lot more in common with them than with us. Nevertheless, we decided to make another special effort to see if we could overcome his hesitations, so Hannah and I went to see him. By then our group had pulled together a few young activists from the CCF Youth who were on our periphery. Attempting to emulate the SWP experience in New York, we had set up our own "regroupment process" and had begun a series of panel discussions with outside speakers on topics we thought would allow us to reach a larger audience than usual.

Our youth forum activity had been in existence for about three months and had been attracting around twenty-five people to each event. We hoped Salsberg would be a speaker. When we phoned him he readily agreed to meet with us, so Hannah and I went to his office on Spadina Avenue, south of College, where he was working selling insurance. I recall him being tall in stature and very friendly and charming, which surprised me a little. He was a little avuncular without being patronizing, intrigued I think more by our youthful enthusiasm than anything else. We didn't discuss the struggle he was going through in the LPP in Ontario because at that time we did not have that much information about it but we let him know we had been to Montreal recently to meet Gagnon. He didn't seem very interested in talking about this, but he questioned us about our experiences in New York because he knew some of the personalities involved there. The fact that Hannah was Jewish also helped because he asked her about her family and some of the people she knew around the American CP. We were very pleased and a little surprised when, after we had assured him the platform would be his alone, he readily agreed to be a speaker. There were not many venues in the city for someone who had been a prominent Communist to air their views and answer the LPP's criticisms of him, something he was clearly anxious to do. It was an important catch for us. We worked hard building the forum, scheduled for February 14th, the fourth in a series, and it turned out to be one of our more successful events that year, with a much better than normal turn out, and, importantly, with broad representation from the left and a very good discussion from the floor. Some of the people who had left in the Pablo split were also in the audience, including Joe Rosenthal and Ross' brother, Murray. It was the only meeting of ours I ever saw them attend.

Despite this success, however, the "regroupment" experience in Toronto did not come to much of anything. In the end, despite our best efforts, we did not get much from it. We were quick to explain our lack of success to ourselves by characterizing Salsberg's evolution as moving towards "reformism," i.e., social democracy, an echo of the diatribe the Stalinists hurled at him in their efforts to inoculate their ranks against his influence. From this distance in time, I now think we were probably a little too impatient and unrealistic in expecting a personality such as Salsberg to jump to Trotskyism so quickly. The personal and political cost to him would have been enormous and it would have been another political barrier against continuing his dialogue with his ex-comrades. It's easy now to see we should have probably come up with more imaginative ways to help him in his political struggle against Buck and to help establish a mutually beneficial relationship with him over a longer period. Nevertheless we put on a bit of a blitz and paid visits to as many ex-Party people as possible. When we evaluated the conversations we had with the few we had visited, we would tend to quickly dismiss them as being "worn out" and wanting to get away from the CP as fast as possible, with not much interest in doing anything that would involve political activity, but I think the sad reality was that we were not a sufficiently large enough organization to appeal to them; we simply did not have the "critical mass" to be an attractive option.

What's interesting is that towards the end of the Sixties, some of these people reappeared in political life, but this time in the Waffle wing of the NDP, where they worked to block our relations with that oppositional grouping. I also think, looking back on it, we tended to expect results too quickly and pushed our ideas too hard. We should have been more patient and allowed people time to change their minds. Another factor, and probably the most important, was that we lacked the intellectual heft to win them over. Ross was the only one amongst us who had the capacity to hold his own in any discussions with them. I remember Hannah and I were assigned once to visit a young Norman Penner, whom we had learned from some of our contacts in the YCL was also challenging the Party line. We took along some pamphlets, including Khrushchev's speech, which he had not seen. We were hoping he would participate in one of our forums. He was very courteous towards us and sat us down for coffee. Hannah and I had a fairly good discussion with him, but I think he was more preoccupied with earning a living than taking on another political commitment and linking up with a small political grouping such as ours.

Not long after that, the "regroupment" forums came to an end and we went ahead and set up a Toronto branch of the Young Socialist Alliance to leverage our connection with the YSA in New York, to see if we could recruit some youth who were around the YCL and a few young people who were disaffected with the CCF. The new organization, however, remained small and seemed to me to have become doctrinaire, which stood in the way of it making any advancement. It was not doing much of anything that would attract youth, not that much was happening yet with that demographic. Its importance to us was that its existence was a testament to our new policy of theorizing the youth issue and looking to providing a political organization that would meet young people's needs, and indeed, in the next few years it was from this sector that most of our new members came.

Chapter 13

Cross-Country with the Workers Vanguard

W E WEREN'T AWARE OF IT THEN, BUT THE LATTER PART OF THE fifties was a time when the CCF had entered its terminal phase, a lingering crisis in the party not publicly talked about much by the Lewis leadership then, but that had precipitated a discussion among the union brass about whether the Party could ever win power in its current form or whether another should take its place. At its national convention in 1956, the CCF had formally codified the pro-capitalist direction it had been on since its founding. It rid itself entirely of its remaining "socialist" baggage and moved to the right ideologically in the hope of breaking out of its electoral impasse to become more acceptable to the media and maybe attract more middle class support. Its founding document, the Regina Manifesto, adopted in 1932—which contained the declaration, "No CCF government will rest until industry has been nationalized," a policy mostly ignored by the party bureaucracy—was replaced with the more moderate Winnipeg Declaration that made no reference whatsoever to public ownership. However, the idea of public ownership had not been totally eradicated in the party and in the thinking of its MPs.

It made a re-appearance once more in the famous Canadian Pipeline Debate in 1955, when the Liberals under Louis St. Laurent used closure motions to cut off debate in Parliament to push through their deal with Lehman Brothers and Texas oil interests, to build a gas pipeline from western Canada to Ontario, part of which would have gone through the United States. During the debate, the CCF's M. J. Coldwell argued that such a pipeline should be publicly owned, a message that became somewhat blurred when three of the Ontario CCF MLAs voted to support provincial Tories in funding it. By the time the election had rolled around, however, and in what was generally regarded as a lacklustre campaign, Coldwell had dumped this position entirely, saying nothing at all about public ownership. John Diefenbaker turned out to be more dynamic and energetic than either the Liberals or the CCF, playing the Canadian nationalism card to the hilt, arguing for a totally Canadian route that would go across Canada's north. A resurgent Tory party swept the Liberals out of office, to form a minority government in what amounted to a massive protest vote.

It turned out to be an ominous result for the CCF. Historically regarded as the "protest" party of Canada, it had been virtually bypassed in the election, its popular vote declining. It only gained two seats and I remember at the time how we marveled at the very large rallies organized by the Tories, especially in the West, with thousands in attendance and wondered if this perhaps signified a kind of political awakening generally in the country and what would be its significance for the left. There was none. Its main effect was to revitalize the Tories and provide the right with a broad populist base. From our contacts in the CCF, we knew there was a high degree of dissatisfaction, although unorganized, about how M. J. Coldwell had performed and a resentful anger mainly in the West about the dumping of the Regina Manifesto, so we thought perhaps some debate might develop about the party's course, but it was not to be. Instead, it seems, most of the discussion took place inside the party and union apparatuses and far away from the ears of the rank and file.

Those were the political circumstances as preparations got underway in Toronto for the SEL's 1958 tour across Canada, that would attempt to make up for the abbreviated and problem-plagued one of the previous year. Part of our thinking was that the feeble results the CCF achieved in the election—only electing ten MPs—would be a major talking point with party activists. At the same time we planned to focus some of our attention on the CP and attempt to meet as many of its members as possible, including those on its periphery or who had walked away, to see if we could work with them. To this end we planned to carry a good supply of the Khrushchev Speech pamphlet along with Peter Fryer's book *The Hungarian Tragedy*,[1] with the intention of getting it into as many hands as possible. Once the tour would reach Vancouver, Ross Dowson said he would fly out to link up with it.

As preparations got underway, Ross proposed that I should participate in it, saying it would be "a very good experience" for me and that it would give me a chance "to get to know Canada," plus apply some of the political experiences I had had in New York talking to people around the CP about our ideas. Initially, I was reluctant to go, primarily because Hannah and I had just arrived in Toronto and it would mean leaving her on her own in what for her was a new city where she barely knew anyone. I could see Hannah wasn't very happy about this prospect either, but when I raised it with her, her loyalty to the group was such she felt she could not object, she later told me. Since coming to Toronto, she had worked hard at integrating herself into the group's activities.

A very good singer and musician, Hannah had become the highlight of our monthly socials, but she would often get frustrated with the group's isolation, which she probably felt more than me. In addition, coming from her relatively comfortable middle class background, living a hand to mouth existence must have been especially hard for her. We were always short of money although she never ever complained about it. She was a very valuable asset for the group. An active member of the branch, she designed all the group's leaflets and produced many of the linoleum-cut caricatures that decorated the pages of the early *Workers Vanguard*. In New York she had worked in book design and now she was working far below her skill level in the publications section of a department store, doing elementary layout work. After talking it over for a few days—"what would be best for the movement?"—she reluctantly agreed to me making the trip.

Ross, who had overwhelming moral authority in the group, had by then inculcated in us such a heightened feeling of responsibility to the organization—with his personal example of sacrificing all material comforts "for the movement"—that, in his words, it was difficult to turn him down. To refuse, especially if someone was in a position of leadership, was like committing some act of betrayal. Later I learned he didn't seem to mind much that members would put their personal relationships under stress, as long as it would serve his idea of the needs of the organization.

The 1958 tour was to be led by Jerry Houle. He and his wife Ruth had been part of the cohort expelled from the CCF in 1954. I remember Jerry as having a very strong but quiet personality. Then in his early thirties, he had given up his university education to work in the rubber industry, and next to Ross, was probably one of our most politically developed leaders. I remember him as a keen student of Marxist ideas. Of medium height, he was of solid physical stature. He always seemed focused, determined, and very methodical in how he went about things, and I remember him being very systematic in how he marshalled his arguments in discussion. As he sat quietly smoking his pipe—it was a cheaper alternative to cigarettes—he always had the look of someone thinking his way through a problem. Stubborn to the point of bull-doggedness, one hesitated to engage him on an issue because he would not relent easily and would always come back to pick up the discussion again and again. His personality was very different from that of Ross in that he did not take on the persona of a leader and was less dramatic on the platform when speaking. He planned to become a full-time organizer when we returned to Toronto, an additional staff person to Ross. His going on the tour annoyed his wife Ruth a lot and caused tension between them because she had not been part of the initial discussion about his going, she told me later. With a small baby, their son Paul, to look after by herself, she felt she should have been part of that consideration. It would mean Jerry would be away for most of the summer. Also on the team that year were Alan Harris, Harry Paine and Pat Brain, who had managed to get a leave of absence from Amalgamated Electric to be on it.

George Bryant, who always pitched in to get the tours underway, purchased an old half-ton Ford truck for us and we went to work to build a structure of plywood on the box where we could sleep and cook meals plus have storage for our personal gear and the literature we hoped to sell. This arrangement was better than a trailer, which might have given us more room but would have had limitations when it came to finding parking space. A truck could be parked anywhere.

We began the tour in May and spent the first couple of weeks going out from Toronto for a few days at a time to some of the main cities of southern Ontario where we sold 350 subscriptions to the paper, a sort of exercise to see what the problems might be when we headed out across the country. Once that phase was completed, Harry came off and I took his place to continue the rest of the trip. We decided to immediately head north and it wasn't long before we had our send-off from the parking lot at the back of the bookstore.

We looked forward to getting clear of southern Ontario, where we usually found the political climate more difficult, to head north where it would be easier to sell subscriptions and talk to people. Our first major stop was the Sudbury Basin with its large Franco-Ontarian population and where Inco and Falconbridge's giant mines and smelters were located. When I first saw it, the countryside around the city was like a moonscape, so much so that when the space programme began, the Americans used it in their training as a stand-in for the moon. No trees anywhere, nothing but black, barren, granite rock. The sulphurous gases from the smokestacks had just about killed all vegetation for miles around and had rendered the surrounding lakes sterile. We didn't have many contacts in the area, aside from a few subscribers to the paper and one sympathizer, a German immigrant who worked on maintenance in the Frood Mine.

Sudbury turned out to be a very good place to sell subscriptions and I remember we sold many, but we had arrived in the area not long after Inco had announced it was reducing production and laying off 1,300 workers, a usual tactic by Inco whenever it entered negotiations for a new contract. Economic conditions were not good in the industry as the U.S. government the previous year, had completed its stock-piling of nickel in preparation for war with the Soviet Union, causing a depression in the non-ferrous metal industry. The employers were refusing to grant any wage increases. Inco and Falconbridge, the main smelters, were organized by the Mine, Mill and Smelter Workers Union, in the largest local in

Canada, representing 23,000 workers. For many years, the union, whose leadership had been purged from the CCF, had been resisting an intense Cold War witch-hunt led by an unholy alliance of the employers, the Catholic Church, the Canadian Congress of Labour, the Steelworkers, the CCF bureaucracy and the RCMP. Mine Mill had rejected the CCL's demand that it purge anyone with LPP associations from its executive board.

Expelled in 1949, its jurisdiction had been handed over to the Steelworkers who had been raiding it ever since, and it was being hammered on all sides at that particular time. When we got there the union was gearing up for a possible strike—their first ever—that would eventually take place in September. But Sudbury was still a better than average place to sell the *Workers Vanguard,* even though it carried a tagline calling for support for the CCF. As we went door to door, some objected to that position, but it was easy to get into discussion with the workers, most of whom worked in the smelters. Because of the heightened political atmosphere, within a few minutes when they heard our criticisms of the CCF, they would become more receptive to our views. It was a lot better than selling subscriptions in southern Ontario. We also made a point of visiting the Steel union and Mine-Mill's offices to see if we could sell some literature there, but the Steel people were very hostile to us, as we sort of expected. Because of Steel's close association with the CCF, they knew our politics very well. The staff at the Mine-Mill office, on the other hand, were much more civil, at least they talked to us but they didn't buy much, I remember. We also sold the paper outside the union's monthly meeting, without any problem. It was usually a huge affair, with several thousands in attendance.

After Sudbury, we headed west to Sault Ste. Marie, site of one of the largest steel mills in the country, Algoma Steel, organized by the Steelworkers Union. For many years, "the Soo" as it was known colloquially, had elected a CCF member to the Provincial Legislature. We were able to sell enough subscriptions to justify the trip there, but it was the first place where we ran into difficulties with the police.

One of our practices when we visited a community with a major industry nearby was to arise early in the morning to distribute our paper.

A large bundle would be shipped to us from Toronto for this purpose. Usually when we showed up at a plant, the security guard would not realize what we were doing until we had distributed most of our papers, and then they would awake to our presence and order us off the plant parking lot. But outside the Algoma plant, as we drove away, suddenly we were halted by a couple of members of the Provincial police who demanded to know what we were doing there, asking in a hostile manner for all of our driver licenses. After questioning we were told to get out of town or they would arrest us. It was a scene that would be repeated many times across the country. In some cases, we ended up in the local jail for a few hours and once we were denounced from the pulpit of a local church whose preacher did not like us.

Relatively new to Canada, travelling into the hinterland in 1958 was an eye-opener for me. I had read about its vastness before emigrating, but coming from an intensely agricultural country like Ireland, to experience the landscape was another matter entirely. Its empty regions took some getting used to. North of Toronto and through the Muskokas, with its abundance of lakes and forests, the province changed dramatically north of Sault Ste. Marie once we reached the Canadian Shield. High granite cliffs of some of the oldest rock in the world towered above the road. Amidst the scrubby jack pine forests, lakes were everywhere, too numerous to appear on ordinary maps, all draining to the Arctic Circle. The land tended to flatten out as we headed north on Highway 11 to Cochrane, a mining town, and to Kapuskasing with its large Kimberly Clarke newsprint pulp mill. This was before the shorter route had been constructed along the north shore of Lake Superior, Highway 17, between Sault Ste. Marie and Thunder Bay (two cities then named Port Arthur and Fort William). Coming from a place where a hundred miles was considered a long distance, the long flat stretches between towns such as Hearst and Longlac seemed to me to go on forever and, since we were driving an old vehicle, I was extremely apprehensive when I saw signs on the side of the road warning drivers there were no gas stations for the next couple of hundred miles.

The social divide between the well-off and the poor was acutely graphic in Ontario's north. It was the first time in my life I had ever seen "tar-paper" shacks, unfinished frame houses, in that state for years, sheeted in with tar-paper and without siding, with the occupants living in poverty. Going door to door trying to sell subscriptions, we could see it everywhere. Scattered along the highway outside small towns, they were a variant of slum housing seen all over the world. Yet in the main town proper, like Kapuskasing for example, in a pattern that could be seen in many places across the north, it looked like a typical southern Ontario community, with neat, well-constructed finished bungalows on grassy lots, well-paved streets and modern facilities such as hockey rinks and modern shopping centres.

As usual, we made a point of visiting the Pulp and Paper Workers' office in the hope of selling a few books to the staff, but most of the time we went up and down the streets selling subscriptions. We discovered that most of the mill's unionized workforce lived in the town and the casual and day labourers and the unemployed lived mainly outside. This was the social divide throughout the north across to Kenora and Dryden, where the stench from the pulp mills could be smelt many miles away across the wilderness.

Northern Ontario also confronted us directly with the sorry conditions of the First Nations people in Canada and the prejudice they suffered. It was in Dryden and Kenora where we witnessed the most open hostility against people from the reserves. From time to time we would hear insults shouted at them and once we saw a couple of native people refused entry into a restaurant. It would be the end of the next decade before people on the reserves would renew their fight and try to reverse the wrongs inflicted upon them since the European occupation.

Indigenous rights were not a big political issue in the 1950s, like they are now. It was not on the political agenda anywhere that I remember, not even in left circles. Certainly I don't recall it being raised as political issue in the CCF or in the unions, for that matter. Nor did we discuss it much in the SEL; it never appeared very often—if ever—as a topic in the *Workers Vanguard*. Of course we were opposed to the oppression and discrimination, but when we discussed the issue informally amongst ourselves, it tended to be within the framework of seeing "the Indians," a word the indigenous people would later reject, as having suffered such a devastating military defeat during the European occupation, it would be a long time before they recovered as a people. Frankly, I think if the question had been put to us then, we would have answered that the best solution would be for the reservation system to be abandoned entirely and that the First Nations people be assimilated into Canadian society while at the same time guaranteeing their rights and cultural identity. It would not be until the end of the Sixties that the First Nations issue would move onto the public agenda, inspired by the Black struggle for equality in the United States and the radicalization around the Vietnam War. They demanded that the Canadian government begin to move ahead with settling the land claims that had been on the books for hundreds of years.

"On tour" was like doing "missionary work" for socialism. Political life for me, I remember, became greatly intensified that summer of 1958, as if time itself was compressed, as we met with hundreds of radicals and labour activists who brought us up to date about what was happening in their communities. There was a sense of adventure about it all, in that we were doing something that had much in common with the early traditions of the socialist movement in the country.

Being "on tour" was no picnic, however, and that year was no exception. Once we arrived in a community, the first thing we did was to head to the post office to pick up our mail from General Delivery, an event all of us looked forward to in anticipation because it was the only way we remained in contact with those close to us. After spending a little time getting caught up with the news from Toronto, we would head out door-to-door selling "introductory" subscriptions, fifty cents for six months. Some places it was especially hard making sales, but Jerry Houle always seemed to do it very well, no matter where we were. Many times we returned to the truck, with Jerry the only one who had had any success. Supper was prepared over a Coleman stove and, in the evening, while two of the team went door-to-door, the other two would drive around the community visiting "contacts" and people who had previously subscribed to the paper. We also attempted to maintain a schedule of political discussions amongst ourselves, usually on a topic from a pamphlet or on some new item, considering ourselves to be a mini-political group. But most times, by the end of the day, dog-tired, we would climb into our sleeping bags in preparation for an early morning start.

Generally, the members of the team got along with each other very well but in the difficult conditions in which we were living and working, occasionally there would be the odd personal conflict, sometimes over very petty issues. I remember once in northern Ontario, at Kakabeka Falls, west of Thunder Bay when after a long day we pulled into the Provincial Park there and Alan Harris grabbed a couple of old *Workers Vanguards*—we had hundreds in the truck—and he headed for the toilets. "What do you want those papers for?" Gerry quizzed him in a somewhat critical tone, already suspecting the answer to his question. "To cover the toilet seat," Alan replied. "You shouldn't use our paper for that," was Jerry's sharp retort, as if the paper was a sacrosanct object, not to be defiled by such an earthly use. A physical conflict almost took place, forcing Pat Brain and me to step in between them. Later on we all laughed and made jokes about it, but it was an example how tiny little issues could easily escalate and come close to getting out of hand.

Selling subscriptions east of Thunder Bay and points west got a lot easier as the tour progressed. We seldom needed to ask Toronto for financial help, always a mark of how well a tour was doing. At pre-arranged communities, we picked up the latest issue of the paper at the local Post Office and those we didn't sell we made a point of distributing to the nearest mine or pulp-mill, usually first thing in the morning. After breakfast, two of us would usually stop at the local library to check the address registry to find the addresses of subscribers who had moved and the other two would visit union halls.

Winnipeg in 1958 was where we first met Gerry Phillips, a black labour activist who worked on the railroads. Unusual for the times, he had an adopted white son. In those early years they would become our main supporters in the city. I think we met Phillips either as we were going door to door selling subscriptions or someone whom we had met casually suggested we should drop in on him because, they said, he might be interested in the literature we were carrying, especially Daniel Guerin's report on black oppression in the United States, *Negroes On The March,* that had been translated by Duncan Ferguson and was being promoted by the SWP. We were trying to get this book into the hands of as many black people as possible, especially black activists.[2]

Suggestions from people we met casually—"this is a person you should really talk to"—was often the way we would meet activists and for me the visit with Phillips turned out to be fateful because of the information he and his son gave me about dealing with the police. Phillips had been a leader of the Sleeping Car Porters' union but his son had been a police constable and had resigned from the force, disgusted with the way the police behaved towards native people. Naturally, when we heard this, we told him how the police had been continually harassing us as we moved across the country, especially when we were doing plant distributions with our paper and that they would often tail us and pick us up for no reason at all and order us out of town.

In the red-baiting culture of the times, with radicals such as us they obviously felt they could get away with anything thing they wished. Clearly, the cops were legally wrong in what they were doing, but we couldn't do much about it but because we were on the move and didn't have the time to challenge them. It would have meant interrupting the tour. Phillips' son wasn't surprised by this police activity, he said, knowing the politically oppressive culture that prevailed within the force, but he pointed out to us that legally, the police had no rights over and above those of an ordinary citizen, and must always have an explanation for their actions.

Not too many people are aware of this, he went on, so they let the police get away with behaving as if they have rights they don't possess. We don't live in a police state yet, he added. My ears perked up when I heard this and it would have meaningful consequences for me at the end of the tour when I arrived back in Toronto in the fall—but more about that later.

One purpose of our tours was to make contact again with our members and supporters scattered across the country, sometimes going out of our way to meet them. In 1958, Joe Burki put us up at his farm west of Edmonton, in Entwistle, Alberta for a few days. Well into his fifties, he had been a member of the group since the thirties. He was in the midst of the haying season when we arrived on his doorstep, yet he gave us a very warm welcome and was eager to hear any news of what was happening in the left across the country, and we talked with him late into the evening. When I met him he was beginning to suffer from a severe form of arthritis and was having difficulty walking. Eventually, it would force him to give up farming. We also met up with Vic Bystrom on that trip, another long-time member. He and our supporters in Lloydminster functioned as a loosely organized supporting group of the SEL. Vic worked in an oil refinery and also farmed a half a section of land, growing wheat.

On that trip I also got to meet George Faulkner, a farmer, for the first time. He and his family lived in a very isolated area of the province, if my memory serves me right, because it was a lengthy drive to reach his place. A long time socialist and supporter of ours, he had joined the Western Federation of Miners in 1899 and the Socialist Party in 1900 and had backed Maurice Spector and Jack MacDonald during the split in the CP. In his eighties, remarkably, he was still a vibrant revolutionary. I would meet him again in 1963 in Vancouver where he was living with his daughter, having the previous year retired and sold his farm. It was two days before his 89th birthday and he had a remarkable story to tell. I interviewed him for our paper.[3] Recently returned from Cuba, he had been enthralled by what he had witnessed. His visit there had come about on an impulse as he was criss-crossing Canada seeing old comrades he thought he would be seeing for the last time, when, he decided he should take a look at what was happening in farming there. When he made contact with the agricultural authorities in Cuba, he was immediately welcomed and given an interpreter and was able to visit many dairy farms. The Cubans seemed to be having some difficulty with cattle they had recently bought from Canada. According to what George had heard, several dairy herds had been carelessly shipped from Montreal, resulting in many of the cattle dying during a storm or aborting and dying after they arrived. In addition, some from earlier shipments were not doing well and were thin and lacking in meat. It appeared to George, who had a long experience raising cattle, that there was an essential element missing from their diet that was causing the problem. He had noticed that the Cubans were having little success in growing clover so he had brought back samples of their feed and was anxiously waiting to get his birthday over so that he could get to Edmonton to have it tested. Cattle were not his only interest. He had raised sheep at one time and, when he left Cuba, he undertook a commitment on behalf of the Cuban government to personally buy for them, out of his own money, a herd in the Fall auctions in Alberta and get them into good condition to take them to Montreal and from there to Havana where he planned to remain for the rest of his life. He was a truly remarkable man and a prime example of that early generation of revolutionaries who had helped build the Canadian socialist movement.

Ralph and Lucy McDonnell of Cranbrook, B.C., of the same generation as George Faulkner, always threw their doors open to us and made us welcome when we were on tour. They also had been founding members of the CP and had supported Trotsky. Both in their eighties by the time I'm talking about, they were among our most consistent supporters and were still active in local politics and seemed to have more energy than people half their age. They owned rental cabins on Christina Lake and it was a unique pleasure for us to spend a few days with them relaxing on their property and swimming in the lake, like true vacationers. When I met him, Ralph's true passion—aside from politics—was prospecting for gold, and even at his advanced age, he would often go into the mountains for weeks at a time hoping to stake a claim. Lucy would worry he might not show up again—but he always did.

On my first tour, I was pleasantly surprised by the number of union staffers in the west who reacted to us positively when we visited their offices. Their reaction was much different from that in southern Ontario where anti-Communism had more deeply penetrated the unions. On the Prairies a few of the staffers would be cool but polite to us. Some wouldn't even let us in the door, but others, a few of whom had been radical in earlier times, happily talked to us, bought our books, and even bought subscriptions to our paper. It was the only way they could get their hands on anti-capitalist literature, of which we carried a broad selection for that purpose. In this respect, I remember we got a very warm reception from Neil Reimer in Edmonton, who was on staff of the Oil and Chemical Workers Union, the main union in the oil industry then. He knew Ross Dowson, who had met him on one of his earlier trips across the country. Reimer was not a supporter of our group. He may at one time have been around the Communist Party, but I remember he was very respectful towards us and he welcomed us into his office and kept us talking there for quite a while. It turned out his family came from Ukraine and he was one of the few people I have ever met outside our group who, as a young person, had personally met Trotsky, something he boasted about not long after we sat down to talk to him.

In addition to union offices, we made a special effort to stop at any construction site we came across. This was easy work for us because these sites were usually off the main highway and in very isolated areas and the workers had little to do in the evening, so they were often happy to chat with us. We had amazing good luck once at a massive construction camp in northern B.C., which housed hundreds of construction workers building a large pulp mill. A supporter of ours worked there, a welder, hearing we were on the road and heading his way, had sent an invitation to Toronto for us to visit him. He smuggled us on to the site where we were fed first class food, three amazing meals a day, anything we wanted, and where we slept comfortably overnight unbeknownst to the company for a few days. We sort of just blended in. Everyone assumed we were part of the regular work force, which was nice for us because it allowed us to meet many workers and sell lots of literature.

The 1958 tour was the first time I met our Vancouver comrades. The city was a great place to arrive in after travelling across the country and after spending many weeks in the cramped living conditions of the truck. That's when I met Ruth and Reg Bullock, two of the main leaders of the group there who, even though they had disagreements with Toronto about how to relate to the CCF, warmly welcomed us into their home in North Vancouver, a remarkable, low, single storey house they had built themselves. In my mind's eye, I can still see it now, a massive stone fireplace arising from the middle of the main floor with a large kitchen on one side and guest bedrooms adjacent to the dining/living room, where in the evening we brought them up to date with what was happening across the country, especially with the CCF, many of whose members Ruth and Reg knew from the CCF's National Conventions. It was a relief to just use their washing machine for our laundry and I remember they fed us very well. Reg took great pride in being a first class cook.

The Vancouver group had about fifteen loosely affiliated members then and the average age-level was a lot higher than Toronto's. They had done a little better out of the CP crisis, however, than we had in the East. Malcolm Bruce, one of the founding leaders, along with Tim Buck, of the Canadian CP, who was then in his eighties and who had been out of the CP for many years, had joined the group along with two other ex-CP workers near retirement age, Fred McNeill and Shelly Rogers, both in the Longshoremen's union. Malcolm was a significant figure in Canadian working class history. The ex-CP people had been won over to the Vancouver group by Ruth and Reg Bullock. Malcolm had publicly identified himself with the Trotskyists in a talk to a Stanley Park CCF meeting in 1956.[4] He quickly became a leader of the branch and I remember he soon acquired a great deal of respect in the group. He was one of the best speakers I had ever heard. He was always critical of the "entry tactic," and tended to side with Toronto on that issue but he could be very mischievous in stirring up trouble between Toronto and Vancouver. For several years he was the B.C. corresponding editor for *Workers Vanguard*, a position that seemed to generate a lot of conflict with Toronto.

Recruitment had been slow in Vancouver compared to Toronto, we were told, but we figured this was because of their nervousness about compromising the "entry tactic" and getting themselves expelled. In addition, despite its small size, the branch was divided into two informal opposing groups. One was led by Ruth and Reg, who had been expelled from the CCF the previous year. The other was led by Lillian and Bill Whitney, leaders of the East Vancouver CCF constituency party. I remember Bill as being very knowledgeable, well read and articulate. It was common for him to quote the Marxist classics to back his opinions, but it seemed to me he talked a lot, and discussions with him tended to go around in circles. It was hard to get anything nailed down. To me, Lillian seemed to be more serious about her ideas than Bill in terms of rolling up their sleeves and getting things done, but I always thought of them as a team. Both the Bullocks and Whitneys were solid working class families—Bill a warehouse worker, and Reg a highly skilled boiler-maker in the Vancouver shipyards. The Bullocks were well known left-wing personalities in the Vancouver area and Reg was active on the Vancouver Labour Council, as was Bill. It was very difficult for an outsider to determine what their differences with each other were, because of the personal animosities, but if you looked hard enough there were clear signs of impatience on the part of Ruth and Reg with Bill's seemingly endless talking. And from my conversations with Lillian and Bill, when I first met them, I detected a measure of resentment about their poorer economic status relative to the Bullocks.

Both groupings considered the CCF to be their main arena of activity and, although they had differences with each other, they were always united in their opposition to Toronto on that issue. Nevertheless they were strong financial supporters and could always be counted upon to meet their quota in our yearly financial campaigns. They had been members since the war and had helped re-establish the group in the immediate post-war period and even though the branch was small, it had suffered a few losses from the Rose split, but not as much as Toronto had in 1953.

Their regular meetings took place in each other's living room— sometimes in the Whitney's home in East Vancouver or in the Bullock's in North Vancouver. There did not seem to be many young people around and those that were, were mainly the children of the older members. And while formally agreeing with Toronto about setting up the SEL, including the launching of the new paper, the *Workers Vanguard,* an agreement that Ross said he had extracted from them when he had been there in 1956 with Alan Harris, in actual practice the B.C. people strongly resisted modifying their "entry tactic" and were reluctant to making any moves towards having a public organization.

The "entry tactic," and how it was applied, had always been a bone of contention between Toronto and Vancouver. Relations deteriorated even more later in the year, 1957, when we ran Ross as a candidate in a by-election in Hasting-Frontenac, near Peterborough, against Sydney Smith of the University of Toronto, a Tory whom the CCF and the Liberals had made a pact not to oppose. Our entering the by-election was another "modification" of the "entry" tactic that Vancouver didn't go along with. (Incidentally, Ross got 266 votes to Smith's 10,513 in that election.) It led to them demanding Ross' resignation as editor of the paper[5] and it didn't improve their mood very much either when, in another modification of the "entry tactic" the following spring, we ran Ross as an SEL candidate in the Federal Election in the Toronto riding of Broadview, in which the CCF had also entered a candidate.

It was as if we had two distinct organizations in the country: a grouping in Toronto where most of its people had been expelled from the CCF, organized in the SEL and publishing its own paper and with its own headquarters; and on the West Coast, a much more loose formation that functioned as "a nameless semi-underground faction of the CCF,"[6] not as ideologically or programmatically defined as we were in the East but yet solidly based in the working class. Vancouver insisted that having some kind of existence as an independent revolutionary organization and publicly selling *Workers Vanguard* would alienate "the broad left forces" they were allied with inside the CCF and risk compromising the "entry tactic" by provoking the Party leadership into expelling the "entered" people. I remember they had a lot more influence in the CCF than we did in the East. Their hopes of being part of a majority left wing in this respect had some reality to it, something they never failed to point out to us. Instead of being a defined organization, the Vancouver group had all the appearance of a broad caucus. They were so loosely structured it was sometimes difficult to determine who was and who wasn't a member.

B.C.'s politics were indeed different, and more radical, than Ontario's. The anti-communist witch-hunt of the fifties had not gone as deep. It was also a bastion of the LPP, which controlled the Fishermen's and the Mine Mill unions and also had a strong influence in the Boiler Makers and Iron Workers unions and on the Vancouver Labour Council. Our B.C. people had not suffered the same isolation from the working class as we had in Ontario. Up to 1950, the B.C. CCF had been under the leadership of its left-wing until the anti-Communist hysteria around the time of the Korean War, when the right-wing took over and lined the party up behind western imperialism in the "Cold War" against the USSR.[7] Unlike in Ontario where the left had never been a major influence in the Party, in B.C. there were still pockets of left-wing resistance throughout the province and they even controlled a few constituencies such as on Vancouver Island and in Burnaby where Ernie Winch, a socialist, was the sitting MLA. Sporadically, right into the Sixties, formidable left wing oppositions, although greatly reduced, would emerge during conventions, led by figures such as Colin Cameron, CCF Member of Parliament from Vancouver Island. In the run-up to the founding of the NDP, the B.C.-CCF, like in Alberta, had moved to the left and demanded that Canada pull out of NATO. It maintained its maverick character by resisting almost until the last minute giving support to the National Council's resolution asking for the Provincial leadership to enter into discussions with the CLC about the new party's formation. While critical of the CLC for dropping its support of the CCF, we in the SEL, in substance, felt no loyalty to the Party, figuring by that time it had exhausted itself as an effective political force in Canada. Differentiating ourselves from a majority of the left in the party on the West Coast, we supported the NC position, in the knowledge that part of the opposition in B.C. was a result of the Ontario CCF and union bureaucracy—most notably in the Steel-workers—campaign to exclude Mine Mill, the main mining union on the coast, and the Fishermen's union, from the new organization.

The CCF in B.C. had a legitimate concern. Without these unions' help, the new party would be unable to get elected in some key constituencies. While eventually voting for the NC resolution, the CCF in B.C. maintained its criticism of the Ottawa leadership, refusing to give up its name for a couple of years.

The 1958 tour was also the occasion when our group held its National Conference. It had been timed to coincide with our arrival in Vancouver. It was a small affair, as I remember it, with about twenty people present, including a few visitors from the SWP branch in Seattle, which was led at the time by Clara Kaye and Richard Fraser, two long-time local leaders of the Party. The four of us on the tour had been elected as delegates by the Toronto branch. Ross, who had flown into Vancouver before the Conference, had prepared the main report on "regroupment" and the CCF, setting out a few immediate tasks for the organization. I remember a discussion about organizing a Vancouver "regroupment" forum with Ross pointing out that there might be a good basis for some kind of ongoing broad left organization coming into existence. Because, he said, there were probably more unattached radicals out there than anywhere else, and because of the crises in the LPP and the CCF. Everyone agreed to work on such a project, but most of the discussion was about what was going on in the CCF and the rumblings about a "new party" and the resistance that was developing to it. The Seattle people, even though they stayed out of the discussion, tended to be discretely supportive of Toronto's attempts at persuading Vancouver to modify their "entry tactic" in the direction of carrying out more independent activity.

In Ross' opinion, the failure to have a "public face" for the group had played into the hands of our opponents on the right who smeared us in the minds of many rank and file activists by characterizing our group as something illegitimate that was behaving in an underhanded fashion, one of the main reasons he had worked hard to set up the SEL.[8] But at times, Ross could barely suppress his frustration with the Vancouver people in their reluctance to move in this direction. Those of us in the tour group could not say much in the discussion, because we simply didn't know enough, but privately Ross told us that in previous "national" gatherings, Vancouver would always agree to set up some kind of office, a headquarters perhaps or agree to publish their own locally produced B.C. paper or even get out a "Ginger group" paper in combination with other leftists. But nothing ever came of these ideas. To avoid rancour, however, these topics were discreetly avoided by Ross in the conference. The Vancouver people were clearly less than enthusiastic about *Workers Vanguard,* telling us they found it "difficult" to use in their work and were very uncomfortable with the changes to the "entry tactic" they saw taking place in Toronto and accusing Ross of "rushing ahead."

Ross, seeing that they had dropped their demand from the previous year that he resign from the paper, had shifted to informally discussing with them individually to see if he could persuade any of them to pick up the bookstore or headquarters idea again. I'm sure that was one of the objectives he had wished to accomplish before he had even set out for Vancouver. In a series of personal discussions with the Bullocks and the Whitneys, he put a lot of pressure on them to move forward, but I remember they appeared to have great difficulty in putting him off because he reminded them they had already agreed to it in previous years. He was very insistent in trying to get something nailed down before we headed back east and finally they gave way. Above all it was their tremendous respect for him that carried the day, recognizing the virtual single-handed role he had played over years in holding the group together in the East. They finally agreed when he told them that Alan Harris would remain behind to manage the bookstore and that the tour group would leave a supply of literature from the truck to help stock it.

Once we had achieved that agreement we spent a few weeks helping Alan to get the bookstore established in the hope that when we left, the Vancouver people would pitch-in and take "ownership" of it. But that turned out to be a bit of a pipe dream. After we left, it turned out that

Alan was virtually left on his own with the project and he, despairing of getting any help, finally threw up his hands and headed back to Toronto. But our efforts had not been in vain. Not long after, on the initiative of the Bullocks, the Vancouver people finally established their own small headquarters and set themselves up as the "Socialist Information Centre."

They also initiated a series of "regroupment" forums, the first one with Hugh Clifford and Rodney Young, prominent CCF left wingers, as speakers, attended by about forty-five people. By the next summer, however, tension in the group between the Bullocks and the Whitneys had become so sharp that with very little prior discussion, they split, confronting Toronto with a "fait accompli." It was totally unclear to us in Toronto what the differences were between them. Each grouping was finally recognized respectively as "Branch Number One" and "Branch Number Two," in the hope they would be eventually overcome their differences and come together.

After helping Alan get the bookstore going, we were anxious to leave Vancouver and head back to Toronto because by that time we were already well into September when it can get very cold in the B.C. mountains and in northern Ontario. In those parts, the temperatures often drop well below freezing at that time of year. For personal reasons, Jerry Houle and Pat Brain had to return to Toronto immediately, so Ross proposed that he and I should continue with the truck back to Toronto. Ross did not know how to drive so I did it all. We moved across the southern route east through the mountains and prairies, stopping to re-visit a few of the people we had met on the way out, but we were in a tricky situation. The truck, on its last legs, was not suitable for sleeping in during the cold nights and we were unwilling to go to a motel, a "needless expense" we felt since we needed to keep a cushion of money in case we ran into mechanical difficulties with the vehicle. By the time we reached northern Ontario, we were confronting a few inches of snow and were experiencing below-freezing temperatures. Finally, after spending a very cold night in Longlac, Ontario, we decided to drive straight to Toronto, close to 800 miles, as quickly as the old truck would take us. After almost six months on the road, I was looking forward very much to seeing Hannah, but before I would finally get home into my own bed, I would be picked up by the police in Toronto and charged with "vagrancy" and held in the Don Jail without she or Ross being aware of what had happened to me.

That last leg of the trip seemed to take forever as I nursed the truck along, hoping it wouldn't conk out on us. We had driven all day and night and had stopped only to eat and gas up, when I arrived and parked the truck at the back of the bookstore on Yonge Street. It was in the early hours of the morning, Thanksgiving, and both of us were so dog-tired we barely spoke a word to each other as I locked the truck and Ross headed into the store. I grabbed my suitcase full of my dirty laundry and headed down Church Street looking forward with great anticipation to seeing Hannah again after being away so many months. She was waiting for me, not knowing the hour when I would arrive. But it would still be a long while before I got to see her.

As I reached College Street, a police cruiser with two uniformed officers pulled up alongside me. They jumped out and asked me for identification. I gave it to them. Where are you coming from, they wanted to know? I told them. Where are you going? Home to see my wife, I replied as I stood there tightly clutching my suitcase, half-expecting the next question. What's in your suitcase? I hesitated, wondering how to answer. Dirty underwear, I said. Open it, they ordered. I refused. Remembering my conversation in Winnipeg with Gerry Phillips' son, the ex-cop, and thoroughly annoyed after having been harassed by police across the country the previous few months, I told them it was none of their business and they had no right to look in my suitcase unless they were alleging I was involved in some kind of criminal activity. They almost went berserk at this, yelling at me to open it and I began to realize the situation could get very serious very soon, but I still refused. Then without hesitation, they swiftly bundled me into their cruiser and took me to the police station. I was still holding my suitcase in a firm grip. In the station, after again ordering me to open it, they and a few other cops jumped on me and wrenched it out of my hands. Opening it in front of me, clearly expecting to find something special and illegal, they got very angry when all they could see were my dirty socks and T-shirts.

Their faces went beet-root red. It was as though I had tricked them into behaving irrationally. Determined to get revenge, they charged me with "vagrancy" and threw me into a holding cell where I got to meet a varied assortment of petty criminals. Most of them seemed to me to be ordinary working class folk caught on the wrong side of the law, and they wondered, when I explained it to them, why I had made such an issue of not opening my suitcase.

My requests to make a phone call home were flatly denied and I was transferred to the Don Jail where I was held for two days because it was a Thanksgiving weekend and the judge was "not available" to hear cases. Finally, as I was getting ready to make my appearance in a court at City Hall, I was allowed to make a phone call and I called Hannah. She and Ross bailed me out immediately. Naturally, they were shocked about what had happened. It was as if I had disappeared from the face of the earth and they didn't know what to expect. It was totally unjustified what the police had done to me, but that wasn't the end of it.

The charge of "vagrancy" was one of those catch-all parts of the criminal code that allowed the police to pick up a lot of people on the street and to hold them. This was despite the fact that I had a bank book showing I had a savings account of over $600—there probably was not that much in the account at the time—and was wearing a wrist-watch which was worth at least a few dollars. I was later to learn the vagrancy law had been used extensively during the Great Depression against labour during its organizing campaigns and even in strikes and as a mechanism to keep the large army of unemployed roaming the country on the move. As I remember it, the "vagrancy" law consisted of three elements: one, the person when confronted by the police was unable to explain their presence in the place where found; two, was "wandering abroad"; and three, "had no visible means of support." Of course it was obvious this did not apply to me and that the police were using the law in this case to punish someone who was questioning their authority. It was a small thing in many respects, but it was an example of how the police dealt with those who are alone and isolated and who don't know how to defend themselves or don't have the resources to do so.

We discussed it in the SEL and agreed we should fight the charge and try and carry out a modest campaign to get support. I quickly got an appointment with Irving Himel, who headed up the Canadian Civil Liberties Association (CCLA) in those years and who was frequently in the news. A tall man with an expansive personality, he was very welcoming when Hannah and I went to see him. He immediately told us that he thought the CCLA would be keen to take up the case. In recent years, he said, they had been looking for openings to challenge the "vagrancy" law, and had had a few test cases lined up, but there always seemed to be complicating factors involved with them, such as the victims being under the influence of alcohol at the time of the arrest or someone who was unwilling to proceed with their case because of job considerations, all of which made it difficult for them to utilize them to make a serious challenge to the law. In my case, he reassured us, the issues seemed to be very clear and, in addition, I had an evident desire to fight it.

By this time we began to receive a little press coverage, which was very encouraging. The minister of the First Unitarian Church on St. Clair, the Reverend P. Jenkins, a friend of Verne Olson, publicly supported us. "If this case stands then the rights of every citizen in the city are in danger," he declared. In the following trial, Irving Himel was successful in getting one of the cops who had arrested me to admit that in his eyes I was a "suspect" because I had been "roughly dressed" and had been walking past an expensive apartment building at the time I was stopped, 5:30 a.m.

We immediately sent out a letter to all the union locals in the area asking if I could appear before their membership to explain the issues in the case and asking for financial support. Invitations came in to speak to a few CCF constituency meetings and from a few union locals, one of which was my old local at Canada Packers who gave us a cheque for $100, as did the Amalgamated Electric local of UE. A local of the International Union of Operating Engineers, which was led by several ex-members of our group, donated $25 and allowed me to write an article about the case for its monthly journal, *The Gauge.*[9]

In the end, enough money came in to cover the costs of a subsequent appeal. We won. I remember Irving Himel being very happy with the outcome, thinking it was an important step in getting the vagrancy law overturned. During the course of our campaign I had gotten to know him a little bit better and as far I could see he was one of those rare individuals in society who toiled away without much recognition, trying to make it a better place to live in. His devotion to defending civil liberties in Canada was limitless. Within a year or so the criminal code was changed so that police could no longer arrest people at their whim and a probable side effect was that panhandling was again legally permitted in public.

After the 1958 tour, I would go on to lead three more—in 1960, 1962 and in 1965. After the 1958 tour, there were many political changes on the left, primarily as a result of the rise of the NDP, and some of the changes were not all positive for us, and probably, in the case of Sudbury, had actually become much worse. I remember in 1960 selling subscriptions there turned out to be more difficult than ever. A bitter strike in the fall of 1958 had lasted for three months and had ended in what was regarded by many as a humiliating contract for the union at Inco, a six percent increase in wages over three years. As a result, a new president, Mike Solski, and a new "reform" slate had taken over the Local and when we got there they were campaigning to have the Steelworkers take over the jurisdiction and Mine Mill was resisting this very strongly. It was as if we had arrived in the midst of a low-grade civil war. We found the community deeply divided on the issue. Because we were outsiders, of course, both sides viewed us with suspicion. I remember that when we dropped in on the offices of the respective unions, we received a very cool reception indeed. Polite enough, but no one would give us the time of day and of course we drew a total blank when we tried to sell them any literature. Going door to door in Sudbury trying to sell subscriptions was equally as difficult. A few days after getting there, we learned the Inco Steelworkers Local was having their regular monthly meeting that was usually attended by a couple of hundred members. We showed up to see if we could sell the *Workers Vanguard* and were immediately confronted by a phalanx of goons who, as if looking for a fight, physically pushed us away from the meeting. The fact that the paper had nothing to do with the Communist Party and was supportive of the CCF had no effect on them. The same was true at a Mine Mill meeting. Totally destructive, the raid was weakening the workers (and thereby strengthened the employers) for the sole purpose, it seemed, that Steel could have a few more dues-paying members.

On those later tours, Winnipeg became one of our major stops and we always made a point of visiting a grouping of socialist activists on the University of Manitoba who were under the influence of Cy Gonick, the editor of the then new radical journal, *Canadian Dimension.* We could count on him organizing a discussion for us in one of his classes on campus. He was a well-known pillar of the left wing on the Prairies. And I also remember us meeting in 1960 with a group of left-wingers in the CCF Youth, organized by Howard Pawley in his home. Howard was then a law student and a radical activist, and, although not a Marxist, was at heart a genuine democrat who was against prohibitions coming from on high and believed that all socialist views should be open for consideration in the party. Again, in 1962, I remember visiting him when he had moved to Stony Mountain to open a law office and build a political base in the community there and where he finally managed to get himself elected as NDP MLA. Many years later he became Premier of Manitoba.

On these later tours, usually when we reached Edmonton, we always made a bee-line to visit Tony Mardiros and Bill Irvine. Mardiros, head of the Department of Philosophy at the University of Alberta, and his wife Betty always made us welcome and generously gave us a bed in their home and fed us for a few days. In the reactionary climate of Social Credit Alberta, they felt their political isolation acutely and they were always very pleased to see us. Irvine, who had a long history in radical politics, was President of the Provincial CCF and was one of founding fathers of the Federal party and a former Member of Parliament. He was very critical of the CCF's dumping of the Regina Manifesto, a sentiment we found increased immeasurably the further west we got from Ontario. At the 1960 provincial convention, he had helped defeat the right wing in having the party take a position opposed to Nato and Norad[10] In 1961, he and Mardiros, apprehensive about the move of the unions and party bureaucracy in dumping the CCF as the NDP was coming into being, set up the Woodsworth-Irvine Socialist Fellowship to argue for a socialist perspective in the NDP and to provide a forum for socialist activists in the Edmonton area. It had not been unusual for left groups in the CCF to organize themselves as "fellowships," an expression of the early influence of the radical clergy, and it is a partial explanation why the CCF was called a "Federation," because such groups had played an important role in founding the party. Historically weak in Alberta, Party members continually felt themselves under siege from Ernest Manning's right-wing Social Credit government.

The Irvine-Mardiros grouping was loosely organized with about thirty members, I remember, and as soon as we arrived, they usually organized a meeting for us so that we could report to their members what was happening in the left across the country. Our aim always was to try and strengthen our relationship with them and perhaps even have a more formal connection, but nothing ever came of this. Ideologically opposed to social democracy, they subscribed to the Marxist concept of replacing the capitalist economic system with a socialist one and "that the fundamental division within capitalist society was between the few who exploited others and the many whose productive powers were exploited." Unlike Marx, however, they believed the farmers should have the same importance as the workers in the struggle for socialism.[11] Their emphasis was on being "democratic" socialists, rather than "social democrats," and they believed that socialism could come by way of Parliament. We, on the other hand, linking ourselves to the experience of the Russian Revolution, believed the most likely way socialism would come about would be through an armed overthrow of the ruling class and the creation of a new kind of state, a much more democratic workers state. They were always a little suspicious of us, I think, especially of our connection to the Fourth International and our "democratic centralism," but despite these differences they always bought a lot of our literature and welcomed us into their midst. Politically we considered them allies in promoting a socialist perspective in the CCF and they were important to us in another sense: by their very existence, they tended to legitimatize the SEL's formation as a distinct grouping within the CCF.

The 1962 tour is exceptional in my memory because it was one of our first efforts to raise opposition in Canada to the Vietnam War. As we crossed the country that summer, we did our best in every major city we visited to organize public meetings about the issue. It was an attempt to get Vietnam on to the left's agenda, but it was early days and few people seemed to be interested in what we were saying. The meetings I remember—in Sudbury, Winnipeg and Edmonton—were not very well attended, with only about half a dozen people showing up to them. Usually one of us would give a prepared talk to these small gatherings and I remember that with some embarrassment, we would show a poorly-produced North Vietnamese documentary about the war, with a sound-track in the Vietnamese language. We thought this was justified because it was one of the first films we had seen that attempted to give the Vietnamese viewpoint about the war. In that stage of the war, most of what people were seeing in the Canadian media was pure propaganda giving the American line, and we hoped the film would help counteract that.

Going on "tour" was one of the means by which we built the SEL in those times as we tried to make up for our small size and extend our influence to the rest of the country. It was a very important activity for the SEL during the decade of the Sixties. One year the tour would cross the country to the West Coast and the next they would be primarily in Ontario and sometimes be composed entirely of women members of the group, and led by women leaders such as Pat Mitchell. A few times we also made the trip to Eastern Canada. It was a unique experience for anyone who ever participated in it, and it became, as Ross Dowson would explain in a letter to Pat Mitchell, an important cadre-building activity.

"So one of the major aspects of the tour," he wrote to her as she was leading one in Ontario, "has been the training of the cadre, of tying in better elements to the movement—and developing their commitment. And the tour has certainly proved to be the best or at least one of the best for just that. All the comrades who went on tour have become cadre element—if not political cadre—leadership cadre in the sense of capacity to explain our ideas—cadre in the sense they have formed a bed rock on which we have built—the comrades you can count on to get a leaflet out—to distribute, to stand up and be counted when needed. I think that has been one of most notable results of the tours—they have been under the direction of persons who were cadre but have numbered comrades really quite inexperienced and to some considerable degree uncommitted. The tour is a terrific education—quitting jobs, dependent on sub sales, meeting police, NDPers, CPers, petty bourgeois. No one goes on the tour to return the same person—almost without exception they come back much more developed—and certainly more committed."[12]

The 1956 SEL campaign. In front is Pat Mitchell (Schulz) and behind her is Peter Metheus (Joe Johnson)

Chapter 14

Birth of the New Democratic Party

*A*FTER MY FEW MONTHS IN NEW YORK, I HAD RENEWED MY CONTACT with the CCF in 1957 and had begun to work with Bill and Mary Temple in the High Park CCF. It was one of the more lively constituencies in the city in that period. Maintaining a modicum of activity in the community, it had regular monthly membership meetings, unlike other CCF constituency organizations. Known in the Party for its independence, the constituency was always critical of the Party leadership. High Park had recently been in the news for publicly criticizing three of the Party's MLAs who had supported Leslie Frost's Tory government in voting funds to build the gas pipeline across northern Ontario. Bill was a long time supporter of the Party's left wing. He and Mary—who was elected to city council a few years later—were very unhappy with the dumping of the Regina Manifesto and the lack-lustre performance of the CCF in the 1957 election. Bill, aside from being on the left, was also well-known as a "prohibitionist" and unfortunately was resented by many trade unionists for his only too-successful campaign over many years to keep alcohol out of Toronto's West End, an issue that tended to cut across him getting support for his criticisms of the Party's leadership. The Temperance movement had a significant influence in the CCF from its very inception, which was only natural I suppose with so many of the clergy helping to found it. Bill, like many Christian socialists, believed "drink was the ruination of the working class," a sentiment prevalent in reform circles in Toronto during the fifties that reeked of Puritanism and Presbyterianism and which was strongly influenced by the large block of Orange Order supporters at City Hall. The city in that period wasn't that much different from Belfast. Restaurants by law were not allowed to open on Sundays and consumption of alcoholic beverages was severely restricted with the pubs closing very early. "Beer parlours," as pubs were called, were segregated with one section for men and another for women. Bill and Mary were determined there would be none of these in the West End and they tirelessly and successfully contested all applications to the Liquor Control Board for liquor permits in their area. Nevertheless, Bill could always be relied upon to lend his name to any cause on behalf of the vulnerable and exploited and he could always be counted upon to be at Provincial conventions of the CCF to support the left wing, including reaching into his pocket to help it financially.

After the 1958 Federal Elections, the Ontario CCF entered a state of mild dormancy with a reduction in activity by many of its constituency clubs, and while High Park was a little more active than most, its meetings seemed to be getting smaller by the month. It was common in those years to hear criticisms within the unions that the Party was at an impasse and what was required was "a new party," a debate that burst out into the open in 1958 when the newly formed Canadian Labour Congress—the product of a unification of the Canadian Congress of Labour, mainly industrial unions, and the Trades and Labour Congress, mainly the craft unions—issued a call for the setting up of a "new party" to replace the CCF. The new CLC had refused to continue with the traditional position of the CCL of endorsing the CCF as "the political arm of labour" and, with the talk of building a "new party" drawn from the ranks of the "liberally minded," it began to look more and more that "independent labour political action," as we characterized it in Canada, was being seriously challenged.

It wasn't as obvious then as it is now, but as the decade of the fifties came to an end we were on the threshold of important changes in the political landscape. We still saw the CCF as being "the form a labour party would take in Canada,"[1] and believed an economic crisis would unfold in which the working class would radicalize and flood into the

Party leading to differences and splits within it around a revolutionary programme. But there was no "economic crisis" in Canada, of course, and instead what we were seeing was that the main impulse in the discussion about a "new party" was coming from the trade union bureaucracy, and not from the rank and file.

What's easy to see now is that the discussion in the labour movement about a "new party," while contradictory, signified that the political world around us was beginning to change, and favourably for the left, which was also true south of the border. At the SWP national convention in 1959, Farrell Dobbs was able to report that the party was beginning to grow and had arrested the impact of the witch-hunt.[2] Yet, as I remember it, one day seemed like the next as we went about our routine activities trying to build the SEL. Attendance at our public forums did not increase dramatically and we still lived under the pressure of a pervading anti-communism and its legacy of witch-hunting that even reached into the labour movement. Nevertheless, important political changes were taking place in the CCF and the unions that would involve thousands of workers in a political discussion about Canada's future and provide revolutionary socialists with new opportunities to promote their views. On top of this, the arrival of the Cuban revolution, with a new non-Stalinist leadership, would allow revolutionaries to find an unprejudiced audience for their ideas for the first time since the Russian Revolution.

A change also took place in my personal life and I would find myself single again. By 1959 my marriage to Hannah had broken down. She had become very unhappy at being so far removed from New York and understandably was questioning the prospect of spending her life with someone who wanted to be a political activist and who was not that interested in raising a family. She had entered our relationship hoping to change me in that respect, and by that time it was obvious I wasn't budging on that issue. It was a responsibility I just didn't wish to undertake then, primarily because, coming from an impoverished background, I was acutely sensitive to what that financial burden would mean. She wanted to settle down and have "a normal existence," she finally told me, but I wasn't interested in this. With each passing day I could see she was becoming increasingly unhappy and I didn't know what to do. It was a kind of emotional paralysis and we both felt miserable. Her folks suggested I come down to New York and, through their contacts, they said, they might be able to land me a job in the printing industry as a linotype operator. That's how the type was set up for printing in those days. It was a tempting and generous offer, but it meant that I would have had to formally apply for immigration to the U.S. But in the end I resisted this idea, not sure whether my relationship with Hannah would last in any case. I wanted to avoid their moral pressure and, furthermore, because of the reactionary political atmosphere in the U.S., I doubted I would be able to obtain a work permit. I just didn't want that kind of hassle. In the end, while on a visit to her parents, Hannah decided to remain in New York. It was over for us and it was probably the best outcome, even though I felt bad about how it had turned out. She later told me that she wasn't too long back in New York when the FBI came to visit her one evening and tried to quiz her about my activities in Canada and in New York. She told them to take a walk. After the divorce, she later remarried and had the children she desired.

By the time I was breaking up with Hannah, I was also trying to change my work situation. Fed up with low paying jobs and always getting laid off because of no seniority, I had decided to try and get a trade and was working to obtain a license as a stationary engineer. Joe Meslin, an ex-member of our group who had been one of its leaders in the pre-war period and was well known in garment unions in the city, had used his connections to give me a leg up with this. He got me an interview with the engineering superintendent in a large building under construction in Toronto's downtown core. They were looking for someone to help operate their heating and air conditioning systems. I got the job, and it led to me getting my license that allowed me to have steady, reasonably paid work whenever I wanted it, for the rest of my life—a very important thing if you are a revolutionary socialist.

Chapter 15

Verne Olson and the Cuban Revolution

THE CUBAN REVOLUTION, I HAVE TO ADMIT, TOOK OUR GROUP BY surprise. Sometimes, as I've discovered, even revolutionaries can be slow in getting off the mark when it comes to recognizing the real deal. I don't remember us paying much attention to Cuba in the years before 1959, because in those matters we tended to take our lead from the SWP. There was not much in *The Militant* at first, as far as I can recall, and only an occasional item in the Toronto papers. Fidel Castro had been in Montreal in 1957—and would return as Cuban Prime Minister in 1959—but that hadn't registered with us much. Our interest was piqued, however, with the appearance of Fidel Castro on television when Herbert Mathews, an editor of the New York Times, interviewed him in the Sierra Maestra mountains and we became aware for the first time of the strength of the guerrilla struggle against the Batista dictatorship. None of us that I recall had ever been to Cuba and I remember especially a couple of people who were close to our group, who had been vacationing in Havana around that time, telling us about a general strike they had seen and that it was obvious something important was going on there. Everywhere you went in Toronto, people were talking about it and public opinion seemed to be supportive of the resistance to Batista. As Robert Wright, a keen student of Canadian-Cuban relations, writes, "editorials and letters in the Canadian dailies—throughout 1958—were overwhelmingly supportive of the guerrillas."[1] "It began as an ill-reported and ill understood revolutionary democratic movement," the SWP's Joe Hansen observed.[2]

Without any hard facts, and not really knowing what was happening on the ground, I remember that in the discussions amongst ourselves we would tend to dismiss Fidel Castro and the July 26 Movement as "bourgeois-nationalist." This was also reflected in our first commentary about the overthrow of Batista, in an unsigned article in our paper. Relying almost entirely on dispatches by the *Globe and Mail*'s Phillipe Deane, the article was very skeptical of the 26th of July Movement and Fidel Castro, whom it saw as a brake on the revolution. "All indications are," we wrote, "that Castro is attempting to control the revolution and channel it into a middle-class reform programme that will leave the source of Cuba's poverty, and misery—imperialism—basically intact. A provisional government has been set up with elections promised a long $1\frac{1}{2}$ to 2 years."[3] And according to the SWP's Lilian Kiezel, writing in *The Militant*, "For the past year Castro has sought in various ways to convince the State Department and plantation owners that he has repudiated the aims announced in 1955 and has no intention of nationalizing industry."[4] A year later, the paper was still maintaining, "The main danger to the Cuban Revolution is in its own leadership. The class background of the Castro forces is petit bourgeois."

These comments by the two main Trotskyist currents in North America were understandably based upon some of the confusion about the aims of the Revolution as expressed by a few of its main leaders, including Castro, but they were nevertheless a mistake that we would have to rectify very soon. And we were not the only ones associated with the Fourth International who were on that track.

The F.I. initially got off to a good start by having, in early 1959, one of its leaders tour the island. She received a warm welcome and was given extensive radio time to promote the F.I., but this opportunity to establish good relations with the new government soon went off the rails and headed in a sectarian direction under the influence of Juan Posadas, a leader of the Fourth International at the time who was co-coordinating the work of the International's Latin American sections. We now recognize that it was a golden opportunity missed, but it was probably the unfortunate by-product of an internal tendency struggle in the International between Michel Pablo and Juan Posadas on the one side and Pierre Frank, Livio Maitan and Ernest Mandel on the other.[5] For a critical period, the views of Juan Posadas and the F.I.'s "Latin American Bureau" set the public tone for the F.I.'s early attitude to the revolution. That could be seen in an appeal it issued three months after the overthrow of Batista in 1959, "on the rising revolutionary struggles in Latin America," reprinted in the Spring issue of *Fourth International,* the theoretical journal of the International Secretariat that referred "to the July 26 movement and similar movements as being led by 'bourgeois parties and agents of imperialism' whose anti-imperialist stance was due to 'the enormous pressure that the masses bring to bear on them.' "[6]

At best, consciousness about the new developments in Cuba was at a low level. A leaflet, for example, put out for circulation in Britain by the International Group in Nottingham, promoting the International Secretariat's "Winter, 1959-1960 *Fourth International*," makes no mention of Cuba whatsoever.[7] But those were the early days. Very soon, as I've said, most of us had corrected our attitude and quickly we became enthusiastic supporters of the Cuban experiment. It was destined to have a profound effect upon socialists everywhere, and defending Cuba against imperialism became a central activity for the radical left in North America, helping it to emerge from the isolation imposed on it as a result of McCarthyism.

It was only after a discussion about Cuba opened up in the SWP, I remember, that we in Canada fully grasped the true significance of the change in Cuba. Farrell Dobbs and Joe Hansen, two of the main leaders of the SWP, had toured Cuba in early 1960 and came away convinced that fundamental change was underway. In a document written in July 1960, Joe declared that "the new Cuban government is a workers and farmers' government..." meaning that while the capitalists still dominated the economy, the workers and peasants had taken control of the government. Five months later, the SWP followed this up by declaring that a workers' state now existed in Cuba, a designation that recognized that the workers and peasants had defeated the capitalists and now controlled the state and economy.[8] The only opposition in our ranks to this view turned out to be in the leadership of the American YSA, led by Tim Wohlforth, Jim Robertson and Shane Mage. Their position was very simple: only the working class could overthrow capitalism, "led by a revolutionary party" such as Lenin's Bolsheviks', preferably with a "Trotskyist" programme, they said. And, since such a party did not exist in Cuba, what was happening in Cuba, according to them, could not be termed a "socialist revolution." They were joined in this view by many Trotskyists of the insular variety in Britain such as Gerry Healy's Socialist Labour League and Ted Grant's grouping, the Revolutionary Socialist League, but in hindsight, I personally shouldn't be too critical about this.

I was initially partial to some of these views myself because I was still locked into a formal way of thinking, and it took me a little while to come around to supporting the majority's views. Indirectly, both Tim and Jim had helped me finally make up my mind because as the discussion unfolded, they began to disagree with each other: Jim believed Cuba had become a "deformed workers state"—a designation in our vocabulary that likened the new Cuban state to those of the authoritarian, Stalinist controlled states of Eastern Europe—and Tim was of the opinion that there had not been a revolution at all. Both were unanimous in calling for the overthrow of the new Cuban government. The SWP, especially through the writings of Joe Hansen, would go on to play an exemplary role in theorizing what had taken place in Cuba and ideologically arming radical activists everywhere for its defense. I know of no other socialist organization anywhere, outside of Cuba, that expended more resources and effort, carried out more internal discussions and debates, or published more articles in its press, about Cuba.

As the Cuban Revolution became more and more anti-capitalist, and with the new government nationalizing key sectors of the economy and implementing a deep agrarian reform, the United States redoubled its efforts to destroy the revolution by imposing a brutal blockade against the country (which lasts to this day) and by resorting to a combination of clandestine and open military intervention. Amidst press speculation about such threats, the SWP moved at full speed to mobilize support for Cuba, not only through the party's press and public forums, but by trying to build as large a united front as possible of all those who supported the right of the Cubans to self-determination and their independence. These were the circumstances under which the Fair Play for Cuba Committee (FPCC) was born. Initiated by Robert Taber, it became for a couple of years the main instrument for spreading the truth about Cuba in North America. Taber, a CBS journalist who had broken the Cuban story to the world when he interviewed Castro in the mountains in 1957, had run a full-page ad defending Cuba in the *New York Times* in April 1960, which was signed by many of the world's leading intellectuals and personalities of that time, among them Simone de Beauvoir, Jean-Paul Sartre, Norman Mailer, James Baldwin, Truman Capote and Robert F. Williams, a militant, black ex-marine from North Carolina who later would create a sensation in the Black civil rights movement because of his book, *Negroes With Guns,*[9] an account of his organizing along with others in his community, armed self-defense squads to protect his community from marauding white racists. Over a thousand letters of support flowed in as a result of the advertisement and Taber had quickly moved to bring into being the FPCC.

The CP and the SWP threw their support behind the new project, with the SWP taking the most active role. "Within six months, the FPCC had 7,000 members—27 'adult' chapters and 40 student councils" and Berta Green of the SWP became one of its main organizers, writes Bill Simpich in a well documented article, summarizing the Committee's work in building solidarity in the critical early years when the revolution was under severe external threat. The FPCC promptly set up a functioning headquarters in New York under the leadership of Richard Gibson, a black journalist. Although Simpich does not mention the internal tensions between the CP and the SWP within the Committee,[10] he nevertheless provides an excellent account of its successes.[11]

The American FPCC lasted barely two years, winding itself up ultimately because of the intense pressure placed upon it by the American government to compel it to register as "a foreign agent" and hand over its membership lists. The final straw was the vicious right-wing smearing of the Committee (think of the "shock jocks" on today's American radio stations) that associated Lee Harvey Oswald with the Committee at the time of John Kennedy's assassination. But in its brief life, because of its hard work and through its publications, press releases, demonstrations and protests—some with many thousands outside the UN headquarters in New York—it was able to have a critical influence on many people's understanding of the illegal activity of their government and at the same time win breathing space for the revolution. The decision by the SWP and the radical left—especially the youth—in the early part of the decade, in making the defense of Cuba their highest priority and through the tactic of building the broadest possible united front around a single issue, on the demand for self-determination, would provide the template for later successful organizing against the Vietnam war, a war that was then in its early stages. And it was an initial entry point for many young people into radical politics. As the Canadian academic Cynthia Wright notes: "In both the United States and Canada, the committees were part of the difficult process of opening up political dissent within the stifling context of McCarthyism and the Cold War consensus; they were also fundamentally linked to the early phases of the civil rights movement, Black Power and the student movement."[12]

The Canadian FPCC was established not long after the founding of the American Committee and was equally as successful, if not more so, and, it turned out, had a much longer life and a more lasting effect. In getting it off the ground, we benefited very much from our close relationship with the SWP. We in the SEL had been following the SWP's initiative on Cuba with great interest, wondering how we could replicate it. Events were moving very fast and all of us believed that our solidarity work should embrace broad forces to persuade working people that Canada should not back up the U.S. Reports were already appearing in the press that the U.S., ominously, had begun threatening military manoeuvres from its base at Guantanamo; we were expecting an invasion at any moment. By then I was on the Political Committee[13] and we began to discuss what possible measures we could take to carry out solidarity activity. One of our first moves—a modest one—was to issue a leaflet in the name of the SEL, "Hands off Cuba!" which we circulated as widely as possible, but that was clearly insufficient. We had to do more. Our first impulse was to organize a picket outside the U.S. Consulate,[14] but we concluded this might be premature and would probably have resulted in something small and ineffectual—a sign of our weakness, more than anything else.

The SEL was a tiny organization at that time, with at most thirty members in Toronto. Although UE and the LPP, many times larger than us, had set up "Aid to Cuba Committees," we noted to ourselves how very passive they had been on the issue, confining their efforts mainly to raising support within their own ranks, perhaps an expression of Moscow's hesitation about what was going on in Havana where the CP, literally, had been pushed aside by the July 26 Movement. We decided that the best approach for us would be to circumvent the CP and set up a "defense committee," similar to that in the U.S. where they had appealed for prominent public figures to become sponsors. We figured we might even be able to do a better job in Canada because of our broad contacts in the labour movement and the CCF. We were also beginning to see that there was some awakening in the labour movement about the issue.

At its Fall convention that year, in 1960, the B.C. Federation of Labour, to overwhelming and thunderous support from its delegates—and to the discomfort of the Canadian Labour Congress, especially its vice-president, Joe Morris—agreed to send all of its top officers to Cuba for a special visit and at the same time urged all of its local unions to elect representatives to accompany them there to make sure it would be a mass delegation to find out the truth of what was going on.[15]

As a first step in getting something going on Cuba, we immediately requested our Toronto and Vancouver branches and our supporters in Montreal to begin the preparatory work for the setting up of a defense committee by contacting sympathetic prominent individuals on the campuses and in the CCF and unions to see if they would be interested in such a project.[16] At the conclusion of the PC discussion, Ross agreed he would approach Verne Olson to see if he would head up the new project, and at the same time we assigned one of our most experienced leaders in Toronto, Pat Mitchell—in the event that Verne agreed—to give him full assistance.

Verne and his wife Ann had recruited me to the SEL a few years earlier and I had always remained in touch with them, visiting them in their home in Swansea from time to time. They were always warm and generous to me and Ann was an excellent cook. I had many suppers there. Verne, who had suffered from polio as a child, making it impossible for him to walk without crutches, came from a poor family in rural Saskatchewan and had remained unschooled in his childhood until a social worker intervened to have him educated. He and Ann became politically conscious in their youth and became active in the F.I. group in Toronto, with Verne becoming one of its leaders. Through single-minded concentration, he had worked hard at overcoming a lack of formal education, and when I knew him he was employed at Ontario Hydro as a certified technologist in hydrology.

It was by no means certain Verne would agree to head up the Cuba project. He suffered periodically from severe depressions—a debilitating affliction that lasted most of his life—and had been on a leave of absence from the SEL for health reasons and also to spend time upgrading his technical qualifications to gain a technologist certification. We were pleasantly surprised when we heard from Ross that not only had he agreed with our proposal, but that he was enthusiastic about the idea. He and Ann had been following events in Cuba very closely with the same great excitement as the rest of us and were also wondering about how we should respond. With his courage, intelligence, and profound sense of moral integrity, he turned out to be ideal for the task, and much of the eventual success of the Committee in Canada was due to his and Ann's single-minded dedication to leading it through its many trials and tribulations. They were central to our campaign in Canada to get the truth out about Cuba, and without them, I doubt it would have had the effect it had.

Towards the end of 1960, because of our contacts with the SWP, we managed to have Verne and Ann included in a large delegation of over 300 visitors to Cuba, organized by the American FPCC. The U.S. broke diplomatic relations with Cuba while the American tour was there; it would be the last tour Americans could join freely, as the U.S. placed a complete ban on their citizens visiting the island. But Verne and Ann's visit was the breakthrough we needed in Canada and we quickly proceeded to set up the FPCC across the country, but independent of the U.S. operation that had been in existence for about a year. This Cuba solidarity work, which lasted from 1960 to 1970, is well described by Cynthia Wright. It's not my intention to give the full story of the Canadian FPCC here—Wright does that very well—but to try to tell how it looked from inside the SEL and its successor organization, the League for Socialist Action (LSA). I will add to Wright's account, however, additional information about some of the difficulties we encountered due to the hostility toward us from Canadian security forces and some of the problems we encountered in the Committee's dealing with those in Cuba who were under the influence of the Popular Socialist Party (PSP), the Cuban version of the CP, and especially about the problems we ran into in dealing with the Cuban governmental organization, the Cuban Institute for Friendship with Peoples (ICAP) that was headed up by Leon Mazzola, whom we came to believe was a PSP member or sympathizer.

The SEL's urgency in defending Cuba arose from the high importance it gave to internationalism, expressed by its membership in the Fourth International whose programme called for the workers in the advanced countries to resist their own capitalist rulers and which placed a high priority on defending the struggles for self-determination and independence in the colonial world. With our limited resources—at that time, as I recall it, we could not have had more than fifty members in the whole country—we believed that the best way to help the Cuban people would be to create a broad single-issue defense campaign to let Canadians know the truth about the revolution and its accomplishments, to counter the barrage of hostile propaganda that was regularly appearing in the Canadian media, as it swung behind American policy objectives. For us, it was the first opportunity since the Russian Revolution to publicize and promote democratic socialism through a concrete example that was unfolding before our eyes. The vehicle for this would be the FPCC.

While Ann and Verne were in Cuba, we busied ourselves with lining-up speaking engagements across the country so that Verne could address Canadians about his experiences there. The response turned out to be greater than we could have ever imagined. Verne even got himself on television and in Toronto we kicked off his cross-country tour with a packed enthusiastic meeting of over four hundred supporters in the First Unitarian Church on St. Clair Avenue West, where we managed to sell approximately 250 memberships for the new committee, such was the excitement in the hall. Alongside Verne on the platform were Professor Leslie Dewart, a Catholic theologian from the U of T, whose family came from Cuba, Farley Mowat, one of Canada's best known Canadian writers on the Canadian north, and keynote speaker Sam Shapiro from the New York office of the FPCC. We also had Richard Gibson, the black journalist and one of the main initiators of the American Committee, on the platform. Verne announced to the meeting a list of prominent sponsors who had quickly rallied to the Canadian Committee. Among them were Kenneth McNaught, a much respected historian at the University of Toronto and the biographer of J. S. Woodsworth,[17] William Irvine, Honourary Chairman of the Alberta CCF, Frank Hanson, editor of the party's Saskatchewan weekly, *The Commonwealth,* Orville Braaten, a leader of the Pulp and Sulphite Union in B.C. and the Reverend John Morgan, a minister of the First Unitarian Church to which Verne and Ann belonged. It was the first of many large meetings across the country about Cuba and an impressive beginning.[18]

Until reading Cynthia Wright's essay, I had forgotten the importance of McNaught in helping to get the FPCC up and running. The same month that the U.S. ended its diplomatic relations with Cuba and while Verne and Ann were in Cuba, an important article by McNaught had appeared in the weekly *Saturday Night,* deeply critical of U.S. policy towards the island and urging Canada to reject it and to formulate its own independent position. McNaught urged readers to contact the New York office of the FPCC and give it support, which hundreds of Canadian did. Those names and addresses were turned over to the Toronto organizers of the Committee. With the successful Toronto event under his belt Verne criss-crossed the country speaking to all kinds of gatherings with hundreds turning out to hear him.

We were riding a wave of enthusiasm. Committee chapters sprung up in Montreal, Winnipeg, Edmonton and Vancouver. Activists in the CCF and the unions were hungry for any reliable news, not trusting what they were reading and hearing in the media. By then we had managed to line up an impressive list of endorsers. On the West Coast, Bob Horne, a student and leading member of our group, moved quickly to get a B.C. wing of the Committee up and running. Soon we had the active support of some key CCF people like Cedric Cox, a CCF-MLA and Dorothy Steeves, a founder of the Party, along with a few prominent trade unionists such as Orville Braaten and Jerry LeBourdais of the Oil and Chemical Workers Union. On the prairies, a young Howard Pawley—who would later become the Province's NDP Premier—became a key member of the Winnipeg Committee. Other active supporters on the prairies were prominent left-wingers in the CCF, of course, such as Bill Irvine, an early sponsor and Tony Mardiros in Edmonton. Hugh Garner, an important Canadian novelist, also publicly backed the Committee. But the biggest boost to our efforts came from Cuba itself. Invariably those who visited the country came back bursting with enthusiasm and wanting to talk about their experiences, underlining the old adage that revolutions can turn ordinary people into the best of revolutionaries.

The Canadian FPCC, as Cynthia Wright notes, became one of the most successful solidarity committees in the English speaking world and, during the course of its ten year history, for many activists in North America it was the main source of information about Cuba, as it went through its many achievements and various crises. Right from the beginning the Committee engaged in a vigourous publishing programme, printing many speeches by Cuban leaders, especially those by Fidel Castro and Che Guevara, and numerous pamphlets and reprints of articles and speeches by Cuba's supporters around the world. Very successful was a pamphlet by Jack Scott (not to be confused with Jack Scott, the Vancouver Maoist), a very popular columnist for the *Vancouver Sun,* comprised of eight of his columns, "Jack Scott Takes a Second Look at Cuba." He had been to Cuba a couple of times before the revolution and his pamphlet about his most recent trip there sold many thousands of copies. Another successful little publication was Leslie Dewar's "A Catholic Looks at Cuba," which also sold many thousands and was distributed widely throughout the country. Eventually, the FPCC would become one of the main suppliers of English-language literature about Cuba to the Cuban Embassy in Ottawa.

It wasn't long before a major activity of the Committee became that of organizing tours to the island so that Canadians could hear first-hand personal accounts about what was going on, and to also persuade prominent intellectuals and artists to go and see for themselves what was happening, especially on important anniversary dates, all to help counter the growing pressure from the U.S. on the Diefenbaker government to line up behind its anti-Cuba offensive that was intensifying by the day.

Dorothy Steeves, a leader of the B.C. CCF until the early fifties and an important B.C. poet, went to Cuba for the first time along with Al Purdy, even then one of Canada's major poets. They were part of a delegation of Canadians from the cultural community in the spring of 1964 who attended May Day celebrations on behalf of the FPCC. Purdy later wrote a very powerful account of the destruction of a sugar refinery by counter-revolutionaries in Oriente province, along with a "Poem to the Sailors on the American Warship, 'Oxford'..."[19] When Purdy returned to Canada, he readily agreed to speak at several meetings about his experiences. I remember in Vancouver, on one of his visits to the city, he spoke to a packed meeting of the YS.

The U.S. State Department's efforts to line Canada up against Cuba were relentless. An ominous sign about what was in store came very early when Senator Croll, a "left" Liberal and powerful influence in his Party, denounced Cuba and came out against trade with it, demanding that a Cuban trade mission then in Canada "should be sent packing." At about the same time, many of Cuba's supporters became very alarmed when the Prime Minister, John Diefenbaker, indicated that he had acquiesced to the Americans' policy towards Cuba. The FPCC promptly issued a press release—one of the many over the course of its life—calling on Diefenbaker to reject the "Kennedy doctrine," pointing out that the U.S. policy also called into question Canada's own sovereignty. And when Cuba was bombed "by unidentified military aircraft" in early 1961, a prelude to the Bay of Pigs invasion, Verne condemned it as "nothing less than a flagrant act of aggression on a member nation of the United Nations"[20] and called upon the Canadian government to denounce it. Just as importantly, when Kennedy launched that invasion, FPCC supporters across the country immediately mobilized to protest. The Vancouver Labour Council, led by FPCC activists in the hall, condemned the action, pledging full support to the Cuban people "in their fight for freedom and for a better life," as did the Regina and Hamilton Labour Councils. During the course of the invasion, the Committee organized a series of pickets of several hundred each outside the Vancouver and Toronto Consulates.[21]

Very soon after it got off the ground, almost in defiance of the growing Diefenbaker hostility to Cuba, the Committee received a warm response for its goals from hundreds of young people in Canada, especially students. Five campus clubs were soon affiliated to it, most of them headed up by members or supporters of the LSA, by then the successor to the SEL. Alongside Bob Horne, Bryan Belfont—who would also become a leader of our group on the West Coast—became prominent in the Committee's activities right up to the end of the decade. A welcome find, prior to that he had spent year studying in Cuba after which he became a very active chairman of the Committee on the University of British Columbia.

In the summer of 1964, the Committee sent a delegation of forty-five students from all over Canada to Cuba, led by a retired Canadian military officer, David Middleton, a left wing leader in the Toronto NDP. The tour had been over-subscribed with 125 students expressing an interest in participating. Plans called for the tour to join several hundred other students from around the world to work "on the construction of the Camillo Cienfuegos School in the Sierra Maestra Mountains during July and August." Ross Dowson, who during the Second World War had been a lieutenant in the Canadian army, had figured Middleton would be an ideal team leader, but we later learned that he had to deal with a rebellion of his young charges who had resisted his attempts to impose a military-like discipline upon them. It all began in Mexico City where the group was waiting for a flight to Havana and continued in Cuba, when a few of the students—who were not connected to the LSA—who, in addition to resisting Middleton's discipline, figured that rather than going into the mountains, they would rather experience the city life of Havana. Ruth Tate, who was a founder of the Vancouver YS and editor of *Young Socialist Forum* at the University of British Columbia, and Hans Modlich, then an engineering student at the University of Toronto and a leader of the YS, both members of the LSA, tried their best to assist Middleton in preventing the tour from falling apart but it became even more difficult once they arrived in Cuba. Ruth and Hans quickly noticed that in addition to the problem of keeping the tour on course, many of the tour group seemed to be constantly engaged with individual Cubans in discussions about the topic of Trotsky.

The views of many of the youth on that tour were not that much different from those of many non-CP activists anywhere in Canada, where the topic of Trotsky was no big deal. It would have been quite natural for them to talk about Trotsky in those days, but we were suspicious that many of these debates had been provoked by PSP people who seemed intent on "setting up" the tour group as a "Trotskyist" enterprise, part of a political operation we suspected to discredit the work of the Committee in Canada. But despite those difficulties, we—and ICAP—considered the 1964 tour a big success, with many of the students later speaking on their campuses about their experiences and bolstering the work of the Committee. "The result of that visit will always be happily remembered by our revolutionary people," Giraldo Mazola, Director of ICAP would later say.[22]

From the very beginning, the Canadian Committee was treated with deep suspicion by the Tory government and soon after its formation it was added to an unofficial blacklist of "subversive" organizations the government deemed a threat to the security of the Canadian state. And the American Committee was coming under similar pressure. Soon after its formation, in the summer of 1961, the right-wing news agency, United Press International (UPI) dispatched a witch-hunting article targetting the American Committee, with the headline, "Pro-Cuba Reds Infiltrating Our Campuses." The article soon appeared in all major newspapers throughout the United States and not long after that the Canadian Committee became the object of a string of virulent, red-baiting articles in the *Toronto Telegram,* a hard-right daily even worse than to today's *National Post,* smearing Verne and FPCC's work.[23] The way the wind was blowing could also be seen when *MacLean's* magazine told Farley Mowat that an article about Cuba that he had been preparing in consultation with their editors was no longer wanted.[24] There was also some red-baiting by the leadership of the Ontario CCF and the United Auto Workers (UAW) against the Committee, and Leslie Dewar and Kenneth McNaught seemed to bend to these kinds of pressure when they publicly withdrew their endorsement of the Committee, precipitating an internal crisis in its ranks.

"We have some intelligence concerning the people who had been appointed officials and to the executive," Dewar told the press. He did not say where his "intelligence" came from, but as far as the LSA was concerned, this was the work of the RCMP, pure and simple. Their filthy fingerprints were all over the affair and could be seen in Dewar's next comment. "McNaught and I put certain questions about policy to the Chairman, Mr. V. O. Olson," he said. "We suggested that all governing officials of the committee should be above reproach in their loyalty to the Queen and Canada's established constitution."[25] It was sad to see these two academics—one of whom, McNaught, was an important public intellectual in his own right and a spokesman for many progressive causes, succumbing to the state's pressures on this issue. Verne, in no uncertain terms, told the two of them where to go with their idea, letting them know that their suggestion would defeat the aim of uniting the greatest number of people behind the goal of fair play for Cuba. "It would require some committee members to investigate the political associations of elected members," he said. "Such a policy would lead to a witch-hunt in the organization."[26] In a later report, Verne expanded on this point, characterizing it as a form of McCarthyism. "I have taken it for granted that all Committee supporters were vigourously opposed to the witch-hunt which has stultified intellectual life on this continent. We have to combat this atmosphere from the word go in order to establish the truth about Cuba. It was in this belief that I declined to become the instigator of a policy to keep the Committee 'above reproach.'"

Backing for Verne's position quickly flowed in from Committee supporters across the country. The Montreal FPCC likened it to "intimidation by thought police reminiscent of (the) twenty year Duplessis Regime." Howard Pawley wrote: "Don't become discouraged. We are with you in Winnipeg." Nevertheless, Dewart and McNaught had supporters in Toronto and in a meeting of the Committee with about sixty people in attendance they proposed that it dissolve itself. The motion was defeated.[27]

In the midst of the furor precipitated by the Dewar and McNaught affair, Verne and Ann were also placed under continuous surveillance and subjected to harassment by the RCMP, with a police car parked twenty-four hours a day outside their home. "Their resignation followed an RCMP statement appearing in the Toronto papers which said that the Mounties were 'watching' the FPCC..." Verne wrote a correspondent.[28] This kind of harassment would continue throughout the Committee's life. In a 1967 letter to the *Toronto Star*, for example, Hans Modlich, on behalf of the Committee, protested a bizarre campaign against it, when media reports appeared saying that the FPCC, "was training 'separatists' in Quebec during Expo."[29]

In September 1961 a new crisis erupted for Verne and Ann, but from a totally unexpected direction. Robert Williams suddenly showed up on their doorstep, on the run from the FBI in the U.S. Williams had been to Toronto prior to this and had helped get the FPCC started, speaking several times in support of the Committee across the country, but now he was on the run from both the FBI and the RCMP. From Monroe, North Carolina, where the Ku Klux Klan was a mass movement, he was a leader of the Black Power wing of the civil rights movement in the U.S. Critical of the pacifist methods of Martin Luther King, he had advocated a policy of armed self-defense and had formed a Black Armed Guard to protect his community against racist violence. During a riot in Monroe, he had been forced to flee under threat of death after the FBI had issued a warrant for his arrest, declaring that he was armed and dangerous. It meant he would be shot on sight.

The SWP had a good rapport with Williams that went back several years from when he was head of the local National Association for the Advancement of Colored People (NAACP) in 1958, when he was in dispute with the national organization about his advocacy for a more militant policy for the civil rights movement, and which led to his expulsion. The SWP had mobilized broad public support for him when he was agitating in the courts and against the police, in what's now known as "The Kissing Case," where two black children had been incarcerated because, while innocently playing, one of them had kissed a young white girl.

The SWP made a major issue of the case that had outraged many in the U.S. and which received headlines around the world. The party would become one of the first of the so-called "white" revolutionary groups in America to fully throw its support behind the "Freedom Now" wing of the civil rights movement. Through the writings of George Breitman, the SWP recognized the significance of Black Nationalism in the struggle for socialism, explaining it from a Marxist perspective and highlighting it as a critical factor in the class struggle. They gave full support to Malcolm X, and Malcolm, for his part, considered *The Militant* to be one of the finest newspapers around. Williams and his supporters, with their tactic of self-defense, were regarded by the SWP as having set an exemplary example of resistance in the black struggle.

When Williams fled to Canada, he could be fairly certain our people would render him assistance. While on his speaking engagements in Toronto—he had been to Montreal and Toronto as recently as the previous May—he always stayed with Ann and Verne. In conjunction with the FBI, a manhunt had been launched in Canada by the Mounties who stated as a fact that he was armed and a "common criminal," a characterization that the FPCC, vehemently protested.[30] It was touch and go whether he would be captured or not. The police and the RCMP harassed many Committee members and supporters in looking for him, searching several people's homes and at one point the basement of the First Unitarian Church.

It was pure chance that Williams wasn't picked up. The Olsons kept him hidden for six weeks while trying to arrange his flight into exile. Finally, they arranged for him to travel to Nova Scotia where a sizable black population lived and where he had a good chance of not being noticed. There he boarded a plane to Cuba and was granted asylum. Mabel, his wife, joined him a few months later. A lot of the details about this event, I didn't know until I read Wright's essay.[31] In the leading committees of the League for Socialist Action (LSA), the successor organization to SEL, and the FPCC it was only discussed in the most general terms and information about it was only given out, correctly so, on a need-to-know basis to protect those involved. The SEL, mainly through the FPCC, maintained very good relations with Williams over the years, with many of our people visiting him from time to time in Havana where the Cuban government had provided him with a radio programme on Havana Radio, "Radio Free Dixie," through which to broadcast to the United States his opinions about current events in the black struggle.

Williams also edited a small journal, *The Crusader,* which Ann and Verne helped him circulate in North America. A few SEL members gathered at their home every month to mail it out to his subscribers, with Ann and Verne's home address on it. We looked upon all this as part of our basic duty of solidarity to help the black liberation struggle in the U. S.

When Verne had met with Dewart and McNaught before they had severed their connections to the Committee, he hadn't been entirely frank about the role of the SEL in relation to it. He had countered their complaint about our influence by telling them that out of an eleven-member executive, only one could be characterized as being in the SEL. But in this he was being a little disingenuous. While perhaps technically correct, he sought to downplay the SEL's influence, trying to protect the Committee against red-baiting. Those were hard anti-communist times, but without the SEL, the FPCC would never have gotten off the ground, which didn't mean it wasn't broadly based. With a lot of support in the NDP and the unions, it was by no means a "front organization," the kind the CPs were infamous for putting in place and which were basically an extension of their own organization, to be used for any purpose they thought fit.

While the SEL had won the respect of many independent activists around the Committee, it very much had a life of its own to the degree that we would occasionally find ourselves in the minority within it. This could be seen early on when we had hoped the Committee would formally affiliate with the American FPCC, something we thought everyone would be in agreement with. However, when we raised this idea, a majority opposed us. They were concerned that membership lists crossing the border might make them vulnerable to the prying eyes of American security agencies, and that possibly money from Canada might be used to publish American literature. The Committee thus decided to remain independent. As Pat Mitchell, a leader of the SEL and the FPCC's membership-secretary later put it, "I don't think this was a good decision because the American committee needs any support it can get but we could not carry our position on this question."[32] Later, Verne, probably trying to make the best of this rejection, spoke positively about the Committee's "independent position," but in the end, happily, it proved to be a wise move because in less than two years, the American organization would be forced to dissolve. It had come under worse attack than we had suffered in Canada. Hauled before various Senate Committees to explain its activities, they demanded it hand over its membership lists and register as a "foreign agent." And there was some falling away of endorsers, among them people like Sydney Lens, then one of the United States' best known labour historians, who was one of the first to buckle, disassociating himself from the Committee because of "Trotskyist influence" in it.

The witch-hunting only served to make us redouble our efforts to expand the work of the Committee, especially in the unions. We were convinced that sympathy by many Canadian working people for Cuba remained strong. This seemed to be confirmed when Hazen Argue, the new leader of the CCF took a firm stand, saying, "... in the last analysis what the Cubans are doing is asserting the soil and resources of their country should belong to them. Threats of intervention from other countries should be opposed, no matter where they come from."[33] "The real reason for the U.S. attitude is economic," pointed out Frank Howard, the CCF-NDP-MP for Skeena, B.C., referring to the Cuban expropriation of U.S. properties.[34] Wherever we had members or contacts in the unions, we would persuade them to try and have resolutions passed in their local membership meetings, asking that their national unions send delegations to Cuba so that the unions could witness for themselves the achievements of the revolution. The CLC sent a delegation, as did the B.C. Federation of Labour and the Vancouver Labour Council. All returned with favourable reports. To this day, there is still a deep sympathy among Canadian trade unionists for Cuba and over one million ordinary Canadians go there every year on vacation, making Canada, amongst all countries, the largest source of tourists for its beleaguered economy.

Typical of the work of the FPCC in those days was that of the Vancouver chapter led by Phil Courneyeur and Cedric Cox. It had a very active life organizing protests, public meeting and promoting Cuba in the NDP and in the unions. Within a couple of years there would be two other "competing" Cuban support committees in the city, one organized by the CP, and the other organized by Jack Scott's small pro-Mao group that had recently emerged from the CP. We deplored this division and at various times reached out to them to try and arrange joint activities with them, but nothing much came of this. Neither was as successful as the FPCC. I remember, when I moved out there in 1962, how impressed I was by its energy, partly due to it being led by young people. Ken Orchard,

Cliff Orchard's brother, a twenty-one year old active in our youth group, was its communications director and Bud Bennet, a leader in the New Democratic Youth, was its secretary.

Every important Cuban anniversary, the Committee would organize a large public event, often attended by Cuban consulate officials—and sometimes the Cuban Ambassador, Americo Cruz—with speeches and talks about Cuba, often followed by a banquet, and attended by close to two hundred people, many of them from the NDP and the unions. It's where I got to practice cooking for large numbers of people, something I had learned while helping Fred Halstead at the SWP's Mountain Spring Camp. Phil Courneyeur, a very bright and precocious teenager, had been recruited to our group by Ruth and Reg Bullock. With a political maturity way beyond his years, he was at the same time secretary of the Burnaby NDP, a centre of the left in the party. He quickly won the respect of the Cuban Ambassador and they became close friends. Cox, also from Burnaby, an NDP-MLA had been inspired by the revolution and had become one of its most outspoken defenders.

During the Cuban missile crisis in October 1962, in addition to organizing several demonstrations outside the U.S. Consulate, the Committee members distributed over twenty thousand leaflets in the Vancouver area, most of them at shopping centres, factories, high schools and at the UBC campus, all within a couple of hours of President Kennedy's October 22nd speech, the closest the world has ever come to all out nuclear war.[35] I remember one particularly scary moment after I had moved out there, during the Cuban missile crisis when we were discussing the launching of a possible protest outside the American Consulate. Against objections, I pushed to go ahead with it even though there had not been much preparation, expecting somehow that our supporters would simply turn out because of the crisis. Unfortunately when we showed up at the U.S. Consulate, we were so few in number that we were immediately surrounded by several hundred hostile Americans spoiling for a fight. They had obviously been mobilized to counter us and I had learned a lesson to listen to others who knew the situation better than me. We were forced to end the protest early at the Consulate, later organizing a demonstration where we outnumbered our opponents.

Both Cedric and Phil, on different occasions, toured Cuba for weeks at a time in 1963. Their experiences and observations were put to valuable use in talks to labour groups, NDP clubs and the constituencies throughout the province. A high point was the NDP's Provincial Convention that Fall that saw a big upsurge in interest about Cuba among the delegates who voted for a resolution "almost unanimously" calling for sympathy and support of the Cuban people "in their struggle to achieve decent living standards' and condemning the U.S. boycott of Cuba."[36] The Committee also rallied to organize material aid to Cuba whenever it suffered natural disasters. In October of that year, in addition to the difficult economic conditions that resulted from the American blockade, two of Cuba's eastern provinces were laid waste by Hurricane Flora. The Committee responded by issuing a public appeal—"Help Cuba!" It urged people to donate generously and asked that its supporters hold social events with the specific purpose of raising money for Cuba.

Among its most popular publications—the product of an FPCC-sponsored tour—was the 1964 pamphlet, "The Real Cuba, As Three Canadians Saw It," by Michel Chartrand of the Parti Socialiste du Quebec, John Riddell from Toronto, a member of our group on the tour representing the Canadian Universities' Campaign for Nuclear Disarmament (CUCND), and Verne Olson. Many thousands were sold across the country. Another popular pamphlet, "Four Canadians Who Saw Cuba," featured accounts by Cedric Cox, who, in opposition to his Provincial leader Bob Strachan, had toured Cuba; John Glenn, a school principal from Ontario and Provincial Council member of the NDP (and a member of our group); Charlie Bieseck, a columnist for the *Prairie New Democrat Commonwealth* and Richard Fidler, chairperson of the U of T Student Committee on Cuba and also a member of our group. As Cynthia Wright remarks, most of these pamphlets circulated widely across the country and today can be found in the archives of many universities throughout North America.

Working with the Cubans was not always smooth sailing, it turned out. For successful solidarity work, of course, their cooperation was essential for us, but sometimes we faced strong headwinds in dealing with them. One of our objectives was to have as many people as possible, from the cultural community, from the unions and the CCF, travel to Cuba to witness the dramatic improvements in health and agriculture and to especially see the spectacular results of a reading and writing campaign that in a very short time had given Cuba a literacy level equal to that of some advanced capitalist countries. Teams of visitors were usually organized in Canada in cooperation with the Cuban Institute for Friendship with Peoples, otherwise known by the acronym, ICAP. Our hope was that once people returned, they would spread the good word about the reforms they had seen, and this usually turned out to be the case. In the early days of the Revolution, things were always a little chaotic in trying to arrange such visits. A tour the Montreal FPCC had organized for the winter of 1960, for example, was called off because the Cubans couldn't provide air travel.

To say that communications with Cuba "were difficult" would be an understatement. A scheduled tour would neither be on nor off and we always seemed to be in limbo, anxiously awaiting word from Havana about this or that project. A tour for the July 26, 1961 celebrations was called off by the Cubans without any explanation. Verne, on one of his trips to Cuba, found that many of the people he met regarded ICAP as a bit of a scandal because of its inefficiencies. ICAP would often be late getting back to Verne in response to his letters and undoubtedly some of the difficulty was caused by the chaos resulting from transforming the bureaucracy, but nevertheless we believed, rather than just "inefficiency," a lot of it was also due to the political influence of the Popular Socialist Party (PSP), the name by which the CP was known in Cuba, which, although reduced by the success of the July 26 Movement, still had considerable presence in the state apparatus and the union movement. Whenever we encountered their people, as we tried to move our projects along, they would invariably be sectarian towards us, often spreading malicious rumours behind our backs and misleading others who often did not know any better into doing their dirty work for them.

In addition to official visits to Cuba, the Committee also had a policy of encouraging supporters to visit Cuba for their holidays. Occasionally they would become a victim of PSP sectarian tactics, we suspected, and be picked up by security forces and held without any explanation or charges being laid, and then released just as mysteriously. Alan Judge, an activist in the Stanley Park CCF in B.C., and supporter of the FPCC, once disappeared for several weeks under such circumstances, as did John Darling, a stalwart of the SEL and the YS, and a founding-member of the FPCC.

In Cuba for a vacation during the dangerous time of the Bay of Pigs invasion, John, an enthusiastic supporter of the Cuban Revolution, on April 17, 1961, was, ironically, picked up in a sweep along with thousands of other non-Cubans and many Cubans who had a history of being opponents of the government. He was held for three weeks in La Cabana Military Prison without any interrogation or explanation or any help from the Canadian Embassy. When he returned to Toronto, in an effort to clear his name, he wrote the Cuban Ambassador that a rumour was circulating in Toronto that he "had been charged and found guilty of black marketing." We figured elements in the LPP were behind this slander. While in Cuba, "I was unable to establish my support for the Cuban government," he wrote, "and my innocence of implied charges of being suspected of counter-revolutionary activity," he stated, requesting from the Ambassador that "you affirm that I have been released clear of all charges or suspicions, and that my detention was an error." The Ambassador replied that his "request has been forwarded to the proper Department in Cuba and as soon as we get a reply, we will call you..."[37]

Bob Silverman, one of the main leaders of the Montreal FPCC also disappeared in similar circumstances to John's, throwing his wife Edith into a state of justifiable panic when she hadn't heard from him for several weeks and was unable to contact him. This led to a flurry of frantic phone calls from Verne to Ottawa and Havana to find out where he was. He too was released without any explanation and we put it all down to a few PSP elements acting in a freelance way to harass anyone they suspected of being associated with us.

Founded in 1925, the Cuban CP (later to become the PSP) had been in its time one of the most formidable CPs in Latin America, a mass party with a strong working class base and a lot of influence in Cuba's intellectual left. We didn't know it at the time, but Raul Castro had joined the youth wing of the PSP in the early fifties while a student at Havana University, later joining the Party. Che Guevara had also joined for a short time in 1957 in the hope of moving it to the left.[38] As loyal followers of Stalin and in a comfortable relationship with Batista before he became a brutal dictator, the CP in its early days had played a leading role in founding the main union federation, the Cuban Confederation of Labour (CTC). In cooperation with Batista—who, the CP stated "was no longer the focal point of reaction, but the defender of democracy"—it helped write the new Cuban Constitution adopted in 1940, and, as part of his "Social Democratic Federation," campaigned for him to be President, electing ten of their members to the Chamber of Deputies and hundreds to city councils throughout the island, including electing the mayors in two major cities and coming close to winning the mayoralty of Havana. In the build up to the Second World War, during the Molotov-Ribbentrop pact, like CPs everywhere else, it had vigourously campaigned against the war and had opposed Cuba's entry into it. But when the USSR declared war on Germany, it swiftly reversed itself becoming a champion of Cuba's participation and changing its name to the Partido Socialista Popular (PSP). "Blas Roca, its leader became the first to volunteer in the army of the Allies."[39]

After Batista seized power in 1952, he banned the PSP and many of its leaders were arrested or went into exile. Yet, curiously, some of its most prominent people—many of whom had been candidates in previous elections—showed up in important positions in his regime, some of them even becoming key advisors.[40] Support for the party declined under Batista's subsequent repression, but it utilized that period to strengthen and re-organize itself. Although weaker, it was still one of the strongest political parties in Cuba at the time of Batista's fall in 1959, but it was fated to end up on the wrong side of history. The PSP had publicly denounced the 1953 Fidelista attack on the Moncada Fortress that had failed but which became the opening shots in an armed struggle that would eventually transform Cuba.

While condemning the repressive methods of Batista—just in case there was any confusion about where they stood—they at the same time publicly disassociated themselves from the new movement, in a position, I must admit, that would have been shared by many Trotskyists: "We repudiate the putchist methods, peculiar to bourgeois political factions of the action in Santiago de Cuba and Bayamo which was an adventurist attempt to take both military headquarters..."[41] But, early in 1958, when the July 26 Movement and the National Directorate were putting plans in place for a national strike, the PSP, softened its position and hurried to get on board giving its support to the action, but the Directorate, for anti-communist reasons mainly, had blocked their involvement, over the objections of Fidel, to whom the PSP had made a special appeal.[42]

Up to the seizure of power—and even after—relations remained tense between the PSP and the Fidelistas. (It is now recognized that some of this was also due to the anti-communist prejudices of some of the Fidelistas.) But as Scheer and Zietlin, point out, "As late as May 1958, the Communists were still referring to the 26th of July Movement as 'those who count on terroristic acts and conspiratorial coups as the chief means of ousting Batista...'" The April 1958 strike was a failure and the Party publicly declared that the strike movement did not have enough support to succeed, a statement that helped Batista defeat the workers as he quickly circulated it throughout the country.[43] And when the CP welcomed the July 26 Movement's "recent espousal of the general strike as a slogan...away from excessive reliance on heroic indecisive guerrilla warfare..." the Fidelistas flat out rejected it and "expressed surprise that the Communist leaders, Blas Roca, Juan Marinello, and others were living peacefully in Havana without interference from Batista's police."[44]

During the lead up to the seizure of power and for a few months after, it's understandable that many socialists around the world would be slow in recognizing the significance of what had taken place. A new phenomenon, it seemed to contradict our traditional notions of how a capitalist system would be overthrown. That was even the case with the International Secretariat of the F.I., which although adopting a position that Cuba was a workers' state, had let itself be out-manoeuvred by the sectarian Juan Posadas and his "Latin American Bureau" to where Posadas, with his crazy positions, was seeming to speak for the entire movement.

Difficulty in understanding what was going on was also true for many of us in North America, as I have already pointed out. Our slowness, however, did not cost us as much as it did the PSP. Its differences with the 26th of July Movement were deeply political and the product of having a two-stage conception of how the working class and peasants would achieve power. In their view, it was first necessary to have capitalist development in Cuba and to support "progressive" capitalists to do this, and then following this phase—who knows how long that would last—a socialist revolution would be on the agenda, a conception similar to that of Canada's LPP which during every election campaigned for an "anti-monopoly coalition" that would include "progressive" capitalists.

The consequence of this policy for the PSP was profound, causing it to lose support in a sharply radicalizing political environment. It initially kept its distance from the new government. "The fact that the CP of Cuba during the first months of the revolution," says Scheer and Zietland, "continued to call for wage increases and improved working conditions, even in the new situation, indicated that it did not expect the Revolutionary Government to fulfill its program and make a revolution and that they did not have close ties to the government."[45] It was as if the PSP was confronting a liberal bourgeois regime of some kind, not recognizing that a fundamental transformation was underway. Seeing their errors, and no doubt having their concentration focused by realizing their support was melting away like snow from a warm spring hillside, combined with the threat of an internal split, they quickly changed course and eventually gave the July 26 Movement full support, fusing with it and the Revolutionary Directorate (R.D.), a mainly student organization based in Havana, to form a new governing party, the Integrated Revolutionary Organization (ORI). Anibal Escalante, who had been a leader of the PSP, became ORI's Organizational Secretary and proceeded to use his position to appoint PSP people to key positions in the party and government, often jumping over revolutionaries from other political backgrounds, and moving to get control of the state's security forces.

The Canadian FPCC tour, scheduled to arrive in Havana for the July 26, 1961 celebrations, plus a proposal to send a delegation from the Canadian arts' community at a later date, seems to have been victims of this factionalism. A list of twenty-five people had been submitted to ICAP by Verne, at the request of the Cuban Consul in Montreal, to arrive in Cuba in time for the celebrations. "(T)he list was an impressive one," Ross Dowson wrote, trying to explain the reasons for the failure of the trip to take place, "prominent persons in the CCF-NDP, the trade union movement and in Canadian letters . . . all persons who in some way or another had signified strong support of the revolution and were prepared to put themselves at the service of the revolution following their return by speaking both here and in the U.S. My name along with the secretary of the FPCC and Olson and his wife were included. At no time was there any exception to the list in any way expressed by anyone, local Cuban officials, Ottawa Embassy officials, ICAP officials in Cuba, etc., etc."[46]

As the time neared when the Committee would have to confirm to those on the list that the tour was definitely on, its leaders became anxious when nothing was heard from ICAP, whose Director, Giraldo Mazola, Verne had learned, was either a member of—or was in the political orbit— of the PSP. In conversations with our contacts in the Cuban tourist bureau in Montreal and in our conversations with the Cuban Ambassador—all of whom we were convinced were supportive of the project—including several phone calls to ICAP in Havana, we would always receive assurances that matters were in good hands. Still nothing happened. Finally Verne persuaded Leslie Dewart, before he had made his spectacular departure from the FPCC and whose father was Spanish and mother Cuban, to get involved. "After several contacts were made, Dewart informed V. O. (Verne Olson) that he was absolutely convinced that the Canadian FPCC was being given the run around Cuban style. He expressed the opinion it was Stalinist sabotage. He told V. O. that he had been noting that the short wave broadcasts from Cuba had been taking on more and more a CP character with more and more coming from Hoy and less and less from the Fidelista press services...he suggested that possibly ICAP had fallen into the hands of the CP and that the list was being sabotaged because there were no CPers on it..."[47]

Although the Committee eventually sent five people to the 26th of July celebrations, we were finally forced to call off the larger tour of twenty-five, much to the disappointment of the prospective participants. And ours, I should add. It was a blow to the Committee and a very demoralizing one at that, not so much because the tour had been cancelled, but because of the manner in which it had happened—with no explanation given. Although we were never directly challenged about it by the Cubans, since then I've wondered that by placing the names of Pat Mitchell and Ross Dowson on the list—two well known Trotskyists—may have been just too much for the Cubans to swallow, making it an easy target for those hostile to us in Cuba, and making it also more difficult for FPCC supporters there to give us their backing. The other tour proposed at the same time, made up of representatives from the Canadian arts world—which we had expended considerable effort on—was also nixed without explanation.[48]

By 1962, Fidel Castro had become so alarmed by the role of some PSP people in ORI, in a major speech he created a sensation by publicly denouncing Anibal Escalante for meddling in government affairs and for creating in ORI a "nest of privilege, of benefits, of a system of favours of all types," and for alienating the party from the masses.[49] Consequently, several PSP people were removed from their positions in the bureaucracy, as was the head of police. With that speech by Castro, and another, "The Revolution Will Be a School Of Unfettered Thought," both of which the

Committee quickly published in English, it confirmed to the world that Stalinist influence in the revolution would be under a watchful eye.

For the next couple of years, the Escalante affair had a major influence on the political life of Cuba and there seemed to be an increasing openness towards the Fourth International's ideas. Normally regarded with anathema in China, Eastern Europe and the USSR, we regarded it as important sign of acceptance when Ernest Mandel, the internationally recognized Belgian Marxist and leader of the Fourth International, whose work *Marxist Economic Treatise* had just been published, received a formal invitation from the Cuban authorities to visit Cuba. "I'm due to leave for Cuba where very favourable developments for us are taking place," he wrote with his typical enthusiasm.[50] "Che has received my book and had whole chapters translated," he wrote a correspondent.[51] To another, he wrote, "On my way to Cuba. Cuban Ambassador has given me many parcels—expect to meet Raul and Che."[52] When he returned, he wrote, "I'm just back from a long trip to Cuba (I stayed there for seven weeks in the course of which I had many long conversations with many leaders of the Revolution)..." I don't remember if he met with Raul at that time but I remember it being reported to us that he had led several long seminars for the economics team around Che Guevara. A few years later, he also received an invitation to visit Cuba that "came through Fidel... they kept me there for six weeks," he wrote.[53]

One of our best sources of information about Cuba in those years was a young intellectual in Havana who was politically close to us, Nelson Zayas Pozos, who many of our people met when they visited Havana. He was one of about fifteen people, some of them in the Ministry of Foreign Affairs, who were sympathetic to the views of the Fourth International. We got along with him so well that at one point one of our Toronto members, Brian Duhig, was dispatched to Havana for a lengthy stay to help him educate the people around him about our ideas. When Verne was there for a five-week trip toward the end of 1963, Nelson told him that the struggle against the CP was continuing. "All the preparations are being made to clean CPers out of the Embassies in both Paris and

London," he said. A supporter of the Fourth International, Zayas "has many, many connections, is widely known and highly respected."[54] When he was in Paris preparing his doctorate and looking for a British publisher for his thesis, Ernest Mandel wrote a letter of introduction for him, calling him "a very good friend of mine"—evidence of his closeness to the Fourth International.[55]

Verne, whenever he was in Cuba, was always very careful in his dealings with PSP people. Even though they were a minority—about a third—in the new revolutionary party that the Castro forces were organizing, they still had considerable influence throughout Cuba. He would occasionally bump into them in the bureaucracy, he told us, and they would very often attempt to frustrate his work. Even in the best of times they would attempt to act as self-appointed "gate-keepers" for the people he wished to see. "Our informant reports that there were apparent efforts to frustrate his meeting and discussing with leading persons," Ross Dowson wrote to the F.I.'s International Secretariat about one of Verne's trips. "However he did succeed in having several lengthy discussions with heads of departments concerned with North America. They apparently have been following our informant's work closely, are amazed, are in complete agreement with its direction, consider it the only really important work being done in the area ..."[56] Verne, on one occasion, managed to meet with Raul Roa, Cuba's United Nations' representative, whom he reported was very supportive of the Committee's solidarity work and insisted that all future tours be arranged through him.[57]

That Verne was able to function so well in such a complicated environment, I'm sure was due to his remarkable political astuteness (although I knew he often harboured inner doubts about his own capacities) and his experience in working class politics, but it must also have been helped by his commanding physical presence. He stood well over six feet tall, and, firmly holding his crutches under his arms, with Ann standing by his side, they exuded such a firm sense of purpose and ethical integrity, I'm sure they were able to have many doors opened to them that would have been otherwise closed.

One of the crosses Verne had to bear whenever he was in Cuba, however, was the sorry reputation of the official Cuban section of the International Secretariat, the Partido Obrero Revolucionario—Trotskyista, known as POR(T). Because of its sectarianism and ultra-leftism, it had become an easy target for PSP factionalists, but in our circles little was known about it. As far as I can remember, the SWP and the LSA at the time of the revolution did not have many, if any, supporters in Cuba, but what news we did have about the POR(T) had certainly alarmed us. This tiny, recently formed organization seemed to be attempting to "be more revolutionary than the revolution." I remember one time in New York in a discussion about the situation in Cuba, Fred Halstead and Richard Garza, a leader of the New York branch of the SWP, pointing out that during a critical period when the revolutionary government was seizing American assets, the POR(T) had been on the streets demanding the takeover of industry. We later learned that it subscribed to the views of Juan Posadas on the question of a possible nuclear war. He looked upon such a nightmare as perhaps being the prelude to social revolution, and even seemed to wish it. Furthermore, the POR(T) had drawn the wrath of the new revolutionary government because of its campaign to have the U.S. naval base at Guantanamo expelled, which would have required Cuba to launch an attack on it. It had even produced a leaflet calling for a demonstration at the base, which the Fidelistas feared, correctly, might act as a provocation and pretext for the intervention of American imperialism, especially in the tense international situation following the Bay of Pigs invasion in April 1961.[58]

Part of our difficulty in assessing the group in those years was that we simply lacked adequate information about it. We were still in the early stages of overcoming the 1953 division in the International and it was hard to find out who was who in some countries. As I've mentioned, the POR(T) was part of a minority grouping within the International Secretariat, affiliated to the "Latin American Bureau" led by Juan Posadas. An F.I. grouping had ceased to exist in Cuba for many years—it had dissolved in 1947—but after the revolution, Posadas, in early 1960, assigned some of his leading people to go there to help get one re-established. It became the official Cuban section at the Sixth World Congress in January 1961, where the position that Cuba was a workers' state was adopted.[59]

That summer, even though our organizations in North America had strong disagreements with the Posadas group, we became very alarmed about its fate when we learned that its weekly publication, *Voz Proletaria*, had been suppressed and the typeface for a Spanish language edition of Trotsky's book, *Permanent Revolution*, which the group had been getting ready for printing, had been destroyed, during a so-called "intervention" by the government to take over the printing industry on the island. We knew nothing of the POR(T)'s circumstance as a result those events and wondered what this signified about democratic rights under the new regime.

Not long after that, Verne used the opportunity of a visit to Cuba for the July 26th celebrations to meet with the POR(T) to see if he could provide them some assistance and get information from them about what had gone on with the suppression of their press. What follows is based upon a report he wrote when he returned to Toronto.[60]

Verne reports that he met with Idalberto Ferrera, the editor of the group's journal, and Jose Lungarzo, who had been assigned to Cuba by Posadas. In Verne's estimation, the organization consisted of approximately forty members, many of them in the militia or in the rebel army, he was told, and was mostly made up of workers along with a few intellectuals and professional people. At no point did Verne discuss their alleged position of calling for the expulsion of the Americans from Guantanamo. It's highly likely he was not aware at the time they had promoted such a position.

According to Verne, the POR(T) had three branches, one in Havana, and the others in Guantanamo City and Santiago de Cuba, respectively. Although *Hoy,* the official PSP journal had carried articles attacking them, and even though PSPers in the unions had been labeling them as "counter-revolutionary," the group had been able to function openly and relatively free from harassment. Not all workers were buying the PSP line, it seems. In one plant, they told Verne, one of their members had been elected three times to a leadership position over fierce opposition from PSP loyalists. The first sign of an escalation of trouble had come just as a May 1961, issue of *Voz Proletaria* was going to press. An eight-page paper larger than tabloid size, it had by then appeared eight times, beginning in April. Just as the ninth issue was about to be printed in one of the few privately-owned print shops in Havana, it was "intervened"—that is nationalized—by the National Print organization, that coincidently, was headed up by a well-known PSP member. It was a harsh action against the group and the editor and the workers in the print shop were told the paper would not be printed any longer because it was "counter-revolutionary." Also in the print shop was the typeface for a Spanish edition of Trotsky's book, *Permanent Revolution,* which was being readied for publication; it was removed by National Print, and presumably smashed. Lacking confidence in their actions, the "interveners" refused to put anything in writing.

A few months earlier, the group's offices in Guantanamo City had been shut down under the pretext of late payment of rent and they weren't allowed to rectify the error, an action carried out against them by a civic official who was a member of the PSP. And just before the July 26 celebrations in Guantanamo City, a PSP led union and a local defense-committee distributed a leaflet calling on the workers to attend a local gathering celebrating the 26th to strike a blow against the enemies of the revolution, and listing the Trotskyists as such enemies. In that instance, the POR(T) responded by quickly rushing out a statement into print, a copy of which they supplied Verne. "Workers and farmers," it stated, "—everyone come to the Civic Square on the 26th of July, the date which commemorates an anniversary of the struggle which was started against the tyranny of Batista and the imperialist Yankee. With our presence we will demonstrate once more our unity in action to advance the Socialist Revolution. We will defeat imperialism and the internal counter-revolution, intensifying our agricultural and industrial production and revolutionary consciousness. For the defense and consolidation of our Cuban Workers State, the first in Latin America.

LONG LIVE OUR SOCIALIST REVOLUTION; LONG LIVE THE COLONIAL REVOLUTION; LONG LIVE THE WORLD SOCIALIST REVOLUTION. Signed: Revolutionary Workers Party (Trotskyist), Cuban Section of the 4th International, Regional Committee of Guantanamo, Dated Guantanamo, 24th of July, 1961." The leaflet was distributed throughout the city, but one of the POR(T) members was arrested a few days later while he was handing it out. He worked on the railways and, subsequently, was arbitrarily removed from his position in his union.

After his meetings with the POR(T) leaders, Verne met with Enrique De La Osa, the editor of *Bohemia*, a current-events journal published in Havana, to see if he could enlist his help. He told Verne that he was familiar with *Voz Proletaria*, but had not known that it had been suppressed. Familiar with the works of Trotsky, he agreed with Verne that it had probably resulted from growing Stalinist influence and said he would meet with Idalberto Ferrera, the paper's editor to see if a meeting could be arranged with Castro's secretary, with the possibility of even meeting with Castro himself. The interview with De La Osa went very well, according to Verne, but we don't know what happened to the possible interview with Fidel. I doubt this took place, because the attacks on the POR(T) seemed to have the backing of Che Guevara, given that he repeated some of the PSP's criticisms of the group in an interview carried in the August 15, 1961 edition of *Ultima Hora*, a Santiago de Chile newspaper. This, despite the fact that Guevara, in an earlier criticism, had referred to them as "Trotskyist comrades," treating them as if they were part of a common struggle. We later learned from our sympathizer Nelson Zayas Pozos that Che's first wife had been sympathetic to Trotskyism and that the only Trotskyists he had ever met were those of the POR(T), that is until he went to revolutionary Algeria in 1964 where he met Michel Pablo and with whom he had been very favourably impressed. Pablo by that time had split from the F.I. and was functioning as an advisor to Ahmed Ben Bella, the new President of Algeria.

Within a year Posadas had split off his Latin American Bureau from the Fourth International to "re-constitute" it as his own "Fourth International."

It lasted a few years before petering out, but I remember running into the remnants of his grouping in Venezuela a few years ago, at the time of an international solidarity conference in Caracas. In my discussion with them they identified themselves to me as "supporters of *Bandera Rosa*," the main journal of Posadas that was no longer being published, and very quickly they revealed themselves to me to be extremely hostile to Hugo Chavez and the Bolivarian Revolution. They seemed to be totally out of sync with the radicalization sweeping Venezuela and I couldn't distinguish their criticisms from what I was reading in the right wing press in Caracas. It seemed to me that from their ultra-left days they had travelled quite a distance to the right.

But in 1966, a few years after the suppression of the POR(T) the SWP's Joe Hansen—who strongly rejected the politics of the POR(T)—spoke for all of the F.I. when he wrote about how it had been badly treated, saying that "It was injurious to the Cuban Revolution to muzzle the Posadas group . . . Was the Cuban Revolution so weak ideologically that it was incapable of answering even a Posadas? . . . The overhead cost of suppressing the group was rather high, for it gave substance to the false charge that the Cuban Revolution is going the way of the Russian Revolution, i.e., becoming *Stalinized* . . . The slowness of the process of setting up democratic institutions of proletarian rule is of concern to many supporters of the Cuban Revolution besides the Trotskyist movement."[61]

Robert Williams, the American black revolutionary to whom we had provided succour in 1961 when he was fleeing the U.S., also had his difficulties with the PSP. When they were in Cuba, Verne and Ann would often make a point of getting together with him and his wife Mabel, as would others from our group when they were in Cuba. Invariably charming and generous, they always gave us a warm reception. In December 1963, Verne and Ann, after several long conversations with Williams, noted that he had undergone considerable political change over the previous couple of years. Referring to when he had first met Williams in 1961, Verne wrote, "it was my impression that Rob was very soft on the Communist Party of the United States as well as the CP-USSR . . . While not a CPer in our usage of the term, he was not receptive to any serious political criticism of the CP ... Now he has evolved 180 degrees and almost breaks out in hives when the word communist is mentioned in front of him."[62]

The American CP, which in those years had an orientation to the most conservative wing of the Black leadership, Williams told Verne, had attacked him in their journal, the *Worker*. It appeared to be a signal to its "Havana branch" to initiate a "Williams Must Go" campaign, as it had begun to circulate a petition among American émigrés in Cuba demanding that he, Williams, be removed from Radio Havana. The reason for the hostility was that Williams' views on the American Black struggle were diametrically opposed to those of the CP. "The most important struggle in the U.S. today is the 'Freedom Now' struggle," he told Verne, "but the CP says that the emphasis upon the race question divides the working class." According to them, "The struggle for socialism should be paramount to the struggle for Negro freedom," he said.

Williams, who had recently been in China where he had been treated like a "head of state," said that China had taken a public stand in support of the "Freedom Now" struggle whereas Cuba—though not Fidel— seemed reluctant and even negligent about taking a position on the issue. He complained that an article he had written for *Bohemia* about his visit to China had yet to appear, which he figured was due to the influence of the CP. When Verne met with Enrique De La Osa, the editor of *Bohemia*, he learned that the article would in fact be published soon, something that happened while Verne was there.

Williams' position in Cuba may also have been influenced by the Sino-Soviet conflict. Early on, Cuba had tended toward sympathy for the Chinese side in the dispute, but by 1966 Fidel had publicly come out with a list of grievances against China, accusing the Chinese of trying to meddle in Cuba's internal affairs by attempting to take advantage of the country's desperate need to import rice, as a tool to pressure political compliance.[63]

As a result of having very little contact with the Cuban people in their everyday lives, Williams, in Verne's estimation, tended to live in "the immediate past" and had a very limited and distorted picture of the Cuban reality, "completely divorced" from the political struggle that was underway between the PSPers, "the sectarians," as Verne called them, and the Fidelistas, the ebb and flow of which may have effected Williams' situation. "He is a true exile in every sense of that word," Verne wrote. "He sees Cuba merely as a vantage point from which he conducts his struggle back home . . . Cuba is good or bad in his mind to the degree that he gets cooperation or hindrance in his efforts to conduct his struggle as he sees fit."

Williams' instrumentalist approach towards Cuba, it turned out, happened to be also true of how he regarded the people in Canada who had helped him the most in getting to Cuba in the first place and who were now circulating his *Crusader* throughout North America. He was not—despite his noble intentions—above careless behaviour, when it came to his dealings with us. This was demonstrated the next year, 1965, when he took advantage of the naiveté of two of our young women comrades, Jess MacKenzie and Joan Newbigging—new members of the YS—by enlisting them to act as go-betweens with his supporters in Detroit. This came about because, at the last minute, the FPCC had received an invitation from ICAP to send two representatives to Havana for the 1965 May Day Celebrations, traditionally a large international gathering of many thousands of people where Fidel usually gave a major address. Jess and Joan were the only ones in the FPCC in a position to make such a trip on short notice and rather than letting the invitation lapse, the Executive Committee recommended they represent the organization. Jess and Joan, aged twenty-two, both fresh out of University, had arrived in Toronto the previous year from Scotland as landed immigrants and were overjoyed at the opportunity to go. Jess and Joan were strong supporters of the Cuban Revolution. Like many young people in Britain in those years, especially students, before they had come to Canada they had begun to develop a social awareness about the world and had been active participants in the anti-apartheid struggle and the 'ban the bomb' movement. Through the happy circumstance of having rented an apartment in the same house where two of our members—Diane Palm and Harry

Paine—lived, they were soon won over to our organization and had become active in the YS, becoming executive members and, not long after, members of the LSA. When they were preparing to leave for Havana, Verne asked them to make contact with Williams, providing them with his phone number and address. They met Williams several times in Havana and were given a warm welcome by him, but they were struck by how paranoid he seemed to be every time they got together with him. He always seemed to be looking over his shoulder, and suggested he was being followed by the security forces or PSP people.

Williams - who was moving quickly to Maoism by this time—may have aroused the suspicions of the Cubans, who began to question his motives. After all, it was the Cuban government that was helping him finance his stay in Havana and had given him a radio programme to speak to black Americans; they were probably wondering what their famous black guest was up to. Jess says she remembers that she and Joan seemed to also be under some kind of suspicion by Cuban authorities at least during some of their visit. Although they were able to participate in the main celebrations without any problems, even being given favoured seats, they were closely followed around by the police and were restricted in where they could go in Havana, unlike other international guests, probably a result of their association with Williams.

Williams, as Verne had noted, was relatively isolated in Cuba and effectively cut off from his supporters in Detroit because of the American travel ban. He was obviously anxious keep in touch with them, and, through the force of his powerful personality, ended up persuading Jess and Joan to become couriers for him between Havana and his supporters in Detroit for the purpose of smuggling money and documents back and forth. He swore them to secrecy about this endeavour, persuading them to keep their new "assignment" hidden from the LSA, including Verne and the FPCC, saying it was probable that the RCMP might have spies in these organizations and it would place him and his supporters in danger.

Another memorable aspect of that May Day visit for Jess and Joan was an unexpected development in Algeria that threw their plans for returning to Toronto into chaos. Houari Boumediene, a military leader in the independence war against the French, overthrew the progressive government of Ahmed Ben Bella in a counter-revolutionary coup d'état. Cuba, which had been in the forefront in supporting that liberation struggle against French colonialism and had mobilized its people to give assistance to the new government, was now compelled, because of fears for their safety amidst the politically uncertainty, to immediately recall its citizens who had volunteered to go to Algeria to assist with health and education. This required the re-routing of all of Cuba's commercial aircraft to Algiers. There would be no planes available, Jess and Joan learned, until all the Cubans had returned from Algeria. As a result, they were stranded in Havana for several weeks, unable to get a flight home.

By the time Jess and Joan got back to Toronto from Havana, they were in a very tense state because of their fears about carrying a large sum of money concealed on their persons through Canadian customs for delivery to Williams' Detroit people. The LSA leadership was ignorant of all these clandestine arrangements with Williams, but had noticed that since Jess and Joan had gotten back, they had been acting unusually reticent about their experiences in Cuba and seemed to be taking their distance from us, prompting Verne to have a discussion with them to find out what had gone on. That's when he learned the details of Williams' actions.

It had clearly been a mistake to have sent such relatively inexperienced people to Cuba to be taken advantage of in this way. After learning what had happened, Verne and Ross Dowson tried to make the best of the situation and decided to help out. A Williams' supporter in Detroit was contacted who immediately drove up to Toronto to get the money, along with the package of documents Williams had sent. Eventually, Williams left Cuba for China, where he remained for several years before returning to Detroit in the 1980s.

Organizing representatives from the cultural community, from the labour movement and universities every year to go to Cuba to get a glimpse of the improvements the Cuban Revolution was making in the lives of ordinary Cubans continued to be a main feature of the work of the FPCC. But this activity virtually came to an end after 1965. During that summer, the FPCC—mainly Verne and Ann—had worked feverishly at organizing something special for the July 26th celebrations. The previous year's students' tour, despite a few difficulties, had come off very well, but the plan for 1965 was more ambitious and much larger, encompassing at least one hundred students from major university campuses across the country. In the end it all came to nothing, and would throw FPCC's relations with the Cuban government into a severe crisis. According to the FPCC, the tour had "been launched early in March after a firm commitment from the Cuban institution ICAP was obtained through the Cuban Ambassador to Canada, Dr. Americo Cruz."[64] Verne had proceeded to organize it in the knowledge that the Ambassador, whom we regarded as a firm supporter of the Committee, had also helped him formulate the original tour proposal to ICAP.

Even though. by this time, we had suspicions there might be a change of attitude by the Cubans toward the Committee—possibly as a consequence of the growing closeness of Cuba to the USSR due to the American embargo—we figured the same arrangements for 1964 would work again this time. It was planned to be the best ever. The intention was to send 100 students for eight weeks. But the Committee was quickly thrown into a huge crisis when, only two weeks before the students were to leave for Havana, Verne received the startling news "that the tour was called off by the Cuban authorities without explanation."[65]

Verne immediately flew to Havana where he spent five days trying to persuade ICAP to reverse its decision. I remember him telling us later that as far as he was concerned he had not received a satisfactory explanation for the plug having been pulled. He had been given the runaround from the Institute's officials when he met with them. Although some of them seemed a little embarrassed about the cancellation, they seemed incapable of giving him a straight answer, only saying that ICAP was in the midst of "discussions" about its relations with all international solidarity groups. As a result, the Committee issued a statement to the public and its supporters, under the signatures of Verne and Andre Beckerman, chairman of the Student Committee on Cuban Affairs at the University of Toronto and a member of the LSA, that stated, "four years' work... has now been jeopardized, not by the external enemies of the Revolution, but by the arbitrary action of an institution of the Revolutionary Government."

The FPCC, for the first time since its formation, aside from taking on ICAP, and throwing all caution to the wind, was also, by implication, pointing a finger at Cuba's revolutionary government. It was something I probably agreed with, but looking back I now have some reservations about the statement. It didn't pull any punches, nor was it very diplomatic about what it thought were the reasons for the cancellation. Using the code word "sectarian" to point to what it thought was the role of the ex-PSP members' influence in the affair, the FPCC asserted—really without any hard facts to back it up—that "the student tour was the victim of sectarian forces within the Revolution itself which have been measurably strengthened in recent months as a result of the critical international situation" and that the cancellation would be "a source of satisfaction only to the sworn enemies of the Cuban Revolution, or to hopeless sectarians." "The Fair Play for Cuba Committee has been struck a harsh blow," the statement concluded, "but our confidence in the Cuban people and their cause, and the pressing need to continue our activities in defense of the Revolution, is unshaken."[66] This was followed up a couple of days later by a joint letter addressed directly to Fidel Castro, the Prime Minister, signed by, among others, Harry Kopyto, Hans Modlich and John Riddell, all members of the LSA but also leaders of several campus Fair Play clubs, stating that while regretting "the strong tone of this letter," the signatories believed that "unjust vilification has been directed toward the Committee serving as an agent for this tour... we suspect the Committee and in turn the students have become victims of pressure politicking and, if so, the exigencies of the issue warrants the immediate attention of the Cuban people" and asking for "a reversal of the unfortunate decision."[67]

Stung by the FPCC criticism, ICAP wasn't long in coming back with a sharp rebuff. In a press release issued under the signature of Giraldo Mazola, ICAP's Director, that received a big play in *Canadian Tribune*, the LPP's weekly, he challenged the assertion that the cancellation had been "left to the last minute." ICAP at any given moment, he stated, "confronts the need to postpone some projects not contemplated in its yearly planning due to strictly budgetary reasons...From the very beginning of the elaboration of this plan," he claimed, "this matter was brought to the attention of the organizers, and it was clearly pointed out to them not to encourage young students about the trip without previously having an affirmative answer." It is not true that "the reasons for the cancellation were not explained and, far from it, that Mr. Olson had the approval from our Embassy." And taking up the direct political attack upon ICAP in the FPCC statement that had alluded to "sectarian forces within the Revolution," Mazola issued a strong reprimand. It was an argument, one can easily see now, that the Committee could never have won, and probably had made a mistake in raising it in the first place. "(T)hey refer to certain matters, which since long ago have been overcome by our Revolution, echoing in a subtle way what the imperialists cry out and pretends to insinuate: the existence of factions, divisions or groups within the Revolution, yet this insinuation crashes against reality, stumble(s) upon the Cuban revolutionaries stern unity who consciously and most decisively break through all difficulties to achieve victory. Regardless of how frequent this pretended division is printed in foreign releases, it will not materialize."

While expressing surprise at Mazalo's assertion that he had been told not to "encourage" students about the tour, in a further comment on the matter, Verne pointed out that he had only proceeded after a "telegram received from Havana on March 6th which we interpreted as leaving in doubt only the numbers..."[68] I don't know if ICAP replied to the "Postscript," but Joe Hansen, who had been copied in on the various statements that had been going to and fro between Toronto and Havana, began to grow alarmed that the matter may have been getting out of hand. "It appears to me that it would be well to drop any further pursuit of the polemic," he wrote to Verne, "even if the last word is left to the other side ... I believe that the Canadian friends of the Cuban Revolution would stand to gain by doing their utmost to reciprocate any efforts from any quarter whatsoever in Cuba to overcome the effects of the setback ... This can be done by dropping the dispute, restraining those who want to pursue it, and accepting in the most vigourous way anything offered to make up for the setback."[69] "Your advice has been digested and acted upon," replied Verne.[70]

Of course, the FPCC's members and supporters were devastated by what had transpired, but I remember we sort of comforted ourselves with what looked like a glimmer of hope in Mazola's reply when he referred to the student tour as having been "postponed to another date, when it would be conveniently feasible." We hoped that might mean that we would have ICAP's cooperation in the future, so we began to discuss a proposal for another student tour and continued with our activities in defence of Cuba. But the Committee's relations with the Institute did not look good, as we found out later that summer when the Committee sent two representatives to Havana to represent it in the July 26th celebrations. "ICAP refused to accept them as part of the Canadian delegation," Verne wrote to Joe Hansen. "They had had several talks with secondary officials in the Institute, who revealed the deep hostility which our statement aroused. On the last day of their visit they were able to see the Director who was full of venom, labeling myself and the Committee as 'agents of imperialism.'"

Despite appearances, things were not going well with the Cuban Ambassador either. A long time supporter of the Committee, we had assumed he had not changed his attitude to us during the whole kerfuffle over the cancellation. He had been in Cuba for three months during the dispute, and when he returned he told Verne that it "was the desire of the Ministry, to repair the damage done to our Committee, and that he was prepared to undertake a tour of Canada under our auspices."[71] And at the FPCC's annual banquet that year, on November 20th, celebrating the fifth anniversary of the Revolution, with close to 200 supporters in attendance, and where he was the featured speaker, "he expressed a warm appreciation of Verne Olson, who launched the Committee, thanked the committee for its efforts to establish the truth about the Cuban revolution in Canada, and pledged himself to help the committee in every possible way in the coming years that he expected to be here."[72]

The Ambassador's words turned out to be a kind of diplomatic double-speak, especially when it came to Vancouver, where a similar banquet had taken place and where FPCC's executive body was made up almost entirely of people not affiliated to the LSA, the exception being Phil Courneyour, its organizational secretary and its main leader alongside Cedric Cox. Cox and several other members, including John Macey, a prominent left-wing Vancouver lawyer, had been upset by the tour cancellation and the dispute with ICAP and were very unhappy with the public statement that Verne and Andre had issued about it.

Hugh Clifford, a major figure in the left of the NDP, who had developed an antipathy to the LSA over the previous couple of years, was of the opinion that the LSA had been entirely responsible for what had happened. According to Phil, he was questioning whether because of it, he should stand again for re-election to the Committee's executive. Despite his reassuring words to Verne, the Ambassador, it seems, during his visit to Vancouver to speak at the banquet, sought to exploit this crisis for his own purposes. He met privately with Cedric, something Phil did not find out about until two months later when he learned from Cedric that the Ambassador had told him directly that "he had been instructed to break off relations with Fair Play by Havana and that he could no longer deal with Cedric or the Vancouver Committee, (and that) he asked Cedric to form a Friends of Latin America Committee ..." Cruz charged that Fair Play was "a Trotskyist organization using its influence to interfere in Cuba's political affairs," and, among other things, that Verne Olson "maintains correspondence with dubious people (who are being watched). He uses his contacts in Havana to pressure the ministry and bypass normal channels. He sends Trotskyist literature to Cuba. He tries to interfere in Cuban politics..."[73] The problem for the Ambassador, however, was that despite his behind the scenes manoeuvring to replace the FPCC with something that he could perhaps exert more control over, he could find no one to go along with his plans and he had to face the hard reality that the Fair Play had more public support, especially on the West Coast, and had been a lot more successful in promoting Cuba than the Communist Party's committee. So Verne, understanding that the Ambassador was smart enough to know that Fair Play was the only game in town, and choosing to overlook his activities in Vancouver, began the difficult work of rebuilding the Committee's relationship with him. But even though the Committee continued to send guests to Cuba for special events, such as anniversary celebrations like May Day and the 26th of July, the 1964 student tour turned out to be the last that the FPCC organized.

The crisis over the aborted 1965 tour would not be the last in the difficult relations between the Canadian FPCC and the Cubans. They would reach another low in early 1966. At the Tricontinental Congress that year in Havana on January 15th, Fidel Castro, whom we came to believe had been influenced by Regis Debray, the French radical intellectual and writer who had been teaching in Havana and who was associated with the top circles of the former Cuban CP, went out of his way to attack *Monthly Review*—an American socialist magazine sympathetic to Cuba— and zeroed in on the ultra-leftism of the Posadists about their irresponsible speculation concerning the disappearance of Che Guevara.

It is now well known that Che had left Cuba because he was preparing for the opening of a guerrilla front in Bolivia, but at the time many in the big business media were speculating—with no basis in fact—that he had been murdered by Castro. This was a slander also repeated by Adolfo Gilly, a main spokesperson for the Posadists in those years, which was also spread by many in the sectarian left who claimed that Che, because of so-called political differences over China, had been "liquidated" by Castro. Fidel, at the Tricontinental Congress, in the process of taking up the speculation about Che, also used the occasion to launch an attack on Trotskyism. In a tone reminiscent of the worst of Stalinism, he characterized the Fourth International as "... a vulgar instrument of imperialism and reaction," referring to it as "mercenaries in the services of imperialism."

Even though we suspected that Castro's comments were influenced by the grievously erroneous positions of the Posadists, the Fourth International was compelled to make a sharp reply defending itself: "The dossier you placed before the participants...is made up of amalgams and links which collapse at the slightest touch..." This response demonstrated that Castro was employing the methods of the Stalinists in attempting to connect statements and actions of individuals and groups—who had long left the organization—with the F.I. "It is shameful, Comrade Fidel Castro, to utilize your prestige and the admiration and affection which the revolutionary masses of the entire world feel for the Cuban Revolution to dig out of the dustbin of history the slanders and lies that no one dares to utter, even in the Soviet Union itself, after the twentieth and twenty-second Congress of the Communist Party of the Soviet Union!" The F.I. demanded that Castro "submit his proofs before a Tribunal of the Cuban people; five of the most representative leaders of the Fourth International are ready to stand before such a public Tribunal and answer the accuser before the people of all Cuba. *Thus the people of Cuba will discover that the entire activities of the Fourth International are devoted to but one aim: the victory of the world socialist revolution!*"[74]

A few weeks later, Pierre Frank, while discussing Castro's attack, went even further and took up some of the limitations that were inherent in the character of the Congress. At a meeting in London, which I reported on at the time, he told us that a basic weakness of the event was that many of the delegations, instead of representing independent revolutionary movements, came from states under CP control or from states that had won a measure of political independence from imperialism and thus were limited by the conservative bureaucratic outlook or passing diplomatic needs of the rulers of those countries. Consequently, despite its many positive achievements and declarations, the Tri-Continental Congress was unable to work out a consistent world strategy of revolutionary struggle and such statements as Castro's on January 15th made against us, Pierre said, would probably remain unchallenged by the delegates.[75]

Because of what they believed was its implication for Cuban solidarity in Canada, the FPCC also responded to Castro's attack against the F.I.

"We are not concerned here," it stated, "with a defense of the Fourth International, Trotskyism or Trotskyists, real or alleged, in an academic sense. We assume they will respond as they see fit. What is of serious concern though, is the integrity of the Fair Play for Cuba and persons associated with the Committee. It goes without saying that the Committee would have to take some actions if known 'mercenaries' or 'agents of imperialism' were active in its ranks." Stressing that the FPCC was a broad non-exclusive organization open to all those who have shown interest in furthering the truth about Cuba, its Executive Committee challenged the Castro charges head on: "For five years of experience of the Committee in Canada has shown," they said, "that persons who are known adherents of, or sympathizers of the organization in Canada known as Trotskyist, have been among the most active, energetic and enthusiastic defenders of the truth about the Cuban Revolution ... We have no evidence to sustain or justify the allegations of Prime Minister Castro regarding Trotskyists, Adolfo Gilly or Monthly Review ... These charges by the most respected leader of the Revolution—charges which are not confirmed in any respect by our experience, but on the contrary are unacceptable to any series political tendency on the North American continent—will make this task unnecessarily difficult and will impede it further development."[76] The FPCC called upon Castro to "reassess" and "repudiate his charges against proven defenders of the Cuban Revolution. "The following year, on the anniversary of Castro's speech, Radio Havana rebroadcast it with the attack upon Trotskyism carefully edited out. We felt a measure of vindication and comfort in our belief that Castro may have been misled on the issue by some of his advisors.

During the dispute with ICAP over the student tour, Verne, it seems, had begun to revise his views about what lay behind the cancellation. In the FPCC's June 3rd,1965 statement issued under Verne's and Andre Beckerman's signatures that did not mention anything about the Castro leadership's role in the affair, Verne had not too subtly ascribed the cancellation as being due to the influence of CP elements within ICAP. But during his five-day visit to Havana as he sought to have the decision reversed, as he told Joe Hansen soon after in a letter on June 8th, he had come to see the cancellation as an expression of a general conservatizing trend within Cuba that had resulted from its growing closeness to the Soviet Union, which had ninety percent of the island's trade. This could also be seen in Castro's March 11th, criticisms of China that year, provoked by its prevention of Cuban arms getting to Vietnam—in which he referred to the "senile Mao."

Two days later Castro called for the banning of *Hsinhua,* a Chinese weekly widely read on Cuban campuses. "Up until this speech," Verne wrote, "the Chinese view was popular and widely read on campus. Today, political discussions are rare on campus and discretion seems to be the better part of valour for all students regarding controversial subjects. This attitude seems to permeate the whole country if my sampling was indicative of a trend..." While there were justifiable concerns about CIA activity on the campus, Verne wrote to Joe, many of his contacts had become alarmed by efforts by the Federation of University Students (FEU) and the Young Communists "to drive from the university all students who are not completely identified with the revolution as well as counter-revolutionary students and homosexuals, etc." "There seems little doubt," he wrote, "that the general situation described is the basic cause of the cancellation of the Student Tour which we had organized. Information gained would suggest that this move was not a high-handed action on the part of conscious Stalinist forces but was taken with at least the knowledge of the tacit approval...(and) could well indicate a qualitative change in the relationship of forces within the revolution itself."[77]

By February 21st of the following year, Verne had come to believe that the negative political trends, "the beginnings of new and profound changes" that he had noted in his earlier letter, had further deepened. In a long, dense, closely-typed six-page letter to Joe Hansen, he wrote that part of the evidence for this change had come from "two comrades who visited Cuba in July," and who were told by two of their contacts "that there was no internal intellectual life in Cuba. The line was set by the top leadership and no discussion or dissent is allowed. In the libraries, Trotskyist publications have disappeared from the news rack and libraries have removed books by the Old Man (Trotsky)." Verne also criticized *The Militant*, the SWP's weekly paper, for taking "at face value" what Castro had said about trade with China and urged the "need for a serious evaluation of the Cuban Revolution" by the SWP in the light of what was occurring. Relying on anecdotal information from people such as Robert Williams—who had told him by phone that "all dissenters are being called Trotskyist"—he had come to the conclusion that there had been a serious shift to the right by the Cuban government. This shift, Verne felt, could also be seen in the pattern of events that included "the removal of Che" by Fidel for political reasons and Che's disappearance from public life; the January 15th, 1966 speech by Fidel attacking the Fourth International; Cuba's support for the Kremlin in the Sino-Soviet dispute; the clamping down on political discussion on the University of Havana campus, and the cancellation of the FPCC student tour.

According to "a Canadian friend"—Fred Brown, who had spent the previous two and a half years teaching at the invitation of Fidel Castro at the University of Havana—"Castro himself was very angry over our statement following the cancellation of the student tour; the decision to cancel being a top level one. Castro has been moving to the right not only in regards to foreign policy but also in regards to internal policy. The result of this, he says, is a growing disenchantment with the leadership of the Revolution among growing layers of the Cuban masses... and was most dramatically expressed in the large, surprisingly large, numbers which our friend reported as having registered with the announcement by Castro that anyone wishing to leave could do so. The report is that 500,000, yes five hundred thousand persons registered to leave ..."[78] Verne was referring here to a recent propaganda offensive against Cuba by the American government when it had offered to accept anyone into the United States who wished to leave the island, an offer it would quickly revoke when the Cuban government turned the tables on it and informed its citizens that anyone who wished to leave the country could freely do so.

Joe Hansen wasn't very long in replying to Verne's February 21st letter, and questioned his conclusions. "The facts you report are of greatest interest," Joe wrote, "and must be given due weight in estimating what is occurring in Cuba and what our attitude should be. I would say, however, that while we accumulate material of this kind, in addition to facts from other sources, and while we should speak out emphatically on any particular event as clear-cut as the attack in Castro's January 15th speech, it would be premature to take the public position that a qualitative change has actually occurred; i.e., that we now face a *degenerated* workers state." Regarding the growth of bureaucratism in Cuba, he wrote, "I do not have the slightest doubt that this has been occurring—and on a dangerous scale." But has this reached the point, Joe asked, "where it can be said that a hardened caste has crystallized out, one that can only be removed by political revolution? If this is so, then we should of course say it. But I am not sure that it is the case. We should recall what happened around Escalante. At that time too, Castro appeared not to be seeing what was happening—if anything it could be concluded from a distance that he was abetting it—and incidents were rife of the kind you cite. But as it turned out the bureaucratic crust was not as deep or as hardened as it appeared to be. The experience should incline us to be all the more cautious for the time being in coming to a definitive conclusion on this."

In taking up Verne's concern about the half million Cuban's who had recently registered to leave Cuba, Joe cautioned against jumping to "one sided or impressionistic conclusions" about the matter. "Whatever the reasons adduced to explain this, they remain meaningless in the absence of a comparable offer from Washington to any other country," he wrote. "How many would register to come to the United States from Venezuela or Brazil, for instance, if they were given the opportunity? Only with at least one control case could the 500,000 figure be seen in the balance— and then it might show Cuba in a favourable light. Despite all the pressure from the U.S., the tightening blockade that has lasted almost six years, the constant threat of invasion, the hardships and absence of an early perspective of substantial relief, only this number wished to leave the beleaguered fortress ... whereas in Venezuela, for instance, virtually the entire population registered" when the Americans made a similar proposal. If some weariness has finally set in, Joe warned, "then it would be a considerable error to interpret this weariness as revolutionary fervor to which the leaders no long respond. It may be the other way around; the leaders are beginning to reflect the weariness of the masses."

Regarding Che Guevara and his disappearance from public life in Cuba, Hansen countered that responsible sources in the capitalist media did not believe that Che was dead, and that the *New York Times, editorially,* was also speculating that he might be in a sanatorium because of ill health, or possibly in Russia. "In the absence of good evidence one way or the other it would be foolish of us to be impressed by or help circulate rumours concerning Guevara's supposed death, particularly the version pinning guilt on Castro."

On the question of the Sino-Soviet conflict, Joe stated that this had "enormously complicated things for the Cubans. Their economic and defense needs compelled them to maintain good relations with Moscow. The Soviet bureaucracy has taken full advantage of this to put the squeeze on them. The Cubans have paid for this in political coin up and down the line. That this has been done generally in an unprincipled way is a mark, of course, of the limitations of the Castroist leadership; but a big share of the responsibility lies at Mao's door. Instead of being designed to help the Cubans maintain a certain distance from Moscow, Mao's policy seems expressly designed to leave no room for Cuba to hold an independent position. By forcing Castro to come out decisively, Mao made him choose Moscow's side. This weakened China. In analyzing this point it is necessary to look beyond the immediate issues in the debate, such as the rice-sugar deal, to the bigger moves in the Sino-Soviet dispute. The actual rift between Peking and Havana began in 1964 and the responsibility was wholly Mao's. When the Cuban delegation ran into this in China, they could not believe what had happened since their sympathies in the dispute were with China."

Joe concluded by restating the SWP's approach to Cuba's internal problems. "During all these years we understood what was involved. The Cuban Stalinists were rabidly anti-Trotskyist; the new revolutionary leaders and cadres were rather sympathetic to us; but they consciously subordinated their own feelings to what they conceived to be the most realistic policy vis-à-vis Moscow. Our policy has been to strengthen the hand of those who incline in our direction, and particularly not to undertake factional moves that would make things difficult for *them*. That is the one reason our rating with them has remained high and why we have continued to be appreciated as a *force* in Cuba and not just a sectarian group."[79]

But by the time of this exchange of correspondence, Nelson Zayas Pozo, a Cuban friendly to our political views who had worked in the Cuban Ministry of Foreign Relations, was in Paris to begin his studies towards obtaining his doctorate. I am assuming he is the "David" referred to in Verne's reply of March 31st to Joe. I couldn't find a copy of his letter in the archives, but from Verne's reply, it seems that Zayas, one of our most reliable sources of information in those years about the internal situation in Cuba, had earlier written to Verne and had questioned the reliability of some of his sources, especially that of the Canadian already mentioned, Fred Brown, the lecturer at the University of Havana.

Although not directly saying so, Zayas had not agreed with Verne's assessment of what was taking place in Cuba, as can be seen from a letter he wrote to him two days after Castro's January 15th speech, in which he provided information about the positive attitude of leading figures in the government—such as Ricardo Alarcon who at the time was Director of North and South American affairs—towards the FPCC and the declining political fortunes of a few leading PSP people he was aware of, including the general receptivity to Trotskyist literature among people with whom he was acquainted.[80] It appears that Joe had shown Zayas Verne's long letter of February 21st. In his March 31st reply to Joe, Verne admits that the assessment of the Canadian, Fred Brown, about what was happening in Cuba may not have been entirely accurate: "It is quite true that Fred's last months in Cuba were most disorienting and I do not doubt that for a period he completely lost his base, particularly under the influence of his wife who was on the verge of an emotional and mental breakdown. It is also true that some of his associates were with persons not completely tied to the Revolution. But for this reason his testimony has a certain value and validity, if properly sifted and interpreted ..." Verne goes on to say that Joe had misread his February 21st letter. "The sharp nature of my comments and possible overstatement of my position was the result of a desire on my part to dramatize my concern with the present course of the movement (i.e., the Fourth International) was on regarding the Cuban Revolution ... I did not intend to suggest that we should draw a balance sheet on the Cuban Revolution as you suggest." It certainly would be wrong, he wrote, to "take a public position that a qualitative change has actually occurred, i.e., that we now face a degenerated workers state . . ." Nevertheless, Verne went on to present further evidence that would go towards substantiating such a conclusion. "An apparatus loyal to the Castro leadership is well on the way to being molded," he wrote, "and will inevitably—through gradual formulation of its own special inter-ests—form the base of a privileged caste ... At the present time Castro is able to make use of his anti-Stalinist past, and the confidence that the masses have in his leadership based on past performance, in order to institute Stalinist type practices and institutions."[81]

Not long after his March 31st letter to Joe, Verne, sadly, resigned from the LSA and the FPCC. His differences with the LSA and SWP about their assessment of the recent changes in Cuba had led him to believe he could no longer support the LSA's viewpoint in the Committee. He had developed strong disagreement, he said, with the LSA team he had been part of from the beginning of the Committee. Much in line with Joe Hansen's understanding of recent events in Cuba, the LSA had maintained its analyses adopted soon after the revolution that Cuba was a workers' state, but as yet lacking in democratic forms of workers' control, and that socialists everywhere had a primary duty to defend it against imperialism.

Verne was not challenging the need to defend Cuba, but his concerns were about the significance of the changes he was pointing to. It's easy to see, now, that there was no reason the discussion could not have continued. Verne was one hundred percent in support of Cuba and no principle was involved in the disagreement. We could have easily agreed to disagree, but by then he had "lost confidence in the movement (i.e., the LSA) at all levels, resulting from deep differences with the comrades," as he wrote in his letter of resignation from the LSA. "The answer which Joe gave to my initial letter," he wrote, "also went a long way towards establishing or re-enforcing this tendency . . . this loss of confidence was under way before Castro's Jan. 15th speech."[82]

Verne's position as Chairman of Fair Play was soon taken over by Hans Modlich. Verne continued to play an important part in the Committee's activities, but not to the same degree as before and not as a member of its executive committee. Hans had been a long time member of its executive and a student leader at the University of Toronto—part of the grouping of the LSA members, such as Pat Mitchell and others, who had originally been tasked with helping Verne get it off the ground. The Committee's relations with the Cuban Ambassador improved to the degree that Ross Dowson, probably Canada's best known Trotskyist, attended the first congress of the Organization of Latin American Solidarity (OLAS) in Havana in 1967, at the invitation of the Cubans.[83] Even though its membership had declined from when it was first formed—to "slightly less than a hundred in the Toronto area"—the Committee maintained a very active chapter in Vancouver and continued to enjoy broad support across the country."[84] And the red-baiting by the right-wing press did not let up. In 1968 the Committee came under a severe witch-hunting attack from Peter Worthington in the right-wing *Toronto Telegram*—no doubt assisted by information provided by the RCMP—with photographs of Hans and other leaders displayed across its pages. As a result, Hans was forced to abandon his engineering career and to return to University because of the difficulty of finding work due to the witch-hunting.

But most people in the broad labour movement saw the red-baiting for what it was. For example, the *Workers Vanguard* reports that at the tenth anniversary celebration of the Cuban Revolution on January 4th,

1969, which Hans Modlich chaired and was attended by some 150 people, the Cuban Consul Humberto Castanedo and his wife formally greeted the guests on their arrival. The Master of Ceremonies was no less than Gerry Caplan, a leader of the NDP, and Verne read greetings to the meeting from Stephen Lewis, then NDP-MPP for Scarborough West. Both prominent NDPers to this day—and no friends of the Trotskyists— must have been well aware of the red-baiting the previous year.[85] The Committee, right into 1970, continued with its successful banquets, which the Ambassador would personally attend and speak at or else send messages of support.

The Committee's activities were reduced, but every month it kept up its commitment to the Cubans by mailing 400 copies of the English edition of the Cuban publication *Granma* to its Canadian subscribers. One of the Committee's last activities was a cross-Canada tour of a photographic exhibit, "Cuba Today," commemorating the tenth anniversary of the Revolution. On display for three weeks at the Sigmund Samuels Library at the U of T, it was displayed at campuses, churches and libraries across the country.[86]

The FPCC remained active for the rest of the decade and into the very early seventies, holding film showings, telling the truth about Cuba to whoever would listen and celebrating its important anniversaries every year. And support for Cuba among Canadians continued to increase, no doubt helped by the Committee's persistent work—for example, in the March 1969 NDP paper, the *Democrat,* the B.C. party's provincial secretary reported to the membership that the following October the party would be sponsoring a two week tour of the island.[87] By the end of the decade, however, the Committee was beginning to run out of steam. There is "overload and fatigue in the members," wrote Phil Courneyour, its secretary in Vancouver. In a letter to Toronto he reported that a film showing about Cuba, which they had promoted heavily, had been far from a success, with only seventy-five people showing up.[88]

Verne died of a sudden heart attack in 1999. A severe depression had forced him to take early retirement from Ontario Hydro and for a long time he had withdrawn from any serious political activity, although many of his friends from the old days would often visit him and Ann to discuss current political events. Whenever we visited, we always came away impressed with his insights and optimism about the future, though sometimes all of us despaired a little about what was happening in the class struggle with the rise of neo-liberalism. When Ann died suddenly, in 1994, I remember well that Robert Williams, although obviously in a state of poor health, made the long journey up from Detroit to stay with Verne and attend Ann's funeral, such was his feeling of solidarity with him. Jess and I helped organize a commemoration at Verne's funeral. Many of his comrades and old friends were there to bid him goodbye and pay tribute to his remarkable life. Even though it had been many years since Verne had been active in defense of Cuba, a delegation from the Cuban Consulate made a point to be there to pay tribute to his memory and to tell the audience about the significance of his contribution in helping Cuba during some of its most difficult days. It reminded all of us that through Verne and the radical left as a whole, we had helped provide critical space so that the Cuban Revolution could be considered by Canadians on its own merits. It was a moving tribute to an exemplary life that had been dedicated to humanity's struggle for a socialist future. In the words of the Cuban Consul who addressed the gathering, Verne's was a life that had found its most creative expression in defending Cuba against American imperialism.

Jess and Joan in Cuba (Photographer unknown)

Chapter 16

New Youth Organization for a New Party

B Y 1960, I HAD BECOME COORDINATOR OF OUR WORK IN THE CCF, but it was more of a nominal position than anything else because it seemed nothing much was happening in the party as the new decade began, at least if the Toronto CCF was a gauge of that. Out of thirteen, only "four clubs of the CCF are holding regular meetings," Ross Dowson observed.[1] The campaign for a "new party" that would become the NDP. had yet to get off the ground. Few of our members were active in the CCF and the SEL's main energy was concentrated on its own independent activities. CCF "fraction" meetings were held regularly, but I remember they were small and only about five or six of us would get together to discuss what was going on in the party. In practice, we had just about written off the CCF in Ontario as an effective working class party, seeing its constituency organizations, that had once had been very active in their communities, evolve from being a social movement to functioning primarily as electoral machines. But this wasn't the case across the country.

In reality, we were somewhat out of touch with the party outside of Toronto, because we were very surprised when its provincial organizations in the West began to move left and edge towards abandoning their support for the Cold War. The Saskatchewan and Alberta provincial conventions of the party passed resolutions opposing NATO and NORAD, as did, by a slim margin, the Sixteenth (and last) National Convention on August 9, 1960 in Regina, a position taken in opposition to its National Council. While the delegates remained committed to the idea of a "new party," there was widespread opposition to the National Executive, who were seen as being responsible for the 1958 debacle. M. J. Coldwell, who had led the party until then and had lost his seat in the election, retired, opening the door to a new leadership. Hazen Argue—the only MP from Saskatchewan to retain a seat and who, with the support of the party's eight remaining MPs, had been Parliamentary Leader—was elected leader of the party, a victory for the left wing.

Despite our "orientation" to the CCF over many years, we had very little influence in those debates and neither had we put much work into preparing for them. Our Vancouver people were still carrying on "regroupment" work and, as a result, we had let our work in the CCF slide. Winnie Henderson from Vancouver was our only delegate to the convention and our cross-Canada tour team that summer, made up of Alan Harris, Cliff Orchard, Joe Rosenblatt and John Darling, made a special effort to be there to give out the *Workers Vanguard*. I couldn't attend myself, as much as I would have wished to. Even though I had been chosen by High Park as a delegate, the National Office had refused to accept my credentials because of my expulsion from the CCF Youth in 1956. Ross, who had flown out to attend as a visitor, found himself very limited in what he could do, because in order to save money he and the tour team had stayed at a campsite far outside the city and so wasted a lot of time travelling back and forth. It was a false economy, of course, and he should have been in a hotel close to the convention.

Even though I was not a member of the CCF Youth, having been expelled at the time of the Suez crises, I was still active in High Park trying to breathe some life into the constituency's almost moribund youth group. I was able to do this because older socialists in High Park, such as Bill Temple, who to his credit considered himself above all to be a democrat and had no difficulty working with others who did not accept the line of the party brass. Moreover, he was smart enough to see that young people were essential to the future of the constituency and he wasn't blind to the reality that youth, with their energy and enthusiasm, were very important at election time, tending to see them mostly as fodder for the party machine. Our CCF fraction in the LSA began to look for ways to increase our influence among the youth who were being attracted to the new party formation. We knew that with "the new party" moving up the agenda of the labour movement, one of the questions confronting those who were organizing the "new party clubs" was what would be the fate of the existing CCF youth when the new organization came into existence?

The answer to that would come when most of the major unions in Ontario, led by the Steelworkers, the Machinists and the Packinghouse Workers Union, began to assign staff to the task of organizing "new party" clubs alongside the CCF constituency organizations, the idea being that they would be "independent" of the CCF, and possibly even to its right. But for us, the immediate question was whether there would be a new youth organization attached to such a "new party." I was fortunate to work with three of these early organizers who had been assigned to Toronto's west end by the International Association of Machinists, two of whom were prime examples of the differing strands of political thought in the unions about the idea of political action. Because of their participation in the High Park CCF, I had gotten to know them very well. As they were both from Belfast and the Shankill Road, they would often talk candidly to me about their outlook and I soon saw they were far to the right of the Lewis leadership and were especially critical of Bill Temple because of his socialist views, a criticism they would always slyly mask under their contempt for his efforts to keep booze out of the riding. It was very clear to us that what they wanted in reality was a new alignment to the right of the CCF made up of some kind of combination involving "progressives" in the Liberal Party, and certainly not the working-class based political party we were hoping for. The third Machinist, a staffer, was much better politically than those two. He wanted to see the creation of some kind of new Labour Party formation in Canada, such as existed in Britain. Very critical of Temple, he believed that High Park CCF should put more of its resources into helping organize the "new party." He was of the opinion that Bill and Mary were dragging their feet on this, which in fact happened to be true, at least initially. They were part of a layer of old CCFers, including many in the West, especially B.C., who were uncertain about the new formation and were deeply suspicious of the union bureaucracy's plans for it.

The Machinist's staffer turned out to be a very useful ally for us. He soon let me know he wanted to do an end-run around Bill and Mary and involve the CCF youth in building the new project. The labour movement was abuzz with discussion about the new party in those months, with a large number of meetings of CCFers, unionists and community activists taking place around the city to discuss what it would look like and talk about how it should be organized. New party clubs were beginning to spring up all over the place, including in a few factories, a move that we supported. These workplace clubs barely got going, however before they were quickly snuffed out by the union brass who redirected them into local constituencies. We quickly saw that our main hope for having an influence in what was going on would be through our work in the CCF Youth, weak as it was, and we posed the question of whether there should be an entirely new youth organization for the "new party" or would it just be a continuation of the existing organization.

Finally, we got the ears of some of the key players in the Toronto unions. For example, Bill Sefton, an International Representative for the Steelworkers and Secretary Treasurer of the OFL, who had high electoral hopes in Davenport in a forthcoming federal election and was sniffing around to see if he could entice some young people to help him. Because of our good contacts with the Davenport CCF Youth, we were well aware of his plans in that respect. Notorious in the labour movement for his inflated ego, he was one of the most preening, narcissistic people I had ever come across. I remember his comb never seemed to be out of his hand because he fancied himself as something of a ladies' man. To me, he seemed to be more interested in getting his hands on the young women who were helping organize the youth, than building the new party and we made a point to alert our people about him. Despite these problems, however, and because we refused to be distracted by what we considered minor issues, we remained firmly focused on our political agenda and managed to win Sefton over to our position. He told us he agreed with us on what should happen in the eventual merger into the new party with the CCF in relation to the youth and that the new political formation should have its own independent organization, of which the existing CCF Youth would be part, but not automatically inherit and dominate. The leadership of the CCF Youth, including a young Stephen Lewis and Gerry Caplan, University of Toronto students at the time, had allowed the organization to wither on the vine, assuming, in their arrogance, that any new youth formation would automatically fall into their laps, like ripe fruit from a tree.

Our group at the same time made a few modifications to its orientation towards youth in general. As I've mentioned, after Hannah and I had returned from New York, with the encouragement of Tim Wohlforth and Jim Robertson, we had set up a Young Socialist Alliance branch, affiliated to the YSA in the U.S. It wasn't very large, with about ten members, some of them young people who had come around our bookstore and who had been referred to us by Ross Dowson. That was how we met a precocious Harry Kopyto. He was about thirteen years old then and would eventually become a leader of our group. Later he came to prominence in Toronto as an activist lawyer in the courts, representing the marginalized and the oppressed, which he continues to this day.

Despite our best efforts however, the YSA in Toronto had been unable to expand much beyond the initial grouping the SEL had assigned to it. Moreover, it was tending towards becoming inward-looking in its activities, comfortable in the LSA, concentrating mainly on running study classes of the Marxist classics. I must confess that because of my involvement in the development of the "new party," I had missed some of its meetings, so I was surprised when I began to meet resistance when I suggested that we re-orient to the new developments around the "new party" youth. Pat Brain, my old work-mate from UE and English Electric let me know in no uncertain terms that he was unhappy with the new direction being proposed, saying I should have consulted with the YSA first before moving on the youth issue in the CCF. That aside, it soon became clear to everyone that what we were confronting was a major opportunity for growing our group, the LSA. It was a no-brainer, as far as I was concerned. With Ross' encouragement, we dissolved the YSA and moved everybody we could into the CCF in preparation for the Founding Convention of the new Ontario youth organization of the "new party."[2]

Some times you can get lucky in politics. As fate would have it, it turned out to be very fortunate that we were in contact with a few rank and file union militants who were active in the Canada Packers Local of the Packinghouse Workers Union, whom I had known from my days when I was secretary of the Packinghouse Workers' local at Maple Leaf Milling. Sefton's support for our organizational perspective helped ease the way for us and through these Packinghouse militants, we were able to meet other rank and file members of other unions and participate with them in a left caucus at the founding provincial youth convention. They liked our ideas and we convinced them that in the process of organizing any new youth organization of the new party, we should try and appeal to new layers of youth to rally around the new party and to facilitate this, that we should create a new youth organization. We argued that it was essential we organize a Founding Convention, in which the various CCF Youth clubs would participate on an equal footing with everyone else, as partners, but not be able to dominate it, ensuring that the new youth organization would be independent of both the CCF and the old CCF Youth organization. We were able to win most of the union rank and file to this perspective. Also key to this work was a new layer of young people we had recruited to our group the previous year, people such as Toni Gorton (nee Foster), John Riddell, Richard Fidler, John Wilson, Jim Onyschuk—all from Toronto—and Peter Schulz from Ottawa. At the Founding Convention in Toronto they formed the backbone of our very effective left caucus. Also involved were close allies such as Paulette Silver, Alan Engler and Jeannie Rands. Jeannie and Alan would later become leaders of the LSA on the West Coast. At the convention we blocked with the trade unionists and in a hard fight with the right-wing, scoring some major victories. If my memory serves me right, we won on NATO—by a handful of votes—and carried the day on nationalization, including electing some our people to its Provincial Executive, positioning the new youth organization much to the left of the NDP. It was a big victory for us and the party bureaucracy was not very happy with what had transpired.

After its Regina convention, the CCF took on a new significance for us, even though we were still telling ourselves that there was "No real motion for the new party as yet."[3] In the run up to the founding convention of the "new party," the right-wing mobilized hard to block the path of Hazen Argue who was taking a run at becoming leader. Their first challenge was to again persuade Tommy Douglas to stand as a candidate, something he had refused to do until then, and for some time after. Andy Brewin and David Lewis, both very powerful figures in the party bureaucracy, were among the first to organize against Argue in Ontario. They could barely conceal their contempt for him; it was as if he had broken some trust with them. At a CCF committee meeting in Brewin's home in downtown Toronto one evening, I remember Brewin very emphatically telling us rather bluntly that "Hazen stood no chance and he should just pick up his marbles and just go home." With the Eastern party establishment and the union bureaucracy beginning to oppose him so vigourously, Argue soon moved even further to the left and in several speeches that were reported in the Eastern press, he began to advocate that the principle of public ownership be included in the new party's platform. This was sufficient for the right-wing to become almost hysterical and to begin mobilizing against him even more intensely, especially in Ontario where the bulk of the votes for the founding convention were located. We watched in amazement as he was virtually shut out of Toronto because the right-wing callously used their position in the party to keep him from speaking. It was shameful. A national leader of the CCF, it was a major public rebuke to have received so few invitations to speak in the city.

When we realized what was going on, we contacted Doug Fisher, CCF-MP for Port Arthur (now Thunder Bay), to see if we could help. Fisher, a bit of a maverick at the time, was heading up Argue's campaign and was eagerly looking for ways to get around the right-wing and find venues for Argue to present his views on the "new party's" future. He quickly gave us the go-ahead to organize a meeting and assured us that, come hell or high water, Argue would be there.

Because of our influence in a few New Party youth clubs in the Toronto area, and mainly because of the hard work of Richard Fidler who headed up the East Toronto New Party youth, we were successful in persuading the latter to give Argue a platform, arguing that it was in the best interests of party democracy that the membership in the Toronto area should be given an opportunity to hear his views. Under their auspices we went on an all out effort to mobilize support for the meeting to ensure it would be successful. Richard—a very intelligent teenager, just graduating from high school—was the main coordinator of this work. He also chaired the event. (He would subsequently become a leader of the LSA and the editor of *Workers Vanguard*) Despite the heat and humidity of a July 18th evening, over two hundred and fifty people showed up for the meeting, made up of what remained of the Left in the CCF, and other party members. It was a hugely successful meeting for Toronto for those days. I don't remember much about what happened there but our paper reported that Richard, on introducing Argue, informed the audience of the recent New Party youth convention that had adopted a general anti-war policy and had come out against NATO. Argue, for his part, called for opposition to the placing of nuclear weapons on Canadian soil, something the Diefenbaker government was considering at the time, but was vague about the question of the public ownership of industry and resources. A few days later he would be more specific on this issue and demand that a policy of nationalization be included in the coming "new party's" programme.[4]

Argue was subsequently defeated by Douglas at the NDP founding convention. Six months later he moved to the Liberals, becoming a Senator, and although there can be no excuse for his betrayal, his brutal treatment at the hands of the bureaucracy bears some responsibility for his desertion. In effect, they drove him out in the most humiliating way, and it was a big loss for the left, but in the dying days of the CCF, the

Argue experience became very important for us, because it began to open the door to some meaningful political activity among the youth of the CCF and it helped to prepare the ground to organize our own independent youth organization. But to get there, we first had to take full advantage of the rising interest in the working class about a new labour party and participate in the debates around it.

Our support to the Argue campaign was the beginning of a new phase in our attempts to build a left wing in the NDP. Less than two years later, however, they kicked most of us out—again There was no democratic process, no hearings or evidence submitted—only a letter to the expelled that they had been kicked out because of "membership in another political party, specifically the Young Socialist Alliance (YSA)." Thirteen were purged in Ontario and eleven in British Columbia. Most were members of our group. But the LSA had just about doubled its membership over the previous year, with some of that taking place in Vancouver where we were also beginning to recruit more youth into our ranks.

Top Harry Stone and Lyle Severin on tour in the Canadian Rockies, 1965. (Photo Ernest Tate)

Bottom Michel Lambeth and camera. (Photographer unknown)

Chapter 17

Vancouver

*B*Y 1961, OUR GROUP IN VANCOUVER, THE SOCIALIST INFORMATION Centre (SIC) had a headquarters at 875 Hastings Street, where it held its weekly meetings and the occasional public forum, a big improvement from the days when the members would meet in each other's living rooms. By then, Bill Whitney and his supporters were no longer formally part of the organization but were negotiating to get back in. The branch had entered another crisis in the summer of 1959 when the Bullocks and their supporters walked out because of their inability to get along with Bill—"out of sheer frustration," they claimed—forming their own grouping and confronting the PC in Toronto with something of "a fait accompli." Because we couldn't see a political basis for the division and because both sides stated they were committed to being in a single organization, we ended up formally recognizing both groupings as legitimate units of the organization, designating the group led by the Whitneys as "Branch #1" and the group led by the Bullocks, "Branch #2." That didn't please Bill one bit; his response was to immediately resign from the National Committee. Apparently he had expected the PC to "order" the Bullock group to go back under threat of expulsion, but we refused to go down that path, because, firstly, we figured the Bullocks wouldn't have listened to us in any case, and secondly, it would have meant that the Bullocks, who we in Toronto thought were keener than the Whitneys to build a more "independent" organization, most likely would have walked away and we might have lost them forever.

For some time we had been pressing Vancouver to agree that the SIC and the SEL become a single organization. In October the previous year we had publicly called in the pages of the *Workers Vanguard* for the SEL and the SIC to come together to "launch the socialist wing of the new party."[1] By the following year we had fused the SEL with the SIC to form The League for Socialist Action (LSA), presenting the face of the "new" organization as a caucus "which would attempt to establish itself as the Marxist, socialist wing of the new party fighting to win the new party to socialism." Bill Whitney and his grouping objected to this move, saying what we were doing was too "mechanical,"[2] but we eventually overcame their objections and they agreed to participate in a coordinating body of the two groups, a "City Executive Committee (CEC)." This meant that despite their differences, they would agree to coordinate their activities and implement the new orientation, with a majority position on the Committee given to the Bullock group because they had the responsibility of implementing the majority line.

This arrangement didn't last very long, needless to say. There were continual arguments over their priorities and their attitude to the coming "new party" and such matters as the operation of the hall and its finances, with Whitney finally boycotting the CEC leading to his group's virtual expulsion from the organization by the PC in Toronto. At bottom, Ross didn't have much use for the Whitney group, thinking that it would never overcome its "deep entrism." It was all a messy business, but if you pushed the personal differences aside, it was easy to see that the Whitney group did not wish to have its comfort level in the CCF affected too much, which the LSA by its very existence threatened. At its core, the differences were essentially tactical, and not about any major programmatic issue that we could see. In an ideal world, the best arrangement would have been to let both sides carry out their respective practices to see which would give the best results, but often the factional atmosphere in groups can become so intense and personal, it's difficult for them to see themselves working together at any level.

That was the situation when I got there in the fall of 1962. It had been long Ross' ambition to have someone from Toronto who had some experience in building an organization outside social democracy, transfer to Vancouver to help the branch there, part of his notion of building the "skeleton" of the future revolutionary party that would be able to eventually attract mass support when a future crisis impelled the working class into action. Ross wanted the group on the West Coast to look as much as possible like that in the East, to have a homogenized practice and organizational form across the country. It should be noted that Ross had worked hard at getting others from Toronto in earlier times to relocate there. A leader of the group, Barry Brent and his companion had transferred there in the early fifties after the split with the Rose group, but had come into conflict with Ross. Eventually Barry dropped out. Ross had tried to persuade Jim and Pat Mitchell to go there after Jim had fallen into his bad graces after the debacle of the 1956 tour, but that didn't go anywhere either and when Bunny and Bruce Batten got fed up with their assignment in Montreal, he urged them to try Vancouver. That didn't pan out; by that time it was too late, both of them were on their way out of the organization in any case. Alan Harris had been there for a couple of months trying to set up a bookstore, but that fell through because our Vancouver people left him on his own so he headed home to Britain. Finally, Ruth and Jerry Houle had agreed to relocate there just before me, but had difficulty getting the cooperation of the Vancouver people, with Jerry managing to get himself isolated in the group and everybody angry at him at the same time, mainly because he couldn't hold back in expressing his criticisms of the "low political level" of the branch. I could understand his difficulties. I knew from experience that he could be difficult to work with at times, and could be very blunt with those who did not measure up to the standard in his mind of what a revolutionary leader should be, but in fairness to him, it could not have been easy. He was working at a full-time job and trying to look after a young family, all the while attempting to get the branch into better shape. Not long after his experience on the west coast, his disagreements with Ross deepened—it's too long ago to remember what they were—and Ruth and Jerry left the organization.

The question of someone going to Vancouver was posed again in the winter of 1961–62 while I was at the SWP cadre school, the idea being to help in the consolidation of the new fused organization, the LSA. It was something I had been thinking about for a while because I was by then in a close personal relationship with Ruth Robertson, who in 1961 had moved out to the University of British Columbia to enroll in its library science programme. A capable young organizer and writer, she had been a leader of the Young Socialists in Toronto before heading west, and I couldn't see myself in a long-distance relationship, so I was keen to join her. It was agreed that I would lead the 1962 tour and that I would remain there once we got to Vancouver.

Despite the messy organizational problems with the Whitney group—who were in negotiations to get back in, as I have mentioned—the Vancouver branch had begun to change, and for the first time in many years was attracting new recruits to it, including, most importantly, young people. In addition to Ruth Robertson (later to become Ruth Tate) and me, there were a few other transplants that year from Toronto to help this process along. Joe Hendsbee and his wife Julie had re-located there. He had been a leader in our Toronto Teamster work, as I've noted in my chapter on the Teamsters, and had been fired from his job there. Unable to find work because of a virtual black-list by the trucking companies, Joe thought he would be better off in Vancouver and had gotten a temporary job shortly after he arrived with one of the unions helping to organize non-union plants. But, the most important recruits came from the Vancouver area, mainly from the NDY. Winnie Henderson's daughters, Jacquie and Margaret, had become active in the group as had Ben Clifford, the son of Hugh Clifford, a prominent leftist in the NDP and who was politically close to Ruth and Reg. Jacquie, who was very young, not much past puberty and very bright, was a leader of the youth, eventually becoming a key figure in the YS nationally. Other youth I remember from that time were Larry Nozaki, who would later became a leader of the Postal Workers Union on the West Coast and Walter Walima, who in the 1970s would become a key organizer in the Vietnam anti-war movement. Ken Orchard, Cliff's younger brother, had moved there from Toronto the year before. He was treasurer of the FPCC and part of the team that helped get it going under the leadership of Phil Courneyour and Cedric Cox. Other key youth we had won over from the NDY were Bob Townsend, Bud Bennet, Sonia Puchalski and Stewart Sinclair. Stewart would become a leader of the branch, eventually moving to Toronto where he also was a leader. Bob, an electrician, eventually moved to Cuba to take a position of superintendent of part of the country's electrical infrastructure system and Bud became the secretary of the FPCC. Sonia, active in the CCFY would become active in the leadership of the branch. All would provide the future nucleus of our new YS organization on the West Coast. We had also recruited a few people from the left wing of the NDP. Among them Nick Shugalo, a very energetic Ukrainian Canadian who had spent some time in Cuba before joining our 1962 cross-country tour in Toronto, and the brother and sister team, Bruce and Sheila Elphinstone. All of this provided the basis for a big boost in activity and growth of the branch.

Ruth Robertson's move to UBC proved to be very fortuitous and helped to provide impetus to establish a base on campus a few years before the explosion of radicalism among students in Canada generally. Very soon she was editing and helping to produce a new campus publication, *Young Socialist Forum,* a monthly mimeographed journal, which in our eyes in the East had become amazingly successful, selling over a thousand copies an issue—a remarkable figure for us in those days and higher than the circulation of *Workers Vanguard* in non-tour years—and even making a cash surplus, over and above its cost of production. It wasn't very long before they learned from their campus supporters that the NDY on campus didn't like the publication very much because it kept poking its finger in their eye, challenging their hegemony on campus. Ian Waddell and Lyle Kristiansen—who would later become NDP-MPs—were students at UBC at the time and, at such an early age, right-wing social democrats; they were among the first to initiate a campaign against us, leading to the purge of all those who were putting out the journal. The expulsion of ten of our members and supporters, among them Ruth Robertson, was an action that had all the appearances of being nationally coordinated because it took place at about the same time as the expulsion of our supporters in the Ontario NDY. Most of those purged would provide the nucleus for the formation of the YS, which would replace the YSA.

The expulsions from the NDP happened before I had gotten there, and when I arrived, I found it rather odd that the branch was not making much of a fuss about the matter, such as we had done in Ontario where we had initiated a public protest against our expulsion, holding forums on the issue and producing a pamphlet to explain our case against them. In B.C., I soon discovered, it had become a well kept secret because the left in the party—which was a fairly influential force—was exerting pressure on us to keep quiet in the hope they could "persuade" the leadership to reverse them. They were also nervous about a public "scandal" just before the Provincial election that year. They had come at an "inappropriate time," it seemed. For me, time was of the essence, and the longer the expulsions remained a well-kept secret, the longer the party ranks wouldn't know about them, letting the matter recede into the background and be forgotten. I considered it essential that as many party members as possible know about them and be informed of the right-wing's undemocratic actions against us and that the leaders should pay a political price, no matter how small, for their actions. That's why we were very pleased when the news broke in *The Province* and it was splashed across its pages for many days, forcing the right-wing to explain to the membership its lack of democratic procedures.

My first few months in Vancouver turned out to be very hectic. I had to quickly orient myself to the politics of the labour movement and at the same time get to know our members and its leadership, especially Ruth and Reg Bullock, all the while participating in our various projects and committees. The FPCC seemed to be a very effective and successful operation and didn't require much assistance from me. Phil Courneyour had that well in hand. I remember each month I worked with Ruth Robertson on the *Young Socialist Forum*, doing my best to write for it and to help produce it. It had become a top priority for us because we felt it might give us the breakthrough we needed to increase our influence among a new generation of young people. The expulsions had made it essential that it continue to come out regularly, even though it required great effort to meet its monthly deadline because of having to cut so many stencils for the mimeograph machine and running them off. It had become an important vehicle through which many of our supporters on campus could express themselves and was a means by which our new young activists became radical journalists. I recall it dealt with issues such as the nuclear test ban treaty that was being negotiated between the USSR and the United States, and which was very much in the news, the Chinese-Indian conflict over the McMahon boundary (we supported the Chinese) and the Sino-Soviet dispute, in which we also sided with the Chinese, except for their position on Stalin, of course.

I had also become branch organizer. Ruth—by then Ruth Tate—in addition to putting out *Y.S.F.* and helping organize our budding youth organization, was also on the branch's Executive Committee, with many of the responsibilities of leadership falling on both our shoulders and Ruth and Reg tending to pull back from day to day activities. They were consciously letting the new generation take over, but we never made any new move without first discussing it with them. We often visited them at their home in North Vancouver.

Not long after I got to Vancouver, I had to involve myself in resolving "the Whitney question." It was an issue that kept poking its head up in left circles, making our life a little bit uncomfortable. It was well known to everyone that Lilian and Bill had been leaders of our group for many years. Our people were continually being quizzed about their status in our organization and we didn't have any easy answers to give. It was an issue that had been left over from the previous LSA convention when Ross and I had been delegated to meet with them to try and work something out to get them back in. When we met with them at that time, they informed us that they had grown in membership and that they were in agreement with the LSA's basic statement of principles and programme and that they wished to be in the organization. As far as I was concerned,

I could see no principled reason for keeping them out. "My position is that we allow the whole bunch in ..." I had written Ross.[3] But it was a different matter with the rest of the branch leadership, especially Ruth and Reg, who, backed up by Malcolm Bruce, Fred McNeill and Shelly Rogers, opposed them even coming to the Convention, saying they should first be made to appear before some kind of commission. For whatever purpose, was never made clear to me, but I saw it clearly as part of a delaying tactic in dealing with the matter, hoping they would just go away and not bother us anymore.

Before I had gotten there, Harold Rosenberg had emerged as a leader of the Whitney group and was acting as its spokesperson. He had had several meetings with Ruth and Reg and me about trying to get back into the LSA. A small businessman, his family owned a restaurant supply store and every time I ran into him, he invariably impressed me with his seriousness, his intelligence and his knowledge of Marxism. From what I could see, he was politically quite astute and I would have liked very much to have had him in our organization. Ruth and Reg on the other hand were always very critical of him, unreasonably so, it seemed to me. He was active in the left of the NDP and it seemed they didn't like some things he had said there, but to me he appeared to have a genuine interest in overcoming the division. Apparently another big issue, according to Ruth and Reg had surfaced to stand in the path of unification. Whitney had recently recruited someone from the NDP, Ken Grieves, whom they perceived was careless about details being spread in NDP circles about the LSA, and they didn't want him in the group. I met Grieves several times and had seen him at some of our functions, and although I could see he could be somewhat tactless in the way he spoke, I was of the conviction that the problems with Ken had their origins in the artificial division between us and the Whitneys in the NDP and that in reality, Grieves' membership was being used as an excuse to keep relations between the two groups frozen. But I was in a difficult position, without much leverage. Ruth and Reg had just about lined up everyone behind their position and I didn't wish to have a serious fight about it. My position was simple: let the group in as it was, but I remained a minority on that. It was an issue that remained unresolved the whole time I was in Vancouver.

For a while, Ruth Tate and I lived in an apartment at the rear of the headquarters, on the ground floor of a small apartment building. I remember it being an unpleasant place, noisome, the home of many giant cockroaches, we soon found out, which would stream across the floor to hide under the fridge when the lights were switched on. We were there solely because of our penurious state. The only benefit, aside from the low rent, was that we didn't have far to travel to get to our meetings. But at times this arrangement could be a bit of a drag because we never seemed to be able to escape the organization. But we told ourselves it was temporary, until we found a better place. Nor were we happy with the headquarters. Aside from being located far from the centre of the city, its main problem was that it did not have street frontage and was in an area of low pedestrian traffic, making it very difficult to establish a fully functioning bookstore, the "Toronto formula" to help pay the rent and afford someone on staff. But after a little bit of coaxing, Ruth and Reg finally agreed we should look for another place and the branch executive went along. I think Ruth and Reg's main concern was about who would take care of the rent if we ran into difficulties, an understandable concern because apparently in the past they had been forced to step in to cover non-payment of rent for the group's previous offices. Almost right away I found an empty furniture store, just south of the Granville Street Bridge at 1208, which, with a little bit of effort could be converted into a suitable premises. I brought everyone from the executive to look at it, and after a little hesitation, they all agreed we should take it. As far as I was concerned, it was ideal. There would be enough space for a bookstore at the front and at the back—with its own entrance—a good sized meetings hall to hold up to 100 people along with a couple of offices for the branch organizer to work out of. We set to work right away to renovate the space, and even before it was finished, we were holding public events in it. Just as importantly, Ruth and I were able to move out of our horrible apartment at the rear of the old headquarters into a flat on the top floor of a house on Eighth Street, near Granville. It was by no means ideal, but it was a big improvement for us. At least it was much cleaner, and less demoralizing, and a little distance separated us from the office.

Looking back on it, I wonder to this day about how we achieved so much under such difficult circumstances. During most of my time in Vancouver, personally I was in a crazy position: I was functioning as a virtual full time un-paid organizer of the group and all the while scrambling around looking for work to make ends meet. At the same time Ruth, who was still at UBC and working at a part-time job, was in the midst of a very difficult pregnancy. She had been ordered by the doctor to give up her part-time job and confine herself to bed, four months into the pregnancy for fear of miscarrying the baby, all the while trying to complete her degree. In addition, the branch had entered a crisis and was on the verge of another split, requiring a lot of my time to deal with it. I missed Ruth's leadership in the group and worried about her constantly as I ran from meeting to meeting. I was frantic and the only relief that came was when I returned home in the evenings to go over what was going on. At the same time we were broke, living only on my unemployment insurance.

British Columbia at the time was in the midst of one of its frequent recessions. There was very high unemployment and I had difficulty finding a job in my trade—stationary engineer—because I wasn't registered in that province and was still in the process of getting a B.C. license, which seemed to take an inordinate amount of time. Now and then Ruth would receive some money from her parents in Toronto, which was a lifesaver, but it wasn't much. Occasionally, I would find a few weeks work as a day labourer in the saw-mills working on the "green chain," usually selecting and stacking lumber after it was sawn. It was heavy work and often I was so tired I could hardly keep my eyes open at our meetings. Fortunately, just as I was about to apply for welfare, I managed, through a contact of Ruth's at UBC, to get hired into the steam-plant at McMillan and Bloedel's paper-mill in Burnaby, which was on the banks of the Fraser River. A novel feature of the job—and a very desirable one from my point of view—

was that it was a "relief" position and I only, on average, had to work three days a week and sometimes more over holiday periods and the summer to allow the full-time operators of the plant time off. The plant's workers were organized by the Paperworkers Union and the pay was sufficient for Ruth and me to live on and let me continue with my political work, but it meant I had to work most public holidays and often on weekends. In the conditions I lived under in our group, I wasn't alone in this. This tended to be the norm for people who were in its leadership.

There was little money for staff so as a consequence sometimes one of a couple would work to support the other going on staff, and many times we persuaded people to go to various parts of the country to try and organize branches, often with their own resources and without providing financial support to them. Ross had set the tone for this. It was a way of making up for our small size by demanding everything we could from our cadre. Without being too judgmental, I now recognize this as a form of "pulling ourselves up by our own bootstraps," an attempt to leap over the difficult political conditions that confront all revolutionaries when the class struggle is at low ebb. And we were only able to do this because of our youth.

The new hall and bookstore at 1208 Granville Street turned out to be very successful from the start and helped establish our group on a new basis. Even before the renovation of the premises was fully complete, we began a series of forums and educational functions that won us an audience much bigger than in the past. Soon Alan Engler and Jean Rands arrived on the scene, a welcome addition and an important strengthening of the cadre who were beginning to lead the organization. Alan and Jean were very hard workers and very disciplined in their approach to the group.

They had come to Vancouver by way of Regina, where Jean's folks lived. I knew of her family from our cross-country tours when we would drop in to see them. They could always be counted upon to make us very welcome. Jean's father, Stan, a very gracious and gentle person, I recall, had been a central figure in the Saskatchewan CCF, and was known to the left across Canada for having been purged from the National Film

Board in Ottawa during the McCarthy witch-hunt. By the early Sixties, he was a key organizer of the community health centre movement for socialized health-care. Jean and Alan were friends with Peter Schulz in Ottawa, who had helped recruit them to the LSA. I had first met them at the founding convention of the Ontario NDY and I remember we would often joke together about how remarkable that experience had been: Alan, extraordinarily articulate and a great debater, but who hadn't said a single word in any of the debates, had been elected to the National Executive, because of the power of the Left Caucus that had included him on its slate. After that, Alan and Jean moved to Toronto and had been active in our Toronto branch. I had gotten to know him quite well because he had been on one of our tours that I had led across the country. In Vancouver, they lived a few steps away from our bookstore and as a consequence, I saw a lot of them.

I got to like them very much, especially Alan's sharp sense of humour and Jeannie's intensity about ideas. He got a job soon afterwards on the railways, on shift work. He had a keen interest in history and he was literally devouring the classics at a very rapid rate. It seemed just about every other day that summer he would be asking to borrow a book from my personal library. Jean and he became an essential part of our new leadership team, and I remember Jean having a great admiration for Ruth Bullock, one of the pillars of the branch, a feeling that Ruth reciprocated fully. A few years later, in 1968 when I was in Britain, I was surprised to hear, almost by accident, that Alan and Jean had broken with the group over our orientation to the NDP, and the perspectives for youth work, the details of which still remain unclear to me. I later heard from others that it was mainly a personality conflict with Ross, and that Ross had initiated their supporters' expulsion over tactics about the trials of those arrested on a demonstration. Later in the 1970s, when I was visiting Vancouver, Ruth Bullock told me this was also her opinion.

Among the first events in the new hall that summer, of which I have a special memory, and there would be many like it, strange as it might seem for a political grouping, was a literary event, a poetry reading, in which Milton Acorn had a big hand in helping to organize. Milton had by then emerged as a major poet—originally from Prince Edward Island—who totally identified himself with the working class. He had been a member of the Communist Party. I had known him in Toronto where he was a sympathizer of the LSA. He had been active alongside Joe Rosenblatt and other artists in a "free-speech" campaign we were helping organize to force Toronto City Council to change the law to allow open-air meetings to take place in Allan Gardens, what we hoped would be a variant of Speakers' Corner that exists in London's Hyde Park. When Gwendolyn McEwan, who would become a poet of equal stature in Canada, if not greater than Milton's, broke off her relationship with him in the summer of 1963, he was immediately cast into deep emotional and psychological crises that led to his hospitalization in the psychiatric ward of the Department of Veteran Affairs in London, Ontario.

After a few months, on being discharged and still in a fragile mental state, Milton mentioned to Ross that he was thinking of heading west to Vancouver—I suppose he wished to get as far away as possible from Gwendolyn—so Ross suggested he get in touch with me as soon as he got there. Ross had alerted me that Milton was on his way, so I wasn't too surprised when one day he showed up at our doorstep, smoking one of the large smelly cigars that always seemed to be in his mouth.

In the best of situations, poetry is a precarious way to make a living—unless one has connections in academia, of course—but Milton had none of those and suffered the additional burden of possessing a radical political outlook towards the world. So he was compelled to survive on a small disability-pension from the army and always lived in a state of near penury. He later told me he had been in the military and had developed a glandular illness—that explained his slightly protruding eyes, he said—leading to his discharge. After our first contact, I spoke to our building superintendent and, within a few days, he ended up moving into a small apartment above Ruth and me.

Milton immediately made the rounds to most of the major poets in the city and was soon out at UBC visiting Earle Birney, who was probably

Canada's most eminent poet in those days, head of the creative writing department at UBC for many years, and the focal point for a group of young West Coast poets who were just beginning to get themselves established. In the early days of the SWP, Birney had been a Trotskyist active in Salt Lake City, Utah, where he had recruited Joe Hansen to the Party, but he had long broken with Trotskyism and had moved to the right politically.

Milton quickly pitched in to help us with our work. I remember one day when he was at the new premises at 1208 Granville Street—which was still in the process of being renovated—on looking it over he casually remarked that such large space would be ideal for a poetry reading. Apparently there were few venues in Vancouver outside UBC for such activity. I immediately seized upon the idea, suggesting if such a thing were to occur in the hall, it should be separate from our normal political forum programme and should be organized on a one-off basis around the need to raise financial support for some as yet unknown worthwhile cause.

With that, Milton got to work to line up a few Vancouver poets—some of them aspiring—to come and read. The first reading was very well attended, I remember—over a hundred people packed the place, which was still in a semi-finished state—with Milton in the chair, to raise money for Malcom X, the Black Nationalist leader in New York. One of the poets I remember from that evening was Red Lane, an intense young man who was serious about becoming a poet and whom Milton thought was one of the best around. Milton soon got to know Lane very well and introduced him to me, but I don't remember having any lengthy conversation with him. I have a feeling he may have been apolitical. I remember Milton laughing about how one morning Red had walked him, both of them in deep discussion, halfway across the city, just to buy a special loaf of bread, totally focused on getting what he wanted, but exhausting Milton.

Lane would tragically die within a year of a brain aneurism leaving a young wife and child, a shocking loss of a bright young star. We sponsored a benefit for his family, a reading at our hall, but I don't remember if we raised much. His death had a severe effect on Milton I recall, throwing him into a deep depression. For days he hardly left his room but eventually he was on his feet again and the poetry readings continued on a regular basis, raising money for the black civil rights movement and other important causes.

One of the more successful was one organized to support Cuba, a joint activity of the FPCC and the Canada Cuba Friendship Society. It surprised many that a political group was behind these kinds of events, but others assumed such things were quite normal. For me, it was a way to reach the artistic community in Vancouver and help build the influence of the LSA, and maybe even recruit a few more members, but without Milton it wouldn't have occurred to us to put them on.

By the end of September 1963, Milton had joined the LSA. He was the one who raised the idea and after he and I talked about it over a couple of weeks, I put it to our branch meeting. He said he agreed with us on all the political questions of the day. Everyone was pleased and we gave him a warm welcome into our ranks. As I've mentioned, he had been in the CP in Montreal, and when he got to Toronto, he had been asked to join the LSA, but had turned that down. I don't know what it was, but his impression of our Vancouver operation, was more favourable. On joining, he never missed a branch meeting and participated in all our activities. I remember a few months after, he would travel back and forth to Seattle to the SWP branch and one day he told me he had met a woman there whom he liked very much and with whom he had formed a close personal relationship. I was very happy for him because it was a sure sign he had recovered from his crisis. I don't know much about poetry, but I think it was a very productive time for him, a period that is strangely absent in the various accounts of his life that I have read over the years. Maybe it's because the information is not known. He was very active when I knew him, writing, doing many readings, including giving interviews and readings on CBC Radio. As I recall it, he worked every day at his poetry, sometimes from the morning well into the night in his smoke-filled room, often bringing the finished work to read to Ruth and me. Invariably we were always impressed, though sometimes we wished he would have left his smelly cigar behind for the occasion.

Not long after Milton had arrived, Al Purdy showed up in the city and came to see Ruth and me. A prominent supporter of the FPCC, he had been recently to Cuba on a cultural tour. He was friends with Ross Dowson who suggested that he contact us once he got to the coast. The Young Socialists Forum promptly organized a reading for him that turned out to be very successful. And not long after that, he helped us greatly in our campaign to raise support for Neville Alexander, a South African anti-apartheid leader and Fourth International supporter who had been imprisoned on Robben Island at the same time as Nelson Mandela. He threw his backing behind a poetry reading we were holding to raise support for Alexander. Chaired by Jean Rands, over 150 people came out for it. On the platform with Purdy were Earle Birney, Milton Acorn and Dorothy Livesay. All of them are now recognized as being among Canada's major poets.

Al Purdy had a reputation as a radical in Vancouver, having lived there at one time and some of his early poems are famously about his days working in a mattress factory. When he came to see Ruth and me, he was on the West Coast making the rounds, visiting Birney at UBC. He told us he had just spent a few hours with Milton. Al knew Milton very well before he came west and had a great admiration for him, as can be seen in one of Purdy's well known poems about the time when Milton, a carpenter, was helping him build his house on the shores of Robin Lake, Ameliasburgh, Ontario. He had just been to visit Milton, he told us he was pleasantly surprised at how well he had recovered. When Milton had been in Toronto, Purdy said, he had been in such a severe personal crisis over his break-up with Gwendolyn, that he, Purdy, had personal fears that Milton could possibly take his own life. I was surprised by these words. On his arrival in Vancouver, Milton had seemed reasonably alright to me, not that I knew him very well. Obviously I hadn't been aware of the true seriousness of Milton's psychological state. Purdy told us he had come to see us specifically to thank us for what we had done to help

Milton and that he was sure his recovery was due in part to his being welcomed into our group. We greatly appreciated what Al said, but for us how we dealt with Milton, was only an expression of our solidarity with him during a difficult time.

As a footnote to my friendship with Milton, I should add that after Vancouver, I lost contact with him almost entirely and didn't see him again until 1969 when I had returned to Toronto from Britain. I had been told that Milton had come from Vancouver and had been initially supportive of the LSA but had become somewhat eccentric in his views and had developed a deep hostility to the pro-abortion campaign that was still in its early stages and which was being led by women from the LSA. One day, quite by accident, Jess and I ran into him on Bloor Street West in Toronto, close to where we were living, so we stopped to chat and went for coffee to a nearby restaurant. He seemed pleased to see me again, wanting to know about my stay in Europe. We exchanged a few pleasantries, but I was very anxious to learn if what I had heard about him was true. We weren't long into our conversation when he burst into a tirade—unprovoked—about the issue of abortion, and how in his opinion, "it was part of a ruling class campaign to destroy the working class." It was incredible to see the change in him from when he was in Vancouver. He went on a crazy-like rant, his face reddening and hands gesticulating, something I had never seen him do before. He was so adamant in his opinions that it was impossible to reason with him. I saw him on several occasions after that and each time he seemed increasingly more eccentric and more difficult to talk to. Eventually I lost contact with him altogether.

Vancouver was a great place to be in those years and very different from Toronto, not only with its beautiful location but also in the laid-back atmosphere where the counter-culture had found a ready home. The saying was that it was the end of the road for many radicals who were unhappy with the rest of the country, which was why the percentage of eccentrics in the population was so high. The mountains, so close to the city, looked truly magical and the easy reach of the beaches gave the place a permanent vacation feeling. The mild winters were a relief from the brutal winters of Ontario but it is about the only place anywhere in the world where I have experienced rain similar to Belfast's. I would often feel very much at home as the rain seemed to go on for days on end.

Vancouver should have been even more fun for Ruth and me, but with little money it was a very difficult time for us, not only financially, but politically as we tried to provide leadership to the group and assimilate many of the new young people who were on our periphery. The news that ten of our people had been expelled from the NDY had been in the Vancouver newspapers that summer, as I've mentioned, and our aggressive defense of them including our protests and public criticism of the Provincial party for its undemocratic actions—the expellees were expelled by decree and were not given any chance to defend themselves—induced an explosion of tensions within our group over our attitude to the NDP, between some of our members who had remained active in the party, led by Winnie Henderson on the one side, and a majority, made up primarily of recent young recruits who saw their primary activity as building the LSA on the other.

Suddenly, in late June 1963, without much warning or discussion, Winnie and her group up and walked out of the organization, but without the support of either Jacquie or Margaret, her daughters. Winnie's group refused to attend branch meetings, telling us they were taking a "leave of absence," omitting to tell us for how long. They were a loose grouping of around twenty or so, some of them barely members who had not attended branch meetings for months at a time.

Coincident with this, George Brown and his wife, recent immigrants from Scotland also informed us they were "taking a leave of absence." Both had been sympathetic to Gerry Healy's organization in Britain, the SLL. In reality, they were a "micro-faction" of the SLL in our group and they had been quietly promoting Healy's criticisms of the Fourth International and Healy's opposition to overcoming the 1953 divisions. They hadn't had much success. George, an electrician, a member of the International Brotherhood of Electrical Workers and "active in the union," as he told me, never ever seemed to be able to discuss with us what he was doing there, keeping it all secret from us. After a suitable period of time, we told all of them that "a leave of absence" was a privilege granted by the organization to a member for personal reasons, and not a right, and that if they did not return, we would consider them no longer members of the organization. None of them came back. Part of their problem was that over the previous period, we had been tightening up the organization from the loose arrangement it had been before, getting it to function on a more disciplined basis, asking the membership to take responsibility for implementing the decisions we agreed to in our weekly meetings, and above all working towards getting them to live up to the ideas they had committed themselves to when they had first joined.

Most of Winnie's group didn't like the change. Nevertheless, it was a blow, reducing us to about twenty members.[4] In comparison, Toronto had grown to forty-two by then, a lot more than when I had joined in 1955.[5] And even though we sought comfort in the old saying usually repeated in those situations, "better few, but better," the split reduced our contacts with the NDP, something we never recovered from while I was there. It was also very difficult personally for Ruth and Reg because many of the people who had departed—especially Winnie Henderson and Hugh Clifford—were close friends whom they had worked alongside in the CCF and had known for many years.

One of my first tasks that year as the branch organizer was looking after Joe Hendsbee who unfortunately had landed up in jail. It was a totally unexpected situation for us. Earlier in the year, Joe had been jailed as a result of violence on a picket line he and I had been on at a factory, Allied Engineering, in downtown Vancouver. Over the course of that winter, the B.C. Federation of Labour had been mobilizing support for the workers there, several hundred, who were in the process of trying to get a first contract. The company was trying to smash the strike by transporting scabs over the picket line. Joe, who was active in the campaign, had kept us informed about what was going on and several of us had been making a point of being on the line every day. One morning the picket erupted into a riot with a series of running battles with scabs and the police at the plant. There were many arrests. Joe, who on pure impulse and throwing caution to wind—something that he was prone to do from time to time—and forgetting about the cops, jumped onto the running board of a truck as it barreled through the picket-line. He grabbed a scab by the head, pulling him out of the cab, stopping the truck. I was appalled by this action because the risks he was taking personally served very little purpose, it seemed to me. The police jumped on him, as was to be expected, and threw him into a waiting paddy wagon, later charging him with assault. Soon after that morning I was also arrested—along with many others—and sentenced to four months for "obstruction," but had the sentence suspended because it was a first offence. Joe wasn't so lucky. He got six months, a very severe sentence indeed.

But the words, "He got six months," by no means described the awfulness of his situation. It immediately became a very difficult time for his companion, Julie, and their little boy. They had very little money to make ends meet. Branch members tried to help out, of course, but I'm sure it wasn't enough. I remember Ruth and Reg bringing Julie and her little boy to their home many times. Once the dust of the strike had settled, Joe in jail however, seemed to be on his own and was forgotten by the B.C. Fed. They had provided the lawyer for the court case but there was very little cash to support his family during his incarceration.

For about four months, every week I travelled up the coast to the Oakala penitentiary to see him. As branch organizer, I felt it was the least I could do and I began to get a good appreciation of what it's like, and the burden it imposes on a small group, when it has a member imprisoned for a lengthy period. It taught me that if one is going to get involved in activity that might lead to a subsequent arrest, the matter should be discussed thoroughly beforehand to make sure people understand the full consequences of their actions.

I was always impressed by how Joe was able to keep up his cheerful demeanour in the awful circumstances of prison life during this period. On every visit, he would relate to me his discussions with his fellow inmates and I never heard him complain once, or even express any regrets about what had happened, but instead he set to work to see who he could convince of his ideas. And I was totally nonplussed one day, however, when two uniformed prison guards showed up at our bookstore, asking for me by name. They said they had been in discussions with Joe and that he had asked them to drop by and pick up some literature for him. Of course I quickly put a bundle together, but when I gently asked the guards if it might not get them into trouble, they replied, "no," with straight faces and that it was part of Joe's "rehabilitation." This happened several times, nonetheless. Joe was out of jail by September 10, 1963, and after a short while, he resumed his activities in the branch.

Attending to Joe while he was in prison and the travelling back and forth to visit him, along with Winnie's walkout, on top of trying to keep the organization together, began to take its personal toll on me. I began to feel totally worn out. The stress I was under had been so great that when our son, Michael was born at the end of June after a very difficult birthing lasting most of the night, I collapsed into a dead faint on the waiting room floor and didn't come around for many minutes, only waking up when the nurses waved smelling salts under my nose. I still have a vivid memory of that experience, awakening to a ring of concerned faces staring down at me on the floor. You're taking this harder than your wife, one of them told me, without much sympathy. It's the first and only time something like that has ever happened to me. But more importantly, it was a grueling experience for Ruth and she was totally exhausted, sleeping for many hours after the ordeal, but totally delighted to have Michael, who was very healthy, in her arms. All of this taught me to try and pace myself a little better because it's easy to suffer burnout if one is not too careful.

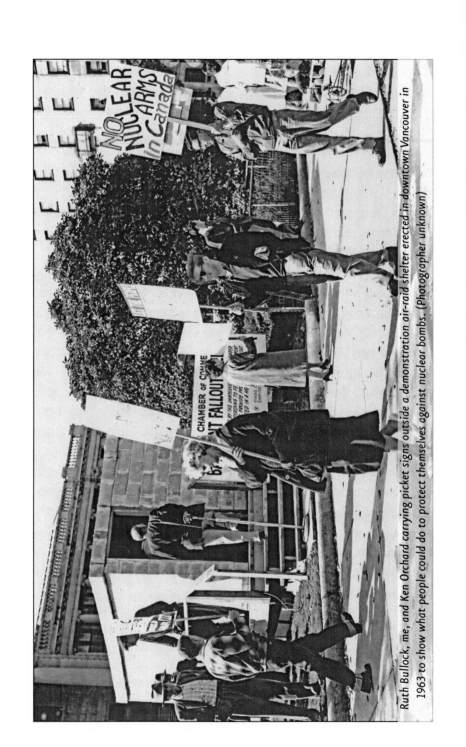

Ruth Bullock, me, and Ken Orchard carrying picket signs outside a demonstration air-raid shelter erected in downtown Vancouver in 1963 to show what people could do to protect themselves against nuclear bombs. (Photographer unknown)

Chapter 18

The Maoists

VANCOUVER WAS ONE OF THE FIRST PLACES IN CANADA WHERE supporters of China, in the growing dispute with the USSR in the early Sixties, broke away from the Communist Party and set up an independent organization. The two main personalities involved were Hardial Bains and Jack Scott. For our part, we had been focused on the Sino-Soviet dispute in the pages of the *Young Socialist Forum* for several months, gleaning most of our information from the air-mail edition of *Peking Weekly*, where new and radical criticisms of Moscow seemed to be appearing every week. The whole left was speculating about how this would play out in the LPP and we were watching for signs of its effects in B.C. where the party had a large base.

Before the dispute had erupted, our group had been in touch with Hardial Bains, a young Punjabi at UBC who was either a supporter of the LPP or a member, but who seemed to have been moving towards a pro-China position for some time. We had had several discussions with him. Ruth Bullock told me she felt he was quickly moving to the left and thought that there was a possibility he might be won over to our group. Ruth Tate had also been in touch with him on campus, but she felt this might be a too optimistic perspective, because she had found him difficult to talk to and he was even a little hostile to her. He always kept his distance from us, she said. Eventually, he became a leading international Maoist, a cult figure in the Stalinist tradition, with strong influence on a few Maoist sects in India and in Britain, especially around Birmingham.

Later, when I was in Britain, I came in contact with a few of them, and found it extremely strange that the young man I had met in Vancouver only a couple of years earlier had a god-like status amongst them. In Canada, his group, which was originally was known as "The Internationalists," named after the place where it held its regular meetings at UBC, the International Student Centre, founded the Communist Party of Canada - Marxist Leninist (CPCML), a grouping that would become notorious for its violence against those with whom it disagreed, which just about meant everybody on the left. It was commonplace for them to show up on demonstrations in Vancouver and Toronto in those days with picket signs stapled onto two-by-fours that they wouldn't hesitate to use on their critics. Bains, who is now dead, went from supporting Mao to embracing Enver Hoxha, the Albanian Stalinist authoritarian, and the last time I checked his supporters were still uncritical admirers of the current North Korean leadership.

The other figure in Vancouver who would lead a Maoist group in those years was Jack Scott who, while not lasting as long as Bains, initially offered the possibility of building an effective left force in the city. Scott at the time was employed as a janitor in the Pender Auditorium, owned by the Boilermakers' Union that was controlled by the LPP, and of which he was a member. Reg Bullock, who had been active in the Boilermakers for many years, alerted us that there had been gossip in the Boilermakers to the effect that Scott might be developing criticisms of the Party and that he had probably "ten to fifteen activists" around him and was moving to the left of the LPP.[1] Lately, Reg noted, Scott had seemed to be much more friendly to him than usual, an important change. Because Reg was well known as a Trotskyist in the local, he was compelled to be very circumspect about being seen talking to Scott. It would have been the kiss of death for him. The party leadership would have used it to politically quarantine Scott, maybe even putting his job at risk. We were very pleased with the prospect of Scott becoming an oppositionist. Even if it only meant the beginning of a friendly dialogue with Scott and those around him, it might bring us into contact, we hoped, with new opposition forces in the LPP. Reg suggested that because I wasn't publicly known in the Vancouver area, I should attempt to meet with Scott and that this would be relatively easy if I went down to the hall where Scott worked in the evenings, when it was usually deserted and when Scott would be there by himself. Reg said he would let Scott know I would be getting in touch with him. I went to see Scott almost right away.

I had many discussions with Jack Scott during the fall of 1963. At first he was a little cool to me, and even a little suspicious, but eventually he opened up and was very frank about his criticisms of the party leadership. He was very pleased, he told me, about the articles on the Sino-Soviet dispute which had been appearing in *Young Socialist Forum,* saying that the *Pacific Tribune,* the LPP's West Coast weekly, had almost ignored the issue, taking its cue from the party leadership in Toronto which was clearly on the side of Moscow. Scott also gave me the impression he was going through a re-evaluation of Stalinism saying that he had generally supported Khrushchev's criticism of Stalin's record at the 20th Party Congress. This was a significant shift in his thinking because on that issue, the Chinese were saying it had been wrong for Khrushchev to have attacked the Stalin cult.

Although never a leader and mainly an activist, Scott had a long history in the Party. An immigrant from Belfast as I was, he had been in the Party since the thirties. He told me he had joined it in 1930, becoming inactive in 1957 for personal reasons (his wife was an invalid) and rejoining again a few years before I had gotten there. Over several meetings, his caution toward me seemed to gradually lift and although cagey, eventually he let me know his group controlled two LPP clubs in the Lower Mainland and that all of them comprised of the Party's NDP "fraction," mainly "sleepers" who were not very active. This aspect about them was important to the LSA because it meant we might be able to work out some long-term collaboration working in the left of the NDP.

He and I quickly developed a good rapport. All this we discussed in our group and we agreed it would be advantageous to try to persuade Scott to pursue the internal debate in the LPP, because we felt, on the one hand, not enough time had elapsed to see what the membership thought about his ideas, and on the other, he needed to really think through some of his own arguments if he was going to do battle with the local party machine. We thought that time would be his friend in the debate, but soon we made a fundamental change in our approach to his group, coming to the conclusion that it would be a mistake to think in terms of his group "joining" the LSA—no matter how desirable that would be—but rather to consider his group as being equal to ours and propose a fusion of the two organizations into something completely new, with even the possibility of others on the left joining in an eventual kind of "regroupment" of the Vancouver left.

We asked him to put this idea to his group and that we should begin the discussions right away. He was very amenable to this and soon we were carrying out joint activity in support of Cuba and other causes and we agreed to campaign for one of their members who was running in the provincial elections on the LPP ticket. But by early December it began to appear he was having second thoughts about joint work and beginning to pull back from collaboration and giving up on the LPP, looking for an excuse to get out of it quickly, it seemed to us. I suspected other issues were beginning to affect his thinking. Beginning to move away from the idea of "regroupment," his focus had narrowed considerably.

Now when we met, he seemed more than anything else to be concentrating on who would get the "Chinese franchise" in Vancouver, not that much different I thought at the time from the LPP in that respect, with its ideological and material connections to Moscow. Scott was quite candid to me about this, telling me that he had already been in discussion with the Chinese Consulate in Vancouver about the setting up of a gift shop through which the Chinese would help fund his group. He saw it as an easy arrangement that could come to fruition fairly soon, but that he was in competition, he told me, with some others who had similar interests—I suspected it was Hardial Bains—and was anxious to settle the matter quickly.

Part of the deal with the Chinese was that the Scott group would set up a "Chinese-Canadian Friendship Committee." Anybody who knew anything about the LPP should have known that this would be highly risky activity for him, but by this stage he did not seem to care. For our part, we were very concerned he was only playing into the Party leadership's hands by not allowing time for the rank and file to enter the discussion. Several of us attempted to persuade him to slow down the process of heading towards a confrontation, but to no avail.

As soon as the local LPP leadership got wind of the fact that he was publicly initiating the setting up of a pro-China committee and taking public positions critical of them, they kicked him and his group out, of course, for "violating democratic centralism." Eventually, he lost his job at the Pender Auditorium and he found a million reasons why he couldn't talk to us anymore. We tried to collaborate with them whenever we could in the ensuing months, but it became increasingly difficult for us to work with them. They immediately set up a "Cuba solidarity committee," for example, obviously in competition with the FPCC but with no justification of why there should be two such organizations in Vancouver.

We were annoyed, of course, but accepted it as just another committee interested in defending Cuba. We proposed common activity, but we were ignored. Within a year, Scott had set up the Progressive Workers Movement and began to try and poach some of our supporters. He recruited a few sorry rejects from around the LSA, people such as Roger Perkins who, despite his pleading, we wouldn't let in. As far as I was concerned, Scott was welcome to them.

He also tried to win over some of our supporters in the broader labour movement. For example, whenever the Chinese Consulate would sponsor a large celebratory banquet, Scott's group handed out many invitations to people whom he thought he might influence, but of course none to anyone from our circles. Cedric Cox and a few sponsors of the FPCC, such as Jerry LeBourdais of the Oil, Chemical and Atomic Workers International Union, were invited, but not Phil Courneyour, its secretary. His relations with us began to deteriorate fast when, at one of their first public forums on China, Nick Shugalo and I took the floor in the discussion period to talk about the mistake of China's support for Stalin and the great damage Stalin had done to the USSR, much to Scott's consternation. Stung by our criticism, obviously, he then resorted to an old Stalinist trick to get revenge.

Out of the blue, the PWM began to publicly circulate defamatory leaflets against us, naming Nick Shugalo and me as "strike breakers" and the LSA as "a gathering of strike breakers."[2] At the same time anonymous leaflets began to circulate around the Vancouver area, accusing me of working for the RCMP and having been trained by them as "a communications specialist." We raised such a storm of criticism about this filth that they were finally forced to back off and did not issue any more. Of course Scott got his wish to put up a wall between his group and ours so that we couldn't influence them anymore with our politics.

Scott's book, *A Communist Life,* does not describe his group's origins as I have above, and I caution the reader not to rely on it for accuracy when it talks about those years.[3] My memories as recorded here of my experiences in Vancouver have been refreshed and re-enforced by looking at the reports I sent frequently to Toronto, sometimes once a week. His book, on the other hand, seems to be based entirely on his memory, serving up to the reader many self-serving statements about his own role and a retroactive projection of his much later formed opinions onto past events, attempting to prettify his own personal history and settling old scores with his political opponents. The LSA features heavily in it but his account is not worth the paper it is written on.

I don't remember him, for example, after his trips to China ever voicing any criticisms—or writing them—about the Cultural Revolution, as he does in his book. To do so at the time would have put an end to such trips. He also tries to play down China's influence upon him and his group, only casually mentioning the existence of his group's China Arts and Crafts Store, for example. He is clearly trying to avoid a charge often leveled against the pro-Soviet CPs, that their material connection to the USSR determined their political line. And his vendetta against me continues in his "history." For example he states that I was in the Socialist Caucus and on a three-person editorial board of its publication, *Socialist Caucus Bulletin,* and that I supposedly had opposed the publication of an article of his about a picket line on the Vancouver docks that had been organized by anti-Vietnam war activists to prevent the unloading of military helicopters.

"I criticized the longshoremen," Scott writes, "saying that it was not good enough for them to honour the picket line. When this stuff comes in they should not unload it. They should put out a call to the community and give the community a chance to do something. They could have put up a picket line and then say we won't unload it. But they want all the protection for themselves, take no chances. So I really criticized this. Tate was down on us. We can't do that, we'll get the union mad at us...Oh, there was quite a discussion about it. The other guy was actually chairman of the board and he was the deciding factor. Tate tried hard to convince him not to run the piece..."

Frankly, I don't remember any of this, but with the facts Scott presents, if they are to be relied upon at all, I can well understand why I would be in disagreement with that kind of ultra-leftism from a group of radicals who were not even members of the union, and who, with no risk to themselves, were urging workers to break their contract, maybe putting their jobs at risk and suffering possible legal sanctions. The article would have been seen by the longshoremen as sectarian grandstanding. The LSA would have had no part of such a thing. But Scott's story is not reliable. His memory failed him. It's sufficient to say that it was highly unlikely I would have even been a member of the Socialist Caucus, never mind a member of the editorial board. By then, most of our people in Vancouver had been expelled from the NDP, including Ruth and Reg Bullock, and I had never been able to regain my membership since being expelled in the fifties. I was never a member of the NDP on the West Coast and, moreover, one could not be a member of the Socialist Caucus without being first a member of the Party. For the Caucus to have allowed non-NDP members to be part of it, especially people such as me, would have invited expulsion from the Party.

So, at best, Scott has me confused with someone else, but I think Scott's purpose here is to try at all costs to justify his factional hostility towards us. The book is littered with this kind of thing. In the early chapters, in an example among many, it can be seen when he targets Stewart Smith, one of the main leaders of the LPP in the pre-war period, for criticism. Scott raises suspicions about Smith's loyalty to the party without producing a shred of evidence to back them up, something I'm surprised the editor of the book, Bryan Palmer, who has a reputation for fine scholarship, would let through and which careful editing should have caught.

"I went through the Party school, eight weeks, I guess, in Toronto," says Scott, writing about the period in the 1930s when the party was underground. "Stewart Smith who was then under the name of George Pierce was director of the school. He had been brought back from the Moscow school. It was known. I wouldn't call him being in hiding, but he was never picked up ..."[4] And again, when he writes about the party being outlawed, resulting in its members being interned under the War Measures Act, he repeats the "never picked up" innuendo again, suggesting that Smith might have been a police agent. "It was the 1st of October, (1939), and I went looking for Stewart Smith," he writes. "I don't know why, but the police couldn't find Stewart Smith. I think maybe they could. I found him and I didn't have their resources."[5] It's obvious that Scott had a personal grudge against Smith for some reason or other—he does not explain why—but his attempt to discredit his memory and settle some old score only exposes Scott's pettiness for anyone who cares to look, including his training in Stalinist methodology which he was never able to overcome and which characterized much of his dealings with us.

Chapter 19

The 1953 Division in the Fourth International

*I*N THE 1953 SPLIT IN THE FOURTH INTERNATIONAL, THE MAJORITY OF the Canadians, as would be expected, sided with the Americans. By the time I joined in the fall of 1955, Murray Dowson, Ross' brother, was in Paris working full-time with the International Secretariat (I.S.) that was led by Michel Pablo, but I have the impression the Canadians did not play any significant direct role in that split or in the earlier period but mainly expressed solidarity with the SWP's positions.

The main dispute had flared up at first over differing interpretations of the 1951, Third World Congress resolutions that had all been supported by the North Americans. But unity began to break down when differences developed over how these resolutions were being interpreted and when the European leadership, led by Michel Pablo, began to intervene in some sections to overturn established majority leaderships who were critical of the "entry tactic" and when he handed these sections over to minorities who supported Pablo's views. This led to what became known as a "cold split"; that is, the political differences didn't deepen and a sort of stasis set in between the two factions. Indeed, towards the end of the faction fight, the SWP leadership began to pick up gossip that their Cochran group did not have majority support from the International Secretariat, and that some of Cochran's supporters had been overheard making derogatory comments about the Pablo leadership.

For its part, the "International Committee" and the leadership of the SWP made no moves to set up an alternative competing organization to the "International Secretariat"; instead of the differences deepening, the two international groupings began to evolve similar views and positions on a series of new world events, some occurring just as the split was unfolding. Common positions began to evolve with both sides supporting the 1956 Hungarian Revolution, the Algerian national struggle for independence, along with a common analysis and perspective on the new wars that were developing in Indo-China at the end of the 1950s. Each side called for these issues to be placed at the forefront of every section's activity. Organizing opposition to the Vietnam War and working to mobilize people on the streets, especially in the advanced capitalist countries to try and counter the imperialist war drive, was the main focus of the great majority of the sections affiliated to both groupings. There was also a majority in both groupings that had evolved a common analysis of the Cuban Revolution and the need for socialists to mobilize opposition to American imperialism's drive to defeat it.

The Canadian's move towards becoming more actively involved in the International, occurred in the late fifties when the Americans alerted us to the possibility of overcoming the differences. Through their contacts in Europe, the Americans had also learned there was a general unhappiness in the International Secretariat with Pablo's leadership and with what they termed, his heavy handed interference in the life of the sections and especially about how he was behaving in regards to the Algerian revolution. There might be a possibility, the SWP thought, of a "rapprochement" to overcome the differences to create a "united" International. In 1957, Cannon had taken the initiative to try to get the two sides together, but it went nowhere. But first the Americans had to get the agreement of its international co-thinkers—the most important being the Socialist Labour League (SLL) in Britain led by Gerry Healy and the International Communist Organization (ICO) in France led by Pierre Lambert. As a result, Ross Dowson was persuaded by Joe Hansen to go to Europe in 1958 to try and help out.

Over the years, the Canadian group's relations with the SLL had always been quite good. Because of the British Parliamentary system being similar to Canada's and our tactic of "entry" into the CCF similar to the Healy organization's earlier relationship to the Labour Party, we had a lot in common with it and as a consequence, we tended to pay close attention to its activities. The British group had become one of the most successful in the International. Starting with only about fifty people at the beginning of the decade, Healy's organization had grown very quickly over the next few years. They had increased their influence in the Young Socialists, the youth organization of the Labour Party, taking leadership control before finally being purged by the Party leadership. Furthermore, of all the International Committee groups, they seemed to have benefited the most from the developing crisis of Stalinism that began with Stalin's death in 1953 and that became more profound with the Khrushchev speech and the subsequent Soviet army's crushing of the Hungarian Revolution resulting in the British Communist Party entering a full-blown crisis.

Healy moved quickly to take advantage of this situation to win some of its major intellectuals over to his side, people such as Cliff Slaughter, John Daniels, Tom Kemp, Peter Cadogan, Peter Fryer and Brian Pearce, who were very unhappy with the role of the British CP's leadership in dealing with the crisis. Peter Fryer, who had been editor of the CP paper, the *Daily Worker,* had been the paper's correspondent in Hungary as the crisis unfolded. On joining the SLL, he had helped it launch a new weekly, the Newsletter, and John Daniels became editor of the organization's theoretical journal, *Labour Review.* As a result, the SLL emerged as the largest far left organization in the country.

The Americans had kept in touch with Healy, mainly through Sam Gordon. Sam, once a leader of the Socialist Workers' Party in the U.S., was living in London and had had his passport lifted by the U.S. State Department, preventing him and his wife Millie returning to the United States. Sam was well known to us for having helped to re-organize the shattered International after the end of the Second World War, when as an American soldier in U.S.-occupied Europe, he had made the first contacts with the International's underground organizations, most of whom had been in the Resistance. Many leading members had been killed by the fascists and many by Stalin's agents.[1]

A delegation from the SWP's leadership came up to Toronto in 1960 to meet with Healy, in an attempt to arrive at an agreement on what to do to overcome the division. This came after Cannon had floated the idea of a possible agreement with the International Secretariat because of a common view about Hungary, but that initiative had gone nowhere. Before they came to Toronto, the SWP had stated they wished to enter into exploratory discussions about the future of their relations with the I.S. The Canadians paid for Healy's trip to Canada. It was one of several donations we made to him around that time. Over the years he had made many appeals to us for money for this or that cause and we always responded positively to his demands.

There were two sets of meetings in Toronto that I recall, when Cannon, Joe Hansen, Tom Kerry and Tim Wohlforth came up from New York to meet with Healy. Ross and I attended, but we were there more as observers than anything else and did not participate in the discussion—not that I would have had much to say in any case—but the SEL used the opportunity of Healy's visit to organize a semi-public meeting for him; I don't remember anything about his speech, but attendance was by invitation only and it was for us a very important event. It was not every day that we had a leading person from the British left in the city, so the people around us were eager to hear him.

In the meetings with the SWP about co-operation with the I.S. to help overcome the division, I remember Healy did not openly express his opposition to the idea and formally gave his support to overcoming the division. He insisted, however, upon the need for "an ideological struggle" against Ernest Mandel, who by then had replaced Pablo as the main spokesperson of the International Secretariat, and the necessity of further discussion about the initial 1953 division on the issue of what Healy claimed, was their "liquidationism" (i.e. a desire to abandon building the International as a revolutionary organization) and their "capitulation to

Stalinism." I remember clearly that he did not make much headway in getting the North Americans on board for this kind of project, but the understandings arrived at with Healy at those meetings about the need for his organization to engage supporters of the I.S. about a possible re-unification, were never carried out. Instead, shortly after these meetings, when he returned to London, Healy moved quickly to try and deepen the division.

The re-uniting of the movement could only take place, he argued, after a full accounting of the 1953-54 differences and an assessment of responsibility and guilt for the split, an approach that was patently designed to push both formations further apart, rather than bringing them together. Not long after a series of articles appeared in his press attacking the I.S. Not about to be deterred by these antics, the SWP decided to move its reunification efforts along, despite Healy and Pierre Lambert's opposition. Instead, they deepened their contacts with the I.S. because of the clear evidence that Ernest Mandel, Livio Maitan and Pierre Frank were committed to making a serious effort to overcome the old divisions and besides, there was a growing body of evidence of an increasing alignment in the political positions of the Europeans and the Americans. But it would be a reunification without Michel Pablo or Gerry Healy.

As the I.S. moved to overcome the old 1953 division, differences began to emerge within it. Pablo was removed as central leader at the 24th Plenum (IEC meeting), which at the same time empowered the I.S. to pursue unification. By then an opposition grouping around Pablo and Sal Santen had emerged that expressed new differences with the Mandel leadership. In regards to Cuba, they argued that it was correct for Khrushchev to have withdrawn the missiles from Cuba during the Cuban missile crisis without consulting Castro; that in the China-Soviet dispute, the Chinese leadership was "the most backward tendency" and had "a long road to cover before it catches up with the level of the Khrushchev or Yugoslav tendency." They also argued that it was possible for the threat of world war to be avoided if imperialism became demoralized by successful revolutions in the colonial world.[2] Pablo, Santen, and their supporters, remained in the I.S. through the re-unification process—they received 15% of the votes—but walked out in 1964.[3]

To help overcome the 1953 division, the SWP proposed the setting up of a "Parity Committee," with equal representation on it from the I.S. and the I. C. This was embraced by the I.S., and Joe became the SWP's main person leading the work in Europe. He and his wife Reba relocated from New York to Paris to begin the preparations for what would be a "re-unification" World Congress. He had also toured Latin America, travelling down the continent's east and west coasts, renewing contacts with supporters and visiting many of the groups who claimed adherence to the Fourth International and getting a sense of their strength and evolution since the 1953 division.

The Americans approached the Canadians to see if we could help out. One of the tasks of a "unified" International, they said would be to try and build a functioning, self-sustaining, openly pro-Fourth International grouping in London which would have the capacity of countering Gerry Healy's sectarian vendetta against us and his distortions of the International's political positions, so that the left in Britain would know what the International actually stood for. We agreed to do whatever we could and Ross Dowson asked Alan Harris if he would be willing to go to Europe and work with Joe and Reba. Alan immediately jumped at the chance. Of all of us, Alan was ideal for the assignment. On one of his vacations to England earlier, before Healy's break from the International Committee, he had gotten on well with the SLL, and had come to know Connie, at one time Healy's secretary and office manager and one of the leaders of the SLL, whom Alan would later marry. Of all of us, he was the one most familiar with left-wing politics in London.

When Alan and Connie had agreed to help the Fourth International in Britain, they had stressed that it would be for a limited time only, for two years at most. And as we approached the Eighth World Congress, an important one because it would be the first since re-unification and scheduled for the end of 1965, the question was posed of who would be available to continue their work. In the early summer of 1965, Ross wrote to me in Vancouver that the SWP enquired if we had anyone who could continue with Alan and Connie's assignment. He said there was no one in Toronto who could go and he wanted to know if I knew of anyone who would be suitable for such a task. He mentioned also that a change was underway in who would represent the SWP; Joe Hansen had fallen suddenly and seriously ill in Paris and had been hospitalized and the SWP had asked Ray Sparrow to immediately fly to France to help Joe get over his health crisis, and that he would likely take over his assignment. Ray had been working and living in the San Francisco area for a few years and had been designated by the SWP to replace Joe at some point, but Joe's sudden illness had accelerated Ray's relocation plans.

Regarding the replacement for Alan and Connie, I discussed the matter with our Vancouver branch executive and they agreed that I was the only one who was in a position to take up the challenge. So I volunteered myself. Luckily, I still had my British citizenship; I had never ever applied for Canadian citizenship because several members of our group, who were from Britain, had been refused citizenship because of their membership in our group we suspected and I didn't want an unfavourable decision on the books against me. I would have no difficulty functioning there, I figured. Besides, I was getting tired of some of the personal difficulties I was in.

After Michael, our son's birth, I'm sure my poor financial situation had put great strain on my relations with Ruth and we had broken up. Earlier, with my encouragement in 1964, she had agreed to lead a student delegation to Cuba, organized from Toronto by the FPCC. On the trip to Cuba, she had obviously re-assessed our relationship and decided to end it. I shouldn't have been too surprised. She and I had been increasingly having squabbles about what we were doing in our personal lives, including money and I couldn't even see when things would improve. The upshot was that she took Michael back to Toronto. I was somewhat bitter at the time, but looking back on it, her actions were perfectly understandable. We were living under the acute pressure of financial and personal difficulties that common political convictions and common outlook about the world could not overcome, especially in midst of the political crisis that had erupted in the branch. In addition, I had been probably less than sensitive to her needs as she cared for our son Michael and struggled to complete her degree at UBC.

After some time, Ross got back to me about my proposal for London. Toronto was a little worried, he said, about who would replace me as branch organizer and what effect my leaving Vancouver would have on the branch. But as far as I was concerned, we had made tremendous progress getting the branch onto its feet and I felt it could get along very well without me. We were growing steadily and attracting new members and, into the bargain, we had established a fairly vibrant youth organization, the Young Socialists, with its own monthly publication. I was confident the organization would be stable and continue to grow, and besides, Alan and Connie had expressed an interest in re-locating from London to Vancouver. In addition, I had a prospective replacement for the position of branch organizer, whom I was sure the comrades would elect, I told Ross, in the person of Alan Engler who by then had become an important part of the branch leadership and who was willing to undertake that responsibility.

After I had suggested myself for the British assignment, Ross consulted Alan and Connie and the Americans and they thought it a good idea, but they suggested that before coming to London, I might consider going to Algeria first where supporters of the Fourth International were preparing to participate in an international youth solidarity congress, in support of the new government of Ahmed Ben Bella. The Fourth International had great hopes for a socialist victory in Algeria and its sections had been on a campaign to popularize its successes.

After a four-year war, the National Liberation Front had defeated French colonialism. Millions had been slaughtered by the French army. The NLF's Tripoli programme, one of the most radical statements to be adopted by a liberation movement in Africa in those years, suggested the revolution would go beyond capitalism, in the tradition of the Cuban Revolution. Indeed the Cubans saw it that way too and mobilized their forces to help the new government consolidate its power. The

American SWP—supported by the Canadians—argued that what we were witnessing with the new regime led by Ben Bella, was the setting up of "a workers' and farmers' government," a characterization that had its origins in the Third International when it envisaged the possibility of the oppressed classes in a society uniquely getting control of the government, while the rest of the state and the economy remained under capitalist control. It was considered that this state of affairs would be highly unstable, transitory, and preparatory to the rest of the state being transformed and coming under the control of the oppressed, as had happened in Cuba.

And the Ben Bella government indeed proved to be "highly unstable." Alarmed at the move of the government to the left, and hostile to socialist revolution, suddenly the military cadres of the NLF under Houari Boumediene seized power in a coup d'état that removed Ben Bella from power, placing him and his team under arrest. This threw the preparations for the international solidarity conference into chaos. The coup leaders ordered the Cubans out of the country. The Cuban government was forced to divert many of its commercial aircraft to Algiers to get the Cubans out, totally disrupting air-travel from Cuba to Canada and stranding hundreds of travelers. As I've mentioned, Jess MacKenzie, now my partner, and her close friend Joan Newbigging who were in Cuba on behalf of the Fair Play for Cuba Committee to attend the May Day celebrations in Havana, found themselves stranded for many days, waiting to return to Canada.

Algeria's abrupt turn to the right quickly obliged the Fourth International to cancel its scheduled solidarity conference there. My plan had been to attend it after a short stay in Toronto, so the pressure was off me to get to Europe right away, and fortunately the delay occurred just as the LSA's *Workers Vanguard* cross-country tour ran into a serious problem: Hans Modlich was coming off it to attend to family matters and someone was needed to replace him. With me now in Toronto and obviously available, it didn't take long to come to a solution. I agreed to immediately head out to join it. Driving Hans Modlich's Volkswagen so he could get back with it, I headed out to Edmonton, Alberta, and found myself once again for several months politicking across the country, my last major activity before leaving for Europe.

I had fully expected my assignment to Britain to last only two years, but as it turned out, it stretched into almost four. It was one of the most exciting periods to be there, when a lot of political and social change was compressed into a relatively short time, especially culturally, from popular music to how people dressed, with the most significant change for revolutionary socialists being the masses of young people who were now questioning political authority. It was a time when the extra-parliamentary left surged in strength against the back-ground of a Labour government under Harold Wilson driving through historic roll-backs against the unions as it imposed its infamous "incomes policy"—a virtual wage freeze—and declared a long seamen's strike illegal, all the while supporting America's vicious war in Vietnam. One consequence of Labour's reactionary policies was the sudden appearance on the streets of a mass protest movement against the war in Vietnam, with the small forces of a re-unified Fourth International playing a key role in it as a deep youth radicalization swept Europe. I'll pick up that story in volume two.

Notes

Chapter One. Arrival in Toronto
1. "Northern Ireland: The Orange State," by Michael Farrell, 1976, Pluto Press.
2. "Inside the USA," by John Gunther, Harper, 1947.
3. Letter to Joe Hansen, Feb. 8th, 1956, Ross Dowson Internet Archive
4. Letter to Haase, May 24, 1956. R. D. Internet Archives.
5. "The Federal Election and the CCF," by Ross Dowson, May, 1957, R. D. Internet Archive.

Chapter Two. The World Party of Socialism
1. "Is War Three Inevitable?" by Joseph Hansen, August/October 1953, www.marxist.org
2. *The History of American Trotskyism,* by James P. Cannon, Pioneer Publishers,1944, 232pp.
3. To Deutscher from Joe Hansen, July 21, 1964, File 50, Deutscher Archives, IISH Amsterdam.
4. R. D. Internet Archive.

Chapter Three. The Club
1. "Poor Michel, committed suicide while you were in the UK, a depressive." Email to me from Joe Rosenblatt, December 17th, 2013.
2. http://www.bac-lac. gc. ca/eng/portrait-portal/Pages/ARProfile. aspx?ArchivalRecordKey=4234215
3. Minutes of the Toronto Branch, October 26, 1955, R10995, Vol. 60, file 60-10, Ross Dowson Fonds, Library and Archives Canada (LAC).
4. Displaced Persons, usually refugees from Eastern Europe.

Chapter Four. The Socialist Education League
1. "Memo on the CCF," by Ross Dowson, June 3, 1957, R. D. Internet Archive.
2. *Workers Vanguard,* January, 1965, Volume 9, No. 9.

Chapter Five. Our American Co-Thinkers

1. "History of American Trotskyism, 1928-1938. Report of a Participant," and "Struggle for a Proletarian Party," by James P. Cannon, Pathfinder Press, 1972.
2. 1955, PC Minutes, R. D. Internet Archives.

Chapter Six. Problems on the 1956 Cross-Country Tour

1. Letter on the end of the tour by R. D., October 27th, 1956, R. D. Internet Archive.
2. "Paddy Stanton" in The LSD Leacock, a selection of poems by Joe Rosenblatt, 1966.
3. *Workers Vanguard,* August, 1956, Vol. 1, No. 9
4. *Workers Vanguard,* September, 1956, Vol. 1, No. 10
5. Pat Mitchell became Pat Schulz after she broke-up with Jim and married an Ottawa member of our group, Peter Schulz, who was tragically killed in 1970 in a car accident while on his way to a meeting in Toronto.

Chapter Seven. Activity in the Unions

1. Even though it was tiny, the organization had all the formal structures of Lenin's Bolsheviks and the American Socialist Workers Party.
2. *Socialism on Trial,* by James P. Cannon, Resistance Books, 1999.
3. *Workers Vanguard,* Mid-November, 1959, Vol. 4, No. 12.

Chapter Eight. The Teamsters

1. Letter to Cliff Cotton, December 28, 1960, R. D. Fonds, MG 28, 1V 11, Vol. 105-16, LAC.
2. *Workers Vanguard,* Mid-June, 1960, Vol. 5, No. 7.
3. *Workers Vanguard,* January,1961, Volume 5, No 12.
4. *Workers Vanguard,* June 1962, Vol. 7, No. 3.
5. *Workers Vanguard,* July, 1962, Vol. 7, No. 4.
6. *Workers Vanguard,* August, 1962, Vol. 7, No. 3.
7. *Workers Vanguard,* December, 1965, Volume 10, No. 6 (114)
8. *Workers Vanguard,* Mid-December, 1965, Volume 10, No. 7 (115)
9. From a telephone conversation with George Bryant, 15th, September, 2012.
10. League for Socialist Action, successor to the SEL.
11. Letter to Art Gray from Ross Dowson, April 21, 1966, MG 28, 1V 11, Cont. 107-1, LAC.
12. *Workers Vanguard,* Mid-January, 1966, Volume 10, No. 8 (116)

Chapter Nine. The Cooperative Commonwealth Federation

1. "Memo on the CCF." January 3, 1957, R. D. Internet Archive.
2. *The Federal Election and the CCF,* by Ross Dowson, R. D. Archive, 1957.
3. op. cit.

Chapter Ten. Crisis in the Communist Party

1. *Hungarian Tragedy* by Peter Fryer, 1956, New Park Publications.
2. Letter to Farrell Dobbs from Ross Dowson, May 18, 1956, R. D. Internet Archive.

Chapter Eleven. Marriage and the Founding of the YSA

1. Formerly, the youth organization of Norman Thomas' Socialist Party, but later affiliated with Max Shachtman's ISL.
2. *The Struggle for a Proletarian Party*, by James P. Cannon, Resistance Books, 2001.
3. *In Defense of Marxism: Against the Petty-Bourgeois Opposition in the Socialist Workers Party*, by Leon Trotsky, Pathfinder Press 1973.
4. Letter to Ross Dowson from E. Tate, Mountain Spring Camp, July 13, 1957, Container 15—File 16, R. D. Fonds, LAC.
5. One of the people who worked with Shachtman to eventually get the ISL into the Democratic Party was Morris Spector, a leader of the Canadian Trotskyists in the Thirties. See Dave McReynold's memoir, *The Evitability of War, Revolution and Socialism*.
6. op. cit. Letter to Ross Dowson from E. Tate, Mountain Spring Camp, July 13, 1957.

Chapter Twelve. Regroupment

1. Family Quarrel: Joe Salsberg, the 'Jewish' Question and Canadian Communism'. *Labour/Le Travail 56*, Fall, 2005.
2. Address of Ernie Tate, Toronto Youth Socialist Forum, to the Council of Socialist Clubs in Quebec, Montreal, MG 28, 1V 28, Cont. 105-21, R. D. Fonds, LAC.
3. Letter to the Tour, from Ross Dowson, July 11, 1963, R. D. Fonds, LAC.
4. Letter to Alan Harris from Ross Dowson, December 30th, 1959, R. D. Fonds, L. A. C.

Chapter Thirteen. Cross-Country with the Workers Vanguard

1. *Hungarian Tragedy*, by Peter Fryer, 1956, Dobson Books, Britain.
2. *Negroes on the March: A Frenchman's Report on the American Negro Struggle*, by Daniel Guerin. American Distributor, George Weissman, New York, 1956.
3. *Workers Vanguard*, May, 1963, Vol. 8, No. 2.
4. Ross Dowson Internet Archive, Branch Minutes, June, 1956.
5. R. D. Internet Archive, from Nov 29, 1957
6. "The Federal Election and the CCF," by Ross Dowson, May 1957. R. D. Internet Archive.
7. "Confronting the Cold War: the 1950 Vancouver Convention of the Co-operative Commonwealth Federation," by Benjamin Isitt, *Canadian Historical Review 91*, September 3, 2010, University of Toronto Press.
8. "The Federal Election and the CCF," by Ross Dowson, May 1957, R. D. Internet Archive.
9. *Workers Vanguard*, Mid-February, 1959, Vol. 4, No. 3.

10. p 261, *William Irvine: The Life of a Prairie Radical,* by Anthony Mardiros, James Lorimer and Company, Toronto, 1979.
11. op cit. p 245, Anthony Mardiros.
12. Letter to Pat Mitchell (later to become Pat Schulz) on Tour, from Ross Dowson, June 11, 1964, MG 28, 1V 11, Cont. 108, File 6, R. D. Fonds, LAC.

Chapter Fourteen. Birth of the New Democratic Party

1. "Memo on the CCF," by Ross Dowson, R. D. Internet Archive, June 3, 1957.
2. Letter to Jerry Houle, from Ross Dowson, July 2nd, 1959, MG28, 1V 11, Cont. 107, File 24 R. D. Fonds, L. A. C.

Chapter Fifteen. Verne Olson and the Cuban Revolution

1. p98, "Three Nights in Havana," by Robert Wright, quoted in Cynthia Wright's essay, "Between Nation and Empire," in "Our Place In The Sun: Canada and Cuba in the Castro Era," edited by Robert Anthony Wright and Lana Wylie, University of Toronto Press, 2009.
2. Review of C. Wright Mills' "Listen Yankee," *International Socialist Review,* Spring, 1960.
3. *Workers Vanguard,* Mid-January, 1959, Vol. 4
4. *The Militant,* "Cuba Ousts Batista Dictatorship," January 12, 1959.
5. *The Fourth International: The Long March of the Trotskyists,* by Pierre Frank, 1979, Ink Links.
6. "How Sectarians Misrepresented Trotskyism in Cuba," by Jose Perez, *Intercontinental Press.*
7. R. D. Fonds, MG, 1V 11, Cont. 109, File19, LAC.
8. *Dynamics of the Cuban Revolution,* Pathfinder Press, 1978.
9. *Negroes With Guns,* by Robert Williams, Wayne State University Press, 1962.
10. The CP "form clubs but do not affiliate to the Committee…they are not sending money," wrote Cliff Cotton who was attending the SWP's study camp that year and was frequently in New York talking to party activists. Letter to Ross Dowson from Cliff Cotton, November 22, 1960, MG28, 1V11, Container 105, File 16, R. D. Fonds, LAC.
11. "Fair Play for Cuba and the Cuban Revolution: How American Antiwar and Solidarity Movements in 60's Impeded an Effective Invasion of Cuba," by Bill Simpich, *Counterpunch.*
12. op. cit., Cynthia Wright, p. 98.
13. Toronto resident members of the National Committee and the leading body of the group between NC meetings.
14. R. D. Fonds, Container 109, File 18, LAC.
15. *Workers Vanguard,* Mid-October, 1960, Vol. 8, No. 10.
16. Letter to Branch #1 and #2, December 29, 1960 from Ross Dowson,. R. D. Internet Archives."Within the next three weeks we anticipate we will have done sufficient preparatory work to establish such a committee here in Toronto."

17. *A Prophet in Politics: A Biography of J. S. Woodsworth,* Kenneth McNaught, University of Toronto Press, 1959, 339P

18. Report to the 1961, (SEL, Toronto) Branch Conference about the FPCC., MG 28, 1V 11, Cont. 109, File 6, R. D. Fonds, LAC.

19. Summer, 1964, *FPCC Bulletin.* The Oxford, a U.S. warship, in the aftermath of the missile crisis of 1962, constantly hovered close to the coast, in full view of Havana, spying on the island's communications system.

20. F. P. C. C. Press Statement, April 15, 1961, Cont. 109, File 20, R. D. Fonds, LAC.

21. *Workers Vanguard,* May 1961, Vol. 6, No. 3.

22. ICAP Press Release, undated, (most likely the summer of 1965), R. D. Fonds, M. G. 28, 1V, 11, Container 110, File 2, LAC.

23. *Workers Vanguard,* Mid-July, 1961, Vol. 6, No. 5.

24. Op. cit. Cynthia Wright, p100

25. *Toronto Telegram,* June 27, 1961.

26. *Toronto Telegram,* June 28, 1961

27. Report from the Chairman, by Vernel Olson, MG 28, 1V 11, Cont. 109, File 16, R. D. Fonds, LAC.

28. Op. cit. p108,"Between Nation and Empire,"

29. Cont. 109, File 20, R. D. Fonds, LAC.

30. FPCC Statement, October,1961, MG 28,1V, Cont. 109, File 20 R. D. Fonds, LAC.

31. Op. cit. p110, Cynthia Wright.

32. Letter to Harold (Vancouver) from Pat Mitchell, January 27th, 1962, MG 28, V11, Cont. 109, File 11, R. D. Fonds, LAC.

33. Undated FPCC statement, possibly 1961, Cont. 109, File 20, R. D. Fonds, LAC.

34. *FPCC Bulletin,* Summer 1962, Cont. 109, File 19, R. D. Fonds, L. A. C.

35. *FPCC Bulletin,* Summer, 1963.

36. *FPCC Bulletin,* Winter,1963.

37. Letter to the Cuban Ambassador, Americo Cruz from John Darling, June 10, 1961, Letter to John Darling from the Cuban Ambassador, June 19, 1961 M. G. 28, 1V 11, Container 110, File 2, R. D. Fonds, LAC.

38. *One Hell Of A Gamble, Khrushchev, Castro, and Kennedy, 1958-1964,* by Aleksandr Furenko and Timothy Naftall,1997, W. W. Norton and Company. See p15: "Fearful of his brother's reaction, Raul said to Blas Roca that he never told Fidel about his membership in the youth league or, later, in the PSP itself." And when Fidel was in the U.S. in April, 1959, "he categorically denied on NBC's "Meet the Press" that Raul or his wife was a communist," p10. And further: "As we shall see, the KGB at least believed that Fidel did not learn of his brother's communist loyalties until 1962, during something called the Escalante affair, which ripped open the PSP." p16. The authors had access to the Soviet archives of the period. See also, p164-165 and p318, of *Che: A Revolutionary Life,* by Jon Lee Anderson, Grove Press, 1997.

39. p124, *Cuba, An American Tragedy,* a Penguin Special by Robert Scheer and Maurice Zietlin, 1964.
40. Op. cit. p 125
41. Cited in the *Daily Worker,* New York, August 5, 1953, p3, from *Cuba: An American Tragedy.*
42. Op. cit, p. 198, Jon Lee Anderson.
43. Op. cit, p. 127, Scheer and Zietlin.
44. Op. cit, p. 128, Scheer and Zietlan, quoting P187 from *The World Today.*
45. Op. cit, p. 119, *Cuba, an American Tragedy.*
46. Letter to Joe Hansen, from Ross Dowson, August 16, 1961, MG 28, 1V, Cont. 109-11, R. D. Fonds, LAC.
47. Op. cit, Letter to Joe Hansen, August 16, 1961.
48. Op. cit, Letter to Joe Hansen, August 16, 1961.
49. *Cuba: How the Workers and Peasants Made the Revolution,* by Chris Slee, Resistance Books, 2008, p 34.
50. Letter to Dear Friend from Ernest Mandel, February 23, 1964, Ernest Mandel Papers, 21-28, International Institute of Social History(IISH) Amsterdam
51. March 1st, 1964, IISH.
52. Dear Alan, March 7th, 1964, IISH.
53. Letter to David Horowitz from Ernest Mandel, July 20th. 1967, File 38, IISH.
54. What looks like an untitled letter to United Secretariat of the F. I by Ross Dowson, under the pseudonym "Kent," containing a summary of his discussions with Verne, January 17, 1964, R. D. Fonds LAC.
55. Letter to Russell Stetler, January 11, 1968, IISH.
56. Op. cit. Letter to International Secretariat, January 17, 1964.
57. Op. cit. Letter to Hansen, August 16, 1964.
58. Op. cit."How Sectarians Misrepresented Trotskyism in Cuba," by Jose Perez, I. P.
59. *The Fourth International: The Long March of the Trotskyists* by Pierre Frank, 1979, Ink Links.
60. "REPORT OF DISCUSSIONS HELD WITH COMRADES FROM THE CUBAN SECTION—FOURTH INTERNATIONAL," August 14, 1961. This report is unsigned and was probably meant for the International Secretariat. I know that Verne often left his name off sensitive documents in case they fell into the wrong hands, wishing to protect the FPCC against factional attacks, and not wishing to compromise its formal independence from the LSA and the SWP. The sensitivity of the political situation in Cuba also demanded this, along with the fear of being red-baited in Canada. The report's point form and the fact that he refers to the LSA also suggests this. It's highly unlikely an SWP member would have made this specific reference. MG 28, 1V 11, Container 109, File 11 R. D. Fonds, LAC.

61. "Stalinism or Trotskyism in the Cuban Revolution?" by Joseph Hansen, *International Socialist Review*, Vol. 27, No. 3, Summer, 1966. Joseph Hansen Internet Archive, 2006.

62. Letter to George Breitman from Verne Olson, January 29, 1964. Cont. 109, File 16, R. D. Fonds, LAC.

63. Op. cit. p644, Anderson.

64. "FPCC Statement On Cancellation Of The Tour," *FPCC Fall, 1965 Bulletin.*

65. "FPCC Statement On Cancellation Of The Tour," *FPCC Fall, 1965 Bulletin.*

66. *FPCC Bulletin, Summer-Fall, 1965.*

67. "Dear Dr. Castro," June 5th, 1965, Cont. 112-2, R. D. Fonds, L. A. C.

68. Student Tour Cancellation: Postscript by the FPCC," July 25th, 1965, Cont. 112-2, LAC.

69. *"Dear Verne" from Joe Hansen, September 21, 1965, Cont. 110-1, LAC.

70. "Dear Joe" from Verne, December 14,1965, R. D. Fonds, Cont. 110—1, LAC.

71. "Dear Joe," from Vernel Olson, August 31, 1965, R. D. Fonds, Cont. 110—1, LAC.

72. "Ovation for Ambassador at Cuba Fair Play Supper," *Workers Vanguard,* Mid-December, 1965, Volume 10, No. 7, (115)

73. "Letter to Verne Olson" from Phil Courneyour," January 28, 1966, R. D. Fonds, Cont. 110—1, LAC.

74. *World Outlook,* February 18, 1966, Chris Arthur Archive, 711/B/1/3, Warwick University.

75. *World Outlook,* Vol. 4, No 8, March 25th, 1966, Chris Arthur Archive, 711/B/1/3, Warwick University.

76. Statement of the Toronto Executive of the Fair Play for Cuba Committee, February 14, 1966, Cont. 109, File 20 R. D. Fonds, LAC.

77. "Dear Joe," from Verne Olson," June 8th, 1965, Cont. 110-1, R. D. Fonds, LAC.

78. "Dear Joe" from Verne Olson, February 21, 1966, Cont. 110—1, R. D. Fonds, LAC.

79. "Dear Verne" from Joe Hansen, March 7th, 1965, Cont. 110-1, R. D. Fonds, LAC.

80. "Letter to Verne and Anne," January 17th, 1966, unsigned, but from internal evidence appears to be from Nelson Zayas Pozo, Cont. 110-1, R. D. Fonds, LAC.

81. "Letter to Joe Hansen," from Verne Olson, March 31st, 1966, Cont. 110-1, R. D. Fonds, LAC.

82. "Letter to Ross Dowson" from Verne Olson, April 14th, 1966, Cont. 110-1, R. D. Fonds LAC.

83. "L. A. Solidarity Congress Faces Che's Challenge," by Ross Dowson, *Workers Vanguard,* Volume 11, No. 11 (131), Mid-July, 1967.

84. "Memorandum on the Fair Play for Cuba Committee in Canada," July 28th, 1967, by Ross Dowson, "submitted to Minrex with a copy to Fidel Castro." Cont. 110-1, R. D. Fonds LAC.

85. "Tenth Anniversary of Cuban Revolution," *Workers Vanguard*, Volume 13, No. 9 (165), January 13th, 1969.
86. Cont. 105, File 17, R. D. Fonds, LAC.
87. *Workers Vanguard*, Vol. 13, No. 18 (174), May 19th, 1969.
88. Letter to Ross Dowson, July 28, 1969, MG28,1V11, Cont. 109, File 6, R D. Fonds, LAC.

Chapter Sixteen. *New Youth Organization for a New Party*

1. "Letter to Alan Harris" from Ross Dowson, December 30, 1959, MG 28, 1V 11, Cont. 105, File 16, R. D. Fonds, LAC.
2. "Some of our youth comrades are comfortable in the YS and LSA and are reluctant to move in and around the NDP youth." Letter to Murry Weiss from Ross Dowson, August 11, 1961, R. D. Internet Archives.
3. Letter to Cliff Cotton from Ross Dowson, December 28, 1960, MG 28, Container 105, File 16, R. D. Fonds, LAC.
4. *Workers Vanguard*, Mid-July, 1961, Vol. 6, No. 5

Chapter Seventeen. *Vancouver*

1. *Workers Vanguard*, October 1960, Vol. 5, No. 10
2. Letter to Joe Johnson, by Ross Dowson, Sept. 28, 1960, R. D. Internet Archive.
3. Letter to Ross from E. Tate, July 1, 1963. Cont. 109, File 3, R. D. Fonds, LAC.
4. Minutes of the Vancouver Branch, July 27, 1963, Cont. 109, File 3, R. D. Fonds, LAC.
5. Letter to E. Tate from Ross Dowson,July 8, 1963, Cont. 109, File 3, R. D. Fonds, LAC.

Chapter Eighteen. *The Maoists*

1. Letter to Ross Dowson from E. Tate, Cont. 109,, File 3, R. D. Fonds, LAC.
2. "To Members of the PWM," letter from the LSA, November 3, 1964, Container 109, File 4, R. D. Fonds, LAC.
3. A Communist Life, Jack Scott and The Canadian Workers' Movement, 1927-1985, Edited by Bryan D. Palmer, Committee on Canadian Labour History, 1988.
4. Op. cit. p. 19.
5. Op. cit. p. 19.

Chapter Nineteen. *The 1953 Division of the Fourth International*

1. Op. cit. Pierre Frank's The Long March of the Trotskyists . . .
2. "For the Seventh World Congress and Reunification," by Pierre Frank, International Bulletin of the I.S. of the Fourth International, No. 37, April, 1963.
3. Draft Resolution of the United Secretariat of the F.I. (U.S. F.I.), undated, Ernest Mandel Papers, 21-28 IISH Amsterdam.

Index of Names

Resistance Books

FORTHCOMING TITLES

May 2014

We the Indians: The indigenous peoples of Peru and the struggle for land, by Hugo Blanco with foreword by Edward Galeano and introduction by Iain Bruce. Published in association with Merlin Press and the IIRE.

This book paints a graphic picture of the essential and central battle for the land in vivid first-hand accounts with historical contextualisation. Blanco's own understated role shines through.

RECENTLY PUBLISHED

Green Capitalism: why it can't work, by Daniel Tanuro, November 2013 Published in association with Merlin Press and the IIRE.

Daniel Tanuro refutes the major proposals currently being advanced to resolve the climate crisis. He argues that these fail to challenge the drive for profit and the dynamic of capital accumulation such as eco-taxes, commodification of natural resources, and carbon trading. Daniel Tanuro rigorously attempts to demonstrate the impossibility of a socially sustainable transition towards "green capitalism".

Dangerous Liaisons—the marriages and divorces of Marxism and Feminism, Cinzia Arruzza, March 2013, £7. Published in association with Merlin Press and the IIRE.

An accessible introduction to the relationship between the workers' movement and the women's movement. The first part is historical, the second theoretical. Historical examples range from the mid-19th century to the 1970s and include events, debates and key personalities from China, Russia, the USA, France, Italy, Spain and Britain. It shows time and again the controversial and often difficult relationship between feminism and Marxism. The theoretical questions discussed include the origins of women's oppression, domestic labour, dual systems theory, performativity and differentialism.

China's Rise - strength and fragility, Au Loong Yu, November 2012, £12. Published in association with Merlin Press and the IIRE.

Au Loong Yu offers a profound analysis of the rise of China in the manner it should be done: through placing front and centre a meticulous examination of its capitalist ruling class and of the variegated ways in which it appropriates a surplus. By starting from the multiple forms of property through which the country's dominant bureaucratic state capitalists sustain themselves, Au is able at one and the same time to lay bare the roots of the Chinese economic miracle and the foundations of its durable authoritarian political order, to expose the politico-economic contradictions that are likely to limit growth and bring crisis to the system, and to illuminate the sources of the fierce class struggles that continue to wrack town and country and threaten, over time, to open the way to political alternatives. Truly a tour de force.

—*Robert Brenner, Professor of history and director of the Center for Social Theory and Comparative History at UCLA, editor of the socialist journal* Against the Current, *and editorial committee member of* New Left Review.

STILL AVAILABLE

Capitalism—Crises and Alternatives, Michel Husson, Andy Kilmister, Susan Pashkoff, Sean Thompson, Özlem Onaran , Eric Toussaint, et al., Özlem Onaran and Fred Leplat eds., February 2012, £7. (Resistance Books and IIRE pub.)

Ireland's Credit Crunch, Kearing, Morrison & Corrigan, October 2010, £5. (Resistance Books pub.)

Militant years - car workers' struggles in Britain in the 60s and 70s, Alan Thornett, February 2011, £12. (Resistance Books pub.)

New Parties of the Left - Experiences from Europe, Daniel Bensaïd, Alain Krivine, Alda Sousa, Alan Thornett et al., May 2011, £7. (Resistance Books and IIRE pub.)

Women's Liberation & Socialist Revolution: Documents of the Fourth International, Penelope Duggan ed., October 2010, £6. (Resistance Books and IIRE pub.)

The Global Fight for Climate Justice – Anti-capitalist responses to global warming and environmental destruction, Ian Angus ed., June 2009, £8. (Resistance Books pub.)

Strategies of Resistance & 'Who Are the Trotskyists', Daniel Bensaïd, November 2009, £6. (Resistance Books and IIRE pub.)

Revolution and Counter-revolution in Europe from 1918 to 1968, Pierre Frank, May 2011, £7. (Resistance Books and IIRE pub.)

The Long March of the Trotskyists: Contributions to the history of the International, Pierre Frank, Daniel Bensaïd, Ernest Mandel, October 2010, £5. (Resistance Books and IIRE pub.)

Building Unity Against Fascism: Classic Marxist Writings, Leon Trotsky, Daniel Guérin, Ted Grant et al., October 2010, £4. (Resistance Books and IIRE pub.)

Socialists and the Capitalist Recession (with Ernest Mandel's 'Basic Theories of Karl Marx'), Raphie De Santos, Michel Husson, Claudio Katz et al., March 2009, £5. (Resistance Books and IIRE pub.)

Respect: Documents of the crisis, Fred Leplat ed., 2008, £3. (Resistance Books pub.)

Take the Power to Change the World, Phil Hearse ed., June 2007, £5. (Resistance Books and IIRE pub.)

The Party: The Socialist Workers Party 1960-1988. Volume 2: Interregnum, decline and collapse, 1973-1988, Barry Sheppard, November 2012, £10. (Resistance Books pub.)

Foundations of Christianity: a study in Christian origins, Karl Kautsky, £12. (Resistance Books pub.)

The Permanent Revolution & Results and Prospects, Leon Trotsky, £9. (Resistance Books pub.)

My Life Under White Supremacy and in Exile, Leonard Nikani, February 2009, £8. (Resistance Books pub.)

Cuba at Sea, Ron Ridenour, May 2008, £7. (Resistance Books pub.)

Ecosocialism or Barbarism (new expanded edition), Jane Kelly ed., February 2008, £5. (Resistance Books pub.)

Cuba: Beyond the Crossroads, Ron Ridenour, April 2007, £4. (Resistance Books pub.)

Middle East: war, imperialism, and ecology – sixty years of resistance, Roland Rance & Terry Conway eds. and Gilbert Achcar (contributor) et al., March 2007, £6. (Resistance Books pub.)

It's never too late to love or rebel, Celia Hart, August 2006, £5. (Resistance Books pub.)

October Readings: The development of the concept of Permanent Revolution, D. R. O'Connor Lysaght ed., October 2010, £4. (Resistance Books pub.)

Living Internationalism: the IIRE's history, Murray Smith and Joost Kircz eds., January 2011, £4. (Resistance Books and IIRE pub.)

Books can be purchased through the website at **www.resistancebooks.org,** or by writing to **Resistance Books, PO Box 62732, London, SW2 9GQ.** Cheques to be made payable to "Resistance" and £2 p&p is to be added for each book.

Resistance Books

contact@socialistresistance.org
PO Box 62732, London, SW2 9GQ; Phone: 020 7346 8889

About Resistance Books

Resistance Books is the publishing arm of Socialist Resistance, a revolutionary Marxist organisation which is the British section of the Fourth International. Resistance Books also publishes books jointly with Merlin Press and the International Institute for Research and Education in Amsterdam. Further information about Resistance Books, including a full list of titles currently available and how to purchase them, can be obtained at **www.resistancebooks.org**, or by writing to **Resistance Books, PO Box 62732, London, SW2 9GQ.**

Socialist Resistance is an organisation active in the trade union movement and in campaigns against austerity and in defence of the welfare state. We oppose imperialist interventions, and help organise solidarity with Palestine. We are eco-socialist – we argue that much of what is produced under capitalism is socially useless and either redundant or directly harmful. We have been long-standing supporters of women's liberation and the struggles of lesbians, gay people, bisexuals and transgender people.

Socialist Resistance is the bi-monthly magazine of the organisation, which can be read online at www.socialistresistance.org. Socialist Resistance can be contacted by email at **contact@socialistresistance.org**. *International Viewpoint* is the English language online magazine of the Fourth International which can be read online at **www.internationalviewpoint.org**.

The International Institute for Research and Education (IIRE) was opened in 1982 in Amsterdam. The IIRE is now also located in Manila and Islamabad. Its main activity has been the organisation of courses in the service of progressive forces around the world. The seminars and study groups deal with all subjects related to the emancipation of the world's oppressed and exploited. The IIRE publishes Notebooks for Study and Research to focus on themes of contemporary debate, or historical and theoretical importance. For a full list visit http://bit. ly/IIRENSR or subscribe online at: http://bit. ly/NSRsub. To order, email iire@iire.org or write to International Institute for Research and Education, Lombokstraat 40, Amsterdam, NL-1094.

Resistance Books

contact@socialistresistance.org
PO Box 62732, London, SW2 9GQ; Phone: 020 7346 8889